MW01148562

INTIMACY ACROSS THE FENCELINES

INTIMACY ACROSS THE FENCELINES

Sex, Marriage, and the U.S. Military in Okinawa

Rebecca Forgash

CORNELL UNIVERSITY PRESS   ITHACA AND LONDON

First published 2020 by Cornell University Press

Library of Congress Cataloging-in-Publication Data

Names: Forgash, Rebecca, author.
Title: Intimacy across the fencelines : sex, marriage, and the U.S. military
    in Okinawa / Rebecca Forgash.
Description: Ithaca : Cornell University Press, 2020. | Includes bibliographical
    references and index.
Identifiers: LCCN 2019046283 (print) | LCCN 2019046284 (ebook) |
    ISBN 9781501750403 (cloth) | ISBN 9781501750410 (epub) |
    ISBN 9781501750427 (pdf)
Subjects: LCSH: Military bases, American—Social aspects—Japan—Okinawa-ken. |
    Soldiers—Sexual behavior—United States. | Soldiers—Sexual behavior—
    Japan—Okinawa-ken. | Intercountry marriage—Japan—Okinawa-ken. |
    Interracial marriage—Japan—Okinawa-ken. | United States—Armed
    Forces—Japan—Okinawa-ken.
Classification: LCC UA26.O53 F67 2020 (print) | LCC UA26.O53 (ebook) |
    DDC 355.10952/294—dc23
LC record available at https://lccn.loc.gov/2019046283
LC ebook record available at https://lccn.loc.gov/2019046284

Contents

Illustrations

Preface

Ralph Dickson was a gifted storyteller. (I use pseudonyms unless otherwise noted to protect the privacy of research participants.) He had lost his wife to cancer two months before I arrived in Okinawa, and while friends spoke fondly of him, no one volunteered to introduce him to me as a potential research participant. Struggling with grief and depression, he spent his evenings drinking at local bars and strumming his guitar. Friends from the village often had to help him home at night. When we finally met, it was at a dinner party hosted by a mutual friend. Learning of my research and interest in Okinawan history and culture, he invited my husband and me to join him on a bike tour of Yagaji Island the following weekend. Soon we were meeting on a regular basis, exploring historical sites in northern Okinawa on bicycle and in his beat-up Daihatsu pickup truck, while he spoke sentimentally of postwar Okinawa in his distinctive Oklahoma drawl.

Ralph had met his wife, Chiemi, at a village festival in Kin in 1967. He was unclear about her role at the gathering. Was she attending the festival with other town residents, or was she working at the club the Americans convened to after it began to rain? Upon inquiring, he was told, "That one, she doesn't go out with anybody. She does her job, and she does what has to be done, but she doesn't date Okinawans or Japanese or Americans. She doesn't date, period." Despite the warning, he approached her. The two gradually developed a friendship, and in 1969, they moved in together. Eventually, they were married. In 1978, Ralph retired from the navy and took a civilian position on Camp Schwab. Chiemi's uncle, a wealthy landowner and businessman, helped the couple buy land associated with a pineapple cannery he owned in Nakijin, and they moved into the top floor of the abandoned factory.

Visiting Ralph's home, one climbed a rusted steel staircase bolted to the outside of the building and then entered a drafty hallway with high unfinished ceilings. To the right, sliding Plexiglas doors hid tatami rooms used for sleeping. To the left, a door opened into a large room containing the family altar and a low table surrounded by floor cushions. The kitchen and makeshift bathroom remained unfinished. Ralph's "house" was considered strange by his American and Okinawan friends alike, and this seemed to add to the common perception of him as a strange individual, neither Okinawan nor American. Neighbors living in the vicinity were initially against the idea of having an American military man for a neighbor. But after twenty-two years, Ralph had become a fixture in the small mountain settlement, despite his continuing difficulty with Japanese.

> RALPH: It's a nice place to live. It's quiet. Everybody knows everybody, and knows everybody's business, but they don't get too personal with you.
>
> AUTHOR: So you don't feel like a gaijin [foreigner]?
>
> RALPH: No, I feel just like one of them. I go on all the old-folks trips, and I belong to the local gate ball team. One time, the mayor of the settlement told me, "Yeah, Ralph-san, you're a gaijin, but you're *our* gaijin."

Ralph's stories of living across Okinawa's military fencelines for thirty years were fascinating. What was his and Chiemi's life like, given the conspicuous nature of intimate relationships between U.S. military men and Okinawan women? What sacrifices had each made, and what benefits did they enjoy due to their relationship? Did Okinawan family and neighbors truly perceive Ralph as "one of them," as he believed? This is a book of stories, stories of men and women like Ralph and Chiemi, living in unusual, hybrid, and often difficult circumstances due to their symbolic association with war and American empire. Their stories reflect the larger historical, economic, and social contexts of postwar and post-reversion Okinawa, but the stories also structure that reality, rendering it identifiable, understandable, and livable. They are therefore a powerful window on the experiences of men and women in Okinawa at a variety of levels.

My own interest in intimate interactions and relationships between Okinawan women and U.S. military men began nearly twenty years ago. At the time, I had little firsthand knowledge of military life, although a respected uncle previously stationed in Okinawa had shared intriguing stories about living off base, participating in community festivals, and swimming and shelling on isolated beaches. Such idyllic-sounding experiences contrasted sharply with the darker images of U.S. military occupation I had encountered while researching a master's thesis on the U.S. military presence in Haiti during the early twentieth century. The dissonance sparked my interest in the history of U.S. expansion, the variety of experiences of U.S. military personnel abroad, and the views of local people in communities that surround U.S. bases. Inspired by my uncle's stories, I took a teaching position at a language school in Japan's Hiroshima Prefecture. My employers were an international married couple, an American man and his Japanese wife. Borrowing the capital from her parents, they had opened two successful English language schools. The husband contributed a foreign face, an American accent, and seemingly boundless enthusiasm, while the wife ran the business and handled communications with students and their families. For her, I became a confidant and interpreter of the often-mystifying behaviors of her American husband. Through whispered conversations, I learned of the excitement, confusion, and tension that pervade intimate relationships between American men and Japanese women. When their marriage broke up, I heard about the whole painful ordeal.

Developing a research proposal to study intimate international relationships, I decided on Okinawa as a field site, with an estimated twenty-seven thousand U.S. troops and consistently high rates of international marriage. Like residents of Hiroshima, Okinawans had suffered unimaginable losses during World War II. Colonized by Japan during the late nineteenth century, sacrificed in order to forestall an American invasion of the homeland, and host today to more than 70 percent of the U.S. military installations in Japan, Okinawa is at the center of the U.S.-Japan security alliance and the antiwar and antibase peace movements. Against this backdrop, sexual and romantic intimacy between local people and U.S. military personnel is unavoidably political.

The individuals appearing in this book are diverse, reflecting the heterogeneous makeup of their communities of origin and their communities of residence, whether small villages on Okinawa's Motobu peninsula, large military housing areas in central Okinawa, or the transnational community of U.S. military personnel and families, moving back and forth between duty stations in Japan, Hawaii, California, Virginia, and North Carolina. Their stories are also varied, expressed through distinctive speech patterns, colorful turns of phrase, details mentioned versus those left out, and emotions conveyed through tone, emphasis, or silence. I have been drawn to the richly detailed content and delivery of these stories. I worry that I might not be able to do them justice. At the end of nearly twenty years of research and writing, I hope that readers will look beyond the weaknesses of my writing and perspective to appreciate the power and richness of these stories and their narrators.

Acknowledgments

My gratitude goes first to the many people in Okinawa who have helped me over the years to understand relationships among individuals living on different sides of the fences that divide Okinawan society. In the interest of respecting their privacy, I refrain from mentioning most by name. However, I hope that this book will go some small way toward expressing the respect and appreciation I feel for all who allowed me to take part in their lives, visit their homes, meet their families, and record their stories. Their many kindnesses, along with their trust that I would represent their experiences and views accurately and honestly, continue to motivate and inspire me professionally and personally. My debt to them far exceeds this project.

While conducting research, I benefited from affiliation with Meio University in Nago City, Okinawa. Professor of English literature and university president emeritus Senaha Eiki helped arrange my research appointments with the Meio University Research Institute in 2001–2002 and 2016–2017. From our initial meeting at Naha airport in 2000, Senaha-sensei has guided my study of Okinawan history and society, patiently answered questions, considered my ideas, and introduced me to local scholars, community leaders, and dozens of international couples. His wife and family have welcomed me into their home on holidays, repeatedly asked after my husband and children, and shared their own stories and insights, all while suffering my imperfect Japanese. They serve as a model for my own interactions with Japanese and American students and colleagues. Thanks also to the current president of Meio University, Yamazato Katsunori and the directors and staff of the Meio University Research Institute, including Yamazato Kiyoshi, Nakachi Kiyoshi, Lee Jinyoung, Nakamura Koichiro, Oshiro Mikio, and Nakasone-san in the office. In recent years, Ja Yung Kim has become a stimulating companion and collaborator. I appreciate her help clarifying the arguments of Japanese scholars on U.S. military marriage. I first became acquainted with Senaha-sensei and Meio University through a chain of introductions that included Takie Lebra and Koji Taira, for which I am grateful.

Over the years, Kakihana Ikuo has offered invaluable assistance, helping me to arrange accommodation and transportation, find volunteering opportunities, and understand the often-sensitive political situation in Nago. While director of the Nago City International House, Kakihana-san took me under his wing and introduced me to dozens of foreign residents, many former U.S. military members, living in the northern region. Also in Nago, Yoshikawa Hideki, Liz Yoshikawa,

Caroline Latham, and Nashiro Yoshihisa extended invitations to professional, community, and family events. Their intellectual companionship, compassion, and readiness to engage in honest dialogue have challenged me to think deeply about the effects of history and local politics on social relationships among the varied residents of northern Okinawa. I appreciate their enduring friendship. Thanks also to Thomas Shimabukuro, Ohshiro Michiko, Kishimoto Takako, and the owners and staff of E-Star for their generous support and assistance.

Hirata Masayo, Nakama Tetsu, Midori Thayer, and Betty Hoffman shared with me their professional experiences working with military international couples and their children. Hirata-san introduced me to studies on military marriage and divorce conducted by Okinawa Prefecture and local women's organizations, as well as documents relating to the U.S. military's first premarital workshop for international couples, all while pushing me to improve my Japanese-language skills in professional contexts. I benefited immensely from Etsuko Takushi Crissey's excellent Japanese-language study of Okinawan wives of U.S. military personnel living in the United States, republished in English translation in 2017, and I appreciate her support of my research. Tsuneko Maria Miyagi Bartruff pulled in favors to assist with gathering stories from retired couples living in Okinawa and the United States. Gil Hoffman, Mike Oshiro, and James Ross generously shared their ideas and introduced me to others in their networks. At the U.S. consulate in Naha, Valda Vikmanis Keller explained U.S. immigration procedures and resources for military international couples.

My access to U.S. Marine Corps installations in Okinawa was facilitated by the late U.S. senator John McCain. In Okinawa, Randy Tulabut, Arnold Amposta, John W. Lynch III, and Barbara Wolcott shared my interest in military international marriage and facilitated participant observation in on-base settings. Mike Gould, Karen Hanovitch, and Sonia Fife gave generously of their time and assistance, enabling me to learn about U.S. military programs for international couples. My gratitude also goes to several extraordinarily helpful Okinawan employees on the U.S. military bases, who tutored me in Okinawan and U.S. military culture and shared with me their own experiences of military sex, romance, and marriage. Their stories figure importantly in this book. Finally, thanks to my uncle and aunt, Everett "Sonny" and Nancy Long, who inspired my initial interest in Japan and Okinawa, and to Fumi Conner, who trusted me with her hopes and dreams, as well as her despair.

The fingerprints of my many teachers, mentors, and colleagues can be detected throughout the book. I first learned about anthropology, ethnography, and academic writing from Naomi Quinn, Richard Fox, Joanne Passaro, and John Jay TePaske at Duke University. At the University of Arizona, Daniel Nugent, Ana Alonso, Brackette Williams, and Jane Hill shaped my thinking about language, culture, society, and power. Ellen Basso, Susan Philips, and Gail Lee Bernstein inspired and challenged me as I began this project. I appreciate Ellen Basso's enthusiastic interest and expert methodological guidance. Susan Philips's incisive comments and questions regarding the role of the U.S. military in Okinawa and in participants' lives pushed me to think in more powerful yet nuanced theoretical terms. Gail Lee Bernstein offered insights into Japanese culture and asked pointed ethnographic and comparative questions, helping me to refine my arguments with respect to Okinawa. Her editorial comments taught me to take pleasure in the writing, and I have often reflected on her description of classroom teaching as a sort of dance. Thanks as well to Drexel Woodson and Norma Mendoza-Denton. Over the years, Drexel has given generously of his time, advice, and friendship to help me grow as a scholar. I am grateful as well for Maribel Alvarez, Betsy Krause, Elea Aguirre, Betsy Harris, Jess Weinberg, Anne Bennett and Meredith Green Kuhn, whose talent and friendship challenged me intellectually and sustained me personally. Linguist Kyoko Masuda helped design the Japanese language questionnaires that I used in Okinawa.

Japanese language teachers at the University of Arizona, Cornell University's Japanese FALCON Program, and the Inter-University Center for Japanese Language Studies in Yokohama (IUC) taught me basic Japanese conversation, reading, and writing. I wish that I had sought their instruction long before my midtwenties. Special thanks to Robert J. Sukle and to Ted and Vickey Bestor, who hosted me in their home during my time at Cornell. IUC classmate Ken Vickery painstakingly reviewed and commented on drafts of various grant applications and journal manuscripts. I am grateful for his friendship and support. A Foreign Language and Area Studies Fellowship from the U.S. Department of Education and a generous grant from the Blakemore Foundation made advanced language study possible.

Anthropologists Christopher Nelson, Masamichi Inoue, James Roberson, and Linda Angst generously offered suggestions and assistance with networking in Okinawa during the early stages of this project and more recently, as I returned to work on the manuscript. Barbara Brooks and my fellow participants at the 2001 SSRC Japan Studies Dissertation Writing Workshop provided critical feedback as I transitioned from initial data collection to analysis and writing. Sue Je Gage, Taku Suzuki, Caren Freeman, and Fran Mascia-Lees encouraged me to think more broadly about the theoretical implications of the research. Many thanks to colleagues at Tokyo Metropolitan University, including Ishida Shin-ichiro, Ayabe Masao, Ito Makoto, and Tanuma Sachiko for inviting me to speak on the project. Their questions prompted me to think about fencelines in new and creative ways.

I could not have asked for a more supportive group of colleagues at Metropolitan State University of Denver. Thanks to Robin Quizar, Jon Kent, and Jack Schultz, who are models of the dedicated and effective teacher-scholar. Rae Shevalier, Melissa Monson, and Julie Reyes read and commented on the proposals, reports, manuscripts, and chapter drafts that culminated in this book. Su Il Kim, my co-leader for MSU Denver's Japan study abroad course, traveled with me to Okinawa multiple times and read and commented on the manuscript in its entirety. I am grateful for his critical perspective and the many good times we have shared. Kayoko Moore, Liz Kleinfeld, and Amy Eckert assisted with a range of language, writing, and publishing questions on short notice. I have also been fortunate to work with a number of highly talented student assistants in the MSU Denver Ethnography Lab. My appreciation goes especially to Erin Moyer and Tracy Ingram, as well as to Eila McMillin, Savannah Powell, Iain Thomas, Kyle Seay, Aya Fukuda, Katrina Geist, Roman Khamov, Nichole Lambert, Liam Price, Leah Bourgoin, Julianna Zellner, and Taylor Daniel.

My initial fieldwork in 2001–2002 was supported by a Dissertation Fieldwork Grant from the Wenner-Gren Foundation. Return field trips were funded by the College of Letters, Arts and Sciences, the Office for International Studies, and the Office of the Provost at Metropolitan State University of Denver. I could not have completed the manuscript without a yearlong sabbatical leave granted by MSU Denver. To James Lance and Cornell University Press, I am grateful for the opportunity to publish this work and for the patient guidance and support I have received throughout the process. Two anonymous readers for the press offered constructive criticism and recommendations that improved the final manuscript. Michelle Witkowski oversaw copyediting and typesetting, answering my questions with quick turnaround. Cartographer Bill Nelson redrew the maps appearing in the book. Amron Gravett created the index. The evocative image appearing on the book cover is the work of Okinawan photographer Kazuo Kunishi. A different version of chapter 4 appeared as "Negotiating Marriage: Cultural Citizenship and the Reproduction of American Empire in Okinawa" in *Ethnology: An International Journal of Cultural and Social Anthropology* 48, no. 3 (2009): 215–37.

Finally, I am forever grateful for the steadfast love and support of my parents, Andrew John Forgash Jr. and Donna Glover Forgash, and the example of my grandparents, Frank and Rachel Glover and Andy and Vicky Forgash. They taught me the value of hard work and commitment and the rewards of taking the road less traveled. My children, Lucas and Ben Ax, have been a source of tremendous joy, as well as a daily reminder of the challenges of balancing an academic career with a young family. I began the project before they were born, and now they are teenagers. They have taught me patience, practicality, humility, good humor, and appreciation for life's beauty. Finally, and of greatest consequence, Bryan Ax's steadfast faith in me and willingness to pick up the slack in all areas of life, from formatting theses to caring for our children, has helped carry me forward through the many years of work and worry that went into this project. I have been blessed to spend nearly the entirety of our adult lives together.

INTIMACY ACROSS THE FENCELINES

THE INTIMATE EFFECTS
OF U.S. EMPIRE

It was a muggy evening in August 2001. I had just arrived in Nago and was still in the process of getting settled. After investigating the local produce market, a well-known soba shop, and the small department store, I had visited the university to complete paperwork and meet with colleagues. But so far I hadn't spied any foreigners and certainly no U.S. military personnel. The staff at the International House had assured me that American servicemen regularly came into town to eat at local restaurants and bars, and that dozens of international couples, many former U.S. military, lived throughout the northern region. They suggested that I attend the Nago Youth Eisā Festival, a popular community event, which I was now about to do. I walked along the beach path into 21st Century Park, an attractive green space built on reclaimed land in preparation for the G8 summit staged in Okinawa the previous year. At the center of the park, townspeople congregated around the entrance of an open-air amphitheater built of limestone blocks to resemble the ruins of an ancient castle. Friends and neighbors exchanged greetings and gossip, remarking on the humidity and the forecasted arrival of a typhoon later in the week. Elderly women led grandchildren dressed in colorful dragonfly-print outfits by the hand. Teenagers waited for friends beside food stalls selling *yakisoba* and roasted corn. Young men hoisted coolers of beer, their dates carrying picnic blankets to spread on the stone seats of the amphitheater. Then I spotted them. Off to one side, ten young marines from Camp Schwab were gathered around their petite Okinawan culture guide for an explanation of the evening's performance. Inside the amphitheater, an announcer took the stage and declared the opening of the festival. I hurried to find a seat, staying close to the

Americans to observe their interactions. A troop of *sanshin* (Okinawan *shamisen*) players moved into position behind the microphone, and costumed dancers entered the stage beating out energetic sequences on drums and performing *teodori* (literally "hand dancing"). The marines made their way into the crowd and took seats next to a group of Okinawan men and women in their twenties. As the performance progressed, the young people offered one another cigarettes, snack foods, and cans of beer. The Okinawan men half-jokingly challenged the marines to an arm-wrestling match, while the girls looked simultaneously flattered and embarrassed by the flirtatious attention they were receiving. This is how it starts, I thought, imagining the possible scenarios that might lead to intimate relationships between U.S. military men and local women, and which might cause friction with their families and neighbors and between the U.S. bases and surrounding communities.

This book explores the intimate effects of the global U.S. military presence through the experiences of U.S. military men and Okinawan women involved in romantic and sexual relationships with one another.[1] The U.S. military has maintained a large-scale presence in Okinawa, the southernmost of Japan's prefectures, since 1945, when the deadliest battle of the Pacific War was fought there. Today, an estimated twenty-seven thousand U.S. troops and more than 70 percent of the U.S. bases in Japan are located in Okinawa Prefecture, which constitutes just 0.6 percent of the country's land area.[2] While some service members cope with the stresses of military life by withdrawing into the familiar world of the bases, with their American-style food courts, movie theaters, athletic facilities, and grocery stores, others are eager to venture outside the barbed wire fences and experience foreign food, culture, and people. The military promotes troop participation in community events, including attending festivals, volunteering at schools, and participating in beach cleanups, in order to provide a social outlet for personnel and strengthen relationships with surrounding towns. U.S. service members also encounter Okinawans at work and during off-duty hours at nearby shopping areas, restaurants, and clubs. These interactions unfold, however, against a backdrop of simmering political tension. Since the reversion of Okinawa to Japanese sovereignty in 1972, Okinawan politicians have struggled to balance the simultaneous objectives of economic development and political autonomy— some courting Tokyo to secure large construction projects like Nago 21st Century Park in exchange for the bases, others openly siding with antibase intellectuals and peace activists against the U.S. military presence. Recent polls show that, prefecture-wide, 83.8 percent of Okinawans oppose a new U.S. Marine Corps facility under construction in Nago City, and 42.9 percent support the withdrawal of the U.S. military from Okinawa altogether (*Ryukyu Shimpo* 2016). Within this charged atmosphere, individual service members attempt to develop meaningful relationships with Okinawans, and intimate relationships, including marriages, are common.

The term *fencelines* in the title of this book refers to the barbed wire fences that surround U.S. military installations and mark them off-limits to local people. While military fences literally block access to inside spaces and resources, fence-lines also have potent symbolic meanings, signaling the unequal relations of power that have historically separated those on the inside from those on the outside. Symbolic fencelines also run throughout Okinawan society, dividing local people and places along lines of gender, race, and class in ways that support militarization. The term *fencelines* is thus used as a heuristic for thinking about the reach of militarization in Okinawa and its impact on the everyday experiences of residents. In recent years, the catchphrase "across the fenceline" has become a favorite of defense planners designing sustainable "bases of the future" through collaboration with surrounding communities.[3] But social and economic fence-crossing by U.S. service members and residents of surrounding communities has been a part of U.S. military culture since its inception. In Okinawa, everyday interactions and relationships between U.S. personnel and local people reflect and transform military fencelines, affecting formulations of Okinawan identity, local base-related politics, and even local U.S. military policy.

Historically, U.S. military and Okinawan community leaders have put considerable effort into monitoring and regulating intimate relationships between U.S. personnel and local civilians, especially women. Marriage has been considered particularly undesirable. Military men who married Okinawan women during the postwar U.S. occupation of Okinawa (1945–1972) spoke of countless bureaucratic obstacles, including commanding officers who encouraged them to "sow their wild oats" but warned against marrying the women they met on Asian tours of duty. Even today, procedures for marrying Japanese citizens are bewilderingly complex and expensive, whereas purchasing sex is condoned as a necessary outlet and method for preventing violence against local women.[4] For their part, Okinawan politicians and citizens groups have appropriated military international couples and their children as shameful symbols of wartime devastation and foreign military occupation, as well as Okinawa's powerlessness to rid the prefecture of U.S. bases. Despite negative pressures, Okinawan women and American men continue to date and marry. Since reversion, Okinawa Prefecture has reported approximately two hundred marriages per year between American men and Okinawan women (calculated from data compiled by the Japanese Ministry of Health, Labour and Welfare). Compared to other Japanese prefectures, Okinawa has consistently high rates of international marriage, the highest rate of marriages between Japanese women and foreign men, and the highest percentage of American grooms.[5] But even these numbers do not capture the true scope of military marriage. Many couples fly to Guam, Hawaii, or the continental United States and marry there to avoid the extensive paperwork required to legalize a U.S. military marriage in Japan. Moreover, records for marriages performed prior to reversion are scattered and incomplete. Okinawan encyclopedias estimate that approximately four hundred marriages took place per year during the occupation (Takushi 2000, 17). Indeed, few Okinawan families remain untouched by military international intimacy.

Okinawan-U.S. military couples have often been marginalized within Okinawan communities, cut off from family and neighbors, their children ostracized or bullied because they speak English or appear different physically. But some American military husbands have managed to gain acceptance. Examining the stories couples tell, the analysis here focuses on individuals' strategies and subjectivities in relation to shifting community norms regarding sex, marriage, and family and changing formulations of Okinawan identity. One set of strategies couples employ involves creatively utilizing their position at the legal and social margins of both the U.S. military and Okinawan communities. Some actively avoid the extensive paperwork associated with military marriage procedures by marrying "out in town." Many couples also have options when it comes to off-base housing and spouse employment that are not available to American or Okinawan couples. They seek benefits and support through military family services while also drawing on the support of Okinawan family and friends. In this way, military international couples tap resources across the fencelines, a move that allows them to "reposition their own identities to bend lines of power and create an altered space for self-configuration" (Knauft 1996, 168). Through their decisions, experiences, and stories, military international couples jointly construct and negotiate the meanings of U.S. military fencelines, suggesting that many of the intimate effects of U.S. empire are negotiated on the ground in specific communities. Importantly, in Okinawa and other locations where the U.S. maintains bases, such encounters and negotiations take place in a social geography indelibly marked by experiences of colonialism, war, and ongoing social and political marginalization.

The Dual Colonization of Okinawa

Okinawa Prefecture encompasses much of the Ryūkyū archipelago, a string of coral islands stretching from the Japanese island of Kyushu south and west to Taiwan. Flanked by the Pacific Ocean to the east and the East China Sea to the west, the Ryūkyūs emerged as an important trading entrepôt during the late fourteenth century under the indigenous Ryūkyū Kingdom. From that point on, the region's central geographical location has attracted the attention of more powerful nations, including China, Japan, and the United States. From its beginning, the Ryūkyū government engaged in a tributary relationship with Ming China and conducted a thriving maritime trade with East and Southeast Asia. In 1609, feudal lords from Japan's Satsuma domain sent a military force to conquer Ryūkyū and profit from its trade. The islands were formally incorporated into the modern Japanese state as Okinawa Prefecture in 1879. As subjects of imperial Japan, Okinawans were compelled to participate in the Meiji-government education system and military conscription.

In 1944, as Allied forces leapfrogged across the Pacific, Japanese High Command in Tokyo developed a plan to forestall invasion of the homeland by bogging down the enemy in Okinawa. Civilians, including young students, were mobilized to build military fortifications and serve as nurses and fighting forces under Japanese commands. American ground troops initiated a full-scale land

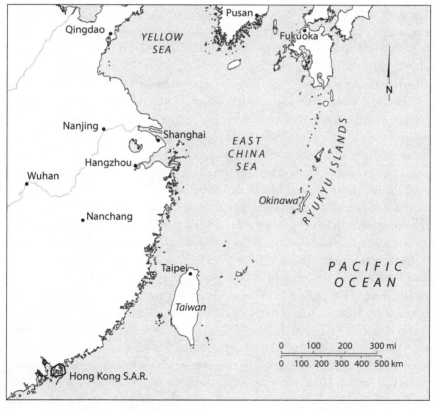

Location of Okinawa in the East China Sea. Cartography by Bill Nelson.

invasion, coming ashore at the Hagushi beaches on the west coast of Okinawa's main island on April 1, 1945. During the ensuing eighty-two-day battle, more than a quarter of the civilian population perished. After the fighting ended, the archipelago was placed under U.S. military supervision, and the islands were transformed into a vast training ground and base for forward-deployed American troops. With Okinawan civilians still living in resettlement camps, the U.S. military appropriated land and shorelines for airfields, fleet anchorage, and troop staging areas. During the 1950s and 1960s, U.S. military installations were enlarged to support operations in Korea and Vietnam. Okinawa became known as the "Keystone of the Pacific," a location of utmost geopolitical importance in containing the spread of communism in Asia. Popular protest against military land seizures intensified in connection with a movement to return Okinawa to Japanese sovereignty. In 1972, after twenty-seven years of U.S. occupation, the islands reverted back to Japan. However, in accordance with the U.S.-Japan Treaty of Mutual Cooperation and Security (1952) and a status of forces agreement (1960), the U.S. military continued to maintain a sizeable presence in the prefecture.[6] Today, the total number of U.S. military personnel, Department of Defense (DoD) civilians, and family members living in Okinawa is somewhere in the neighborhood of forty-seven thousand people.[7] The prefecture hosts the III Marine Expeditionary Force (III MEF) and Eighteenth Wing of the U.S. Air Force, along with associated units from other air force and navy commands and the DoD.

In 1995, popular protest erupted following the rape of a twelve-year-old Okinawan girl by three U.S. servicemen, prompting the U.S. and Japanese governments to establish the joint Special Action Committee on Okinawa (SACO). In its final report, SACO concluded that a phased reduction and realignment of the U.S. bases in Okinawa would best solve existing problems. The report announced the eventual return of eleven facilities, including Marine Corps Futenma Air Station in Ginowan City, contingent upon the relocation of training exercises and other functions to less populated areas of Okinawa. Plans to build a replacement facility in the Henoko district of Nago City were rejected in a popular referendum, even as conservative local politicians indicated their acceptance of the base. The U.S. military and Japanese government plan has evolved to include the reclamation of 160 hectares of sea from Henoko's Oura Bay, two 1,800-meter runways, and a 272-meter dock (McCormack 2016, 3). This so-called Futenma Replacement Facility, currently under construction, would be a land-sea-air base with its own deepwater port, with serious consequences for nearby residential areas and the coastal zone, home to rare species of coral, snails, fish, and marine mammals, including the critically endangered dugong. From 1996 to early 2018, protestors successfully blocked construction of the facility by organizing sit-ins and kayak protests and by taking legal action. A "protest tent" erected on the beach

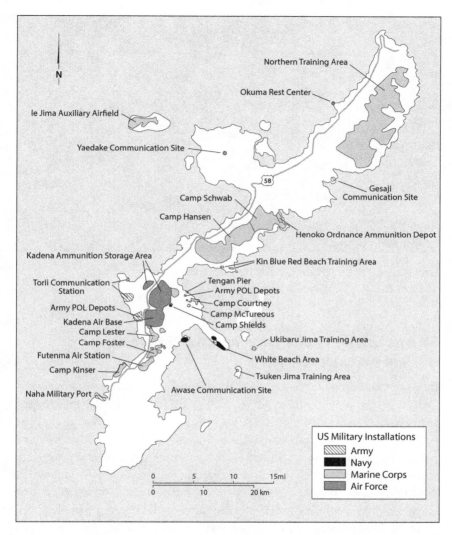

U.S. military bases in Okinawa. © Military Base Affairs Division Okinawa
Prefectural Government. Cartography by Bill Nelson.

next to Henoko's fishing port and Camp Schwab is now in its fourteenth year.
Yet many Henoko residents actually support the new base, believing that it will
help revitalize the economy. Increasingly, Henoko's contentious base-related politics have attracted international attention, adding to the visibility and contro-
versy surrounding intimate military-Okinawan relationships, particularly in
northern Okinawa.

Satellite view of Camp Schwab and new base construction, Henoko.
Imagery © 2018 Google, Map Data © 2018 ZENRIN

Theorizing Intimacy in the Spaces of American Empire

Intimate romantic and sexual relationships between U.S. military personnel and Okinawans confound the taken-for-granted spatial logic of the U.S. military and antibase activists. Emblemized by miles of barbed wire fences enclosing large tracts of land, U.S. military fencelines structure access to land, resources, and people. They also operate as diffuse sites of symbolic negotiation and struggle involving gender, race, class, and nation. Approaches that focus solely on physical fencelines tend to assume a self-evident distinction between on-base and off-base spaces and lives, confusing the effects of military spatial ideology with the messier realities of cohabitation and interaction. The concept of fencelines developed here is intended to capture the dual nature of military fences, as both physical barriers and conduits of militarization.

The U.S. military is depicted by policymakers and scholars alike as a national institution made up of discreet particle-like bases and installations. Military training, organizational hierarchies, and codes of conduct are contrasted with their civilian counterparts. Guarded entrance gates, standardized uniforms and housing, and even recreation and shopping all mark military spaces and lives as distinct and separate from civilian ones. Until recently, ethnographies of overseas U.S. bases have supported this insular model of the military, describing daily routines and relationships that are virtually identical to those one might find on bases in the United States (for example, Hawkins 2001). Experiences of living abroad, having special immigration status, being stationed far from friends and loved ones, encountering language barriers, trying new foods, and developing friendships with local people are absent from such accounts. Moreover, there is little discussion of how the global network of U.S. bases came into being. Despite contributions to the study of life within the confines of U.S. installations, work in this genre generally disregards the historical, political, economic, and social processes that shape relationships between on-base and off-base localities and people. Often such research ends up reproducing military spatial ideology and inadvertently reinforcing the claims of U.S. militarism.[8]

In Okinawa, too, it has been claimed that American service members and local people live in widely divergent social worlds (Yoshikawa 1996; Inoue 2007). Yet, more than eight thousand Okinawans work on the bases, where they come into daily contact with U.S. personnel and their families (LMO/IAA 2013).[9] Thousands more work in the off-base service economy catering to U.S. military consumers. Approximately thirty thousand receive rent money from the Japanese government for land occupied by U.S. forces (Arasaki 1986; Maher 2008).[10] Okinawans also encounter U.S. personnel at community events and family gatherings, since many have relatives who have dated or married U.S. military men. Indeed, many Okinawan bases sit in the midst of densely populated local communities, resulting in noise and frequent and sometimes deadly accidents. Nevertheless, their image as spaces apart is rarely questioned, having been created through what Mark Gillem calls the military's avoidance model, in which "simulacrums of suburbia" are constructed, "with guards and walls designed to keep out troublemakers . . . (and) avoid the entanglements of interaction" (2007, xvi).[11] Gillem's concept of "spillover" represents an attempt to track the impact of U.S. military culture on local host communities (including building codes, noise and accidents, and consumption patterns), yet the term evokes one-way flows of people and culture, from on-base to off-base locales, rather than the multilateral exchanges and interactions that characterize intimate relationships. Feminist scholars (e.g., Cheng 2010; Höhn and Moon 2010; Kina 2016) have taken a different approach, conceptualizing overseas bases as "borderlands," "contact zones," and "hybrid spaces," where U.S. service members and local people engage in the "coproduction of cultures," contributing to "the awkward, unequal, unstable, and creative qualities of interconnection across difference" (Cheng 2010, 27, quoting Anna Tsing). The latter approach encourages a consideration of military fencelines as more than just physical barriers.

Catherine Lutz's formulation of "militarization" directs attention to the porousness of military fencelines, as well as the historically contingent and unequal conditions that govern interactions between U.S. service members and local civilians. Lutz defines militarization as "the contradictory and tense social process in which civil society organizes itself for the production of violence" (2002, 723). Processes of militarization involve an intensification of labor and resources allocated to military purposes, but also "a discursive process, involving a shift in general societal beliefs and values in ways necessary to legitimate the use of force" (723). Lutz's approach integrates military and civilian sectors and paves the way for an examination of discursive and political-economic processes that permeate society. Ronni Alexander's (2016) discussion of U.S. military fences in Guam is another important precursor of the concept of fencelines developed here. Extending the term beyond the physical chain-links that surround U.S. installations, Guamanians refer to "the fence" when talking about militarized space in the abstract. For Guamanians, "the fence" "refers to a multiplicity of lines, most of which recreate a dichotomous view of military/local relations, and help to make invisible the complex web of identities and interactions that pass through, over, and beyond their real and imagined spaces" (Alexander 2016, 870). Using the phrase "the fence" explicitly marks a space as gendered, colonized, and militarized. Building on Alexander's formulation, fencelines here refers to sites of social and cultural negotiation and transformation by Okinawans and U.S. military personnel in interaction with one another. Military fencelines are shifting and permeable, sensitive to larger social, political, and economic trends, and a site of individual and group maneuvering.

In Okinawa and other places that host U.S. bases, intimate encounters and relationships are an important arena for such maneuvering. The term *intimacy* evokes a cluster of ideas including privacy, familiarity, love, sex, informality, and personal connection (Pratt and Rosner 2012). Although the term suggests emotions and experiences hidden away from the larger world and shared only by those on the inside, intimate relationships are in fact a useful vantage point for viewing the dynamics of power that pervade society at large. Within intimate relationships, it is possible to observe how the structuring of difference privileges some and marginalizes others, how social and legal institutions shape obligations and opportunity, and the extent to which interpersonal violence and abuse exist as mechanisms of control. At the same time, intimate relationships present opportunities for emotional connection, shared pleasure, personal commitment, and negotiation and compromise. Intimacy is ultimately a domain of power, permeated by repressive and emancipatory forces that construct private, proximate, and personal domains, while also extending into the public spheres of government and economy (Wilson 2012, 2016). Intimacy between U.S. service members and Okinawans is regulated by multiple state bureaucracies, which cooperate in establishing individuals' legal rights, statuses, and responsibilities, including eligibility to marry, residence options, and work opportunities. National and international citizenship law, the status of forces agreement, and U.S. and Japanese immigration and family law outline basic rights and responsibilities. General Orders of conduct, military marriage procedures, and military family regulations further empower local commanders to manage such relationships. The military thus actively structures and regulates opportunities for sexual and romantic encounters, desire for local-national Others, and interpretations of intimate relationships. Centered on disciplining the bodies, behaviors, and emotions of U.S. servicemen, these efforts amount to an impressive allocation of political and economic resources for purposes of biopolitical governance over U.S. personnel and host-country civilians. Yet neither the military nor the Japanese and U.S. governments are entirely successful at establishing control over intimate practices and emotions, particularly when these government bureaucracies overlap and compete with one another jurisdictionally. Military international couples manipulate existing contradictions and enjoy considerable flexibility due to their ambiguous status on either side of the fencelines.

Ann Stoler's work on European colonialism (e.g., 1989, 2002) highlights the use of biopolitical techniques of governance, including sexual prescriptions by race, class, and gender, to support colonial rule in Dutch Indonesia and French Indochina. Colonial officials scrutinized sexual behaviors and domestic arrangements—where and with whom people lived, what they ate, how they raised their children, and what language(s) they spoke within the home—as a means for distinguishing the categories of colonizer and colonized. Historically, distinctions between U.S. military personnel and Okinawans have been influenced by Japanese colonial discourses on civilization and development and American racial and class ideologies embodied in U.S. military protocols and practices. During the Vietnam War, for example, segregated military entertainment districts linked popular concepts of race to the regulation of sexual encounters with American GIs. Women working in entertainment districts were warned by bar owners and American customers to confine their relationships to either black men or white men. Many identified the women racially as well, as either black or white. Today, Okinawan women tend to emphasize their racial similarity to white Americans, while considering African Americans to be racially different. Yet, for many individuals and families, intimate experiences and emotions across the fencelines bridge or blur these racial distinctions. Within intimate encounters, as the stories in this book demonstrate, notions of race and class, self and other are reformulated as individuals strategically invoke the language of intimate interpersonal connection and commitment. Indeed, talk about intimacy—including stories of fate-filled first encounters, declarations of love (or worry or pain), disagreements with parents, frustration with bureaucracy, differing expectations for marriage and children, and the limits of compromise and commitment—is integral to the crafting of individual and social identities (Wardlow and Hirsch 2006). By invoking the trope of romantic love, for example, Okinawan women position themselves as agents capable of choosing partners who will help with the housework, support them in their careers, and value their sexual satisfaction, contrary to traditional gender and sexual norms. Embracing such modern identities, however, represents more than an emerging feminist awareness. It also suggests their capacity to join public debates on a range of sensitive issues, from the education of Amerasian children to relations between the U.S. bases and surrounding communities. Relationships that cross social boundaries thus create possibilities for political engagement and change. Okinawan women's and U.S. military men's stories about intimacy across the fencelines illustrate and intervene in the complex and changing connections between the broad-scale dynamics of rule and resistance and the intimate sites of implementation—what Stoler has referred to as "the affective grid of colonial politics" (2002, 7).

Researching Okinawa from the Margins

One week after the *eisā* festival described above, on the evening of September 11, 2001, as the first major typhoon of the season came ashore, U.S. military bases on Okinawa were placed on lockdown after the World Trade Center in New York and the Pentagon were attacked. The U.S. military television channel overlaid news coverage from the United States with a message that all installations were at Force Protection Level Delta, the highest state of alert. The message instructed all personnel to return home and await orders. The following weekend, the streets were devoid of U.S. service members. Okinawans discussed the impact of the events on islanders' safety and the local economy. Tourists from mainland Japan were canceling vacations in droves because they believed the prefecture to be a significant military target. They absolutely stayed away from the bases, heeding warnings and voicing concern about possible anthrax attacks. Before leaving the United States, I had secured permission from the U.S. Department of the Navy to conduct research on Marine Corps bases, but that approval was now in jeopardy. Worried that I would not be able to collect data in on-base settings, I stepped up networking in the Okinawan community and among retired and other former-military couples. As the International House staff had promised, I met dozens of international couples living in the northern region.

Six weeks later, groups of marines reappeared at community events, and soon after I was able to apply for a guest pass for Camp Schwab.[12] In late November, I made contact with the staff of Marine Corps Family Team Building at Camp Foster. After possibilities for on-base observation and interviewing opened up,

I was faced with what had developed into a two-pronged project: parallel investigations of younger active-duty couples and older retired or former-military couples—two groups of people who at first seemed very different. The active-duty families I met were in Okinawa temporarily, while the older couples were permanent. The active-duty couples were directly tied to global U.S. military networks, while the retirees were legal residents of Japan. Tracing the connections and tensions that existed between these two groups led me to examine the actual permeability of military fencelines that divide on-base and off-base spaces and lives. Ultimately, I conducted fieldwork throughout the main island of Okinawa, concentrating in Nago City and the northern region. Due to the unique history, culture, and political economy of Yanbaru (the sparsely populated and naturally abundant north) and Nago's status as center of the antibase struggle, my analysis likely reflects a different perspective on Okinawa and the U.S. military presence than one might acquire while residing in the more urbanized and heavily militarized central region. In northern Okinawa, military international couples are fewer in number. They are therefore highly conspicuous when visiting the grocery store or attending town meetings. However, their lives are also characterized by greater connection and reliance on the local community. Some American husbands are active-duty servicemen who have opted to live "out in town" rather than commute back and forth from the closest military family housing at Camp Courtney. Many are retired or separated from the U.S. military, having chosen not to reenlist. They have settled in the north in order to be close to their wives' families, take advantage of cheaper land and housing prices, or simply because they enjoy the laid-back pace and natural beauty of Yanbaru. Although generally known to each other and local townspeople, these couples tend to live outside of Okinawa's military base culture. They therefore represent a lacuna in studies of contemporary Okinawan society.[13]

Taken as a whole, the participants in this study have a wide range of experiences spanning five decades, much of the main island of Okinawa, and in some cases, years of living in the United States as well, reflecting the considerable diversity of intimate heterosexual relationships between U.S. service members and Okinawans. The following chapters explore differences across branches of service, rank, race, class, and historical era, along with discussions of military relationships versus other types of international marriage and marriage to mainland Japanese persons. The U.S. Army, Air Force, Marine Corps, and Navy all maintain installations and personnel in Okinawa, and Okinawan women are aware of such distinctions insofar as they affect funding for military family services and the treatment of foreign spouses. Thus airmen may be deemed more desirable marriage partners than marines because the Air Force offers higher stipends for married personnel and more programs for military families (such as ESL classes). Rank stratification, the gendered composition of forces, marital status, presence or absence of dependents, and length of tour further differentiate U.S. service members in local people's eyes. These factors, too, shape the symbolic fencelines that divide Okinawan society. The participants in this study were without exception involved in heterosexual relationships. I did gather anecdotal evidence of same-sex relationships between U.S. military personnel and Okinawans, but the resulting data and analysis reflect the predominant heteronormative relationship mode I encountered. Additional research is needed on other relationship modes and on the rare cases of U.S. military women who are intimately involved with Okinawan men.

Finally, while the stories in the book frequently touch on the experiences and concerns of Amerasian children fathered by U.S. servicemen, I conducted only limited firsthand research among such individuals. The insights offered here regarding biracial children are based on library research and limited interviews with social workers, educators, parents, and adult children. Interested readers are encouraged to consult the considerable English- and Japanese-language literature to learn more about the experiences and identity politics surrounding Amerasian children and others so intimately affected by the U.S. military presence (e.g., Uezato 1998; Murphy-Shigematsu 2002, 2012; Noiri 2003).

On Remaining Neutral

The element of research that I have struggled with most concerns the ways in which I have expressed (or failed to express) my stance with regard to the proposed new Marine Corps facility in Henoko. In recent years, I have led American undergraduates to Okinawa for short-term study abroad. In June 2016, our group arrived at a particularly sensitive time, following the rape and murder of a young Okinawan woman by a U.S. military contractor earlier that spring and a drunk-driving accident the previous week in which a sailor had collided head-on with two other vehicles. Anticipating popular outrage, the military had instituted curfews, movement restrictions, and a ban on drinking alcohol off base. While the timing enabled my students to learn about Okinawa's precarious political situation, I worried that any behavioral misstep might damage the relationships that I had worked to build with local people and organizations.

Midway through the visit, our group spent the afternoon at Henoko Beach with a prominent antibase activist, a longtime friend and colleague. We discussed the construction plan for the proposed Marine Corps facility and how it would impact nearby residential districts and the coastline. Then, prompted by curiosity about the antibase movement itself, I asked, "How does a hometown boy like yourself survive in this town in the midst of the base debate? How does one oppose (or support) the base without losing friends, without cutting yourself off from family members?" Taking a moment, he answered: "Well, I think, perhaps, you need to have a thick face . . . I mean a thick skin." He talked about the many times that he has overheard whispering as he entered the room and the not-so-kind remarks about his putting politics before family. He told us that he regularly backs away from arguments and softens his stance in order to preserve relationships. Once he was even asked by probase organizers to help translate their materials into English—and he agreed. The students chuckled at the slip, "thick face" instead of "thick skin," assuming that it was merely a momentary misremembering of an English idiomatic expression by a non-native speaker. I suspect, however, that the slip was due to the simultaneous recall of a Japanese expression, *tsura no kawa ga atsui* ("to have thick face-skin"). A person is said to have thick face-skin if they are cheeky, impudent, audacious, impossible to embarrass, or attention seeking, much like the English term brazen (Ervin-Tripp, Nakamura, and Guo 1995, 54). The phrase can be used to describe a person who borrows money but never returns it, a person who accepts food on the first offer, a person who doesn't notice when it's time to leave, or a student who participates too much in

Camp Schwab fence, Henoko. Photo by the author.

class. The slip—"thick face" rather than "thick skin"—it turns out, tells us quite a lot about social norms in northern Okinawa.

At the start of my research, I was extremely sensitive to community prohibitions against having a "thick face." Having grown up in a rural community on the east coast of the United States, I recognized (or imagined that I did) the clues that others provided, observing the frequency of indirect communication and strong rebukes leveled at those who expressed their opinions too assertively. I observed especially how the base issue turned easy conversations into social minefields, and I often felt pressure to appear politically neutral. After a number of uncomfortable encounters, I developed what was to become my routine response to base-related talk, based on my upbringing: I smiled and nodded, and kept my opinions to myself. This turned out to be a productive research strategy that allowed me to elicit data from individuals on both sides of the issue. Moreover, it was a strategy that was familiar and acceptable to local people, who also held their tongues in order to avoid conflict.

However, remaining neutral also implies support for the status quo, a status quo in which the voices of Okinawans are routinely silenced or ignored by the Japanese and U.S. governments and the U.S. military. In the introduction to *Anthropology and the Colonial Encounter*, Talal Asad argued, "The process of European global power has been central to the anthropological task of recording and analyzing the ways of life of subject populations, even when a serious consideration of that power was theoretically excluded. It is not merely that anthropological fieldwork was facilitated by European colonial power . . . ; it is that the fact of European power, as discourse and practice, was always part of the reality anthropologists sought to understand, and of the way they sought to understand it" (1991, 315). Thirty years later, Engseng Ho (2004) suggested that Asad's critique be extended to American anthropology conducted in the context of U.S. empire. Although I still find it utterly dissatisfying, the reality is that in Okinawa, anthropologists and local people must negotiate relationships within the framework of multiple and overlapping exclusions that characterize local base politics and community life. This is inescapable. I have tried to be fair to all who spoke with me, while taking a critical approach to the politics involving intimate military relationships and popular representations of such intimacy—all the while recognizing that my own positionality, worldview, and influence as a white American female anthropologist have shaped the research and manuscript in elusive ways.

Layout of the Chapters

The chapters of this book analyze narratives of U.S. military-Okinawan intimacy against the backdrop of Okinawan history, culture, politics, and economy. Chapter 1 explores military international intimacy in Okinawa in relation to military fencelines and changing community norms, especially regarding marriage, family, and community membership. Since the nineteenth century, Okinawan families and communities have undergone tremendous change due to modernization and assimilation programs initiated by Japan's imperial government, displacement due to war and U.S. military land expropriations, and recent integration into global economic and communications networks. Opportunities for intimacy, notions of appropriate romantic partners, residence and household membership, and responsibilities for childcare and eldercare have shifted accordingly. In connection with this history, marriages to individuals from different villages, Okinawa's outlying islands, and mainland Japan have been frowned upon. But since 1945, hostility to marriages involving U.S. military personnel has been especially acute. The discussion situates military international marriage with respect to other types of "marrying out" in Okinawa, as well as international marriage in mainland Japan. I explore community perceptions of military international marriage in relation to symbolic fencelines that shape changing distinctions among insiders and outsiders and notions of appropriate marriage partners. Through an examination of common themes and narrative strategies that Okinawans employ when speaking of military international relationships and other forms of "marrying out," including the trope of romantic love, the analysis reveals spaces for creative self-fashioning as couples assert the legitimacy of their relationships and challenge existing social boundaries.

Chapters 2 and 3 explore the impact of Okinawan memories of war and occupation on popular stereotypes of American men, Okinawan women, and military international intimacy. Racialized historical imagery is often used to police the boundaries that separate Americans, Okinawans, and mainland Japanese and is also key to the negotiation and reproduction of contemporary understandings of race, class, and sexuality. Chapter 2 explores Okinawan discourses on race and military men's sexuality, with a focus on how Japanese and American racial discourses have shaped local understandings of difference. During the prewar period, Okinawans were gradually incorporated into Japanese imperial hierarchies of race, ethnicity, and nation to claim an ambiguous membership in the Japanese *minzoku* (race, ethnic group, nation). Imperial rhetoric positioned Okinawans and other Asians—and at times all "colored peoples"—alongside the Japanese in unified opposition to Europeans and Americans. During the postwar occupation, the U.S. military and its personnel introduced into Okinawa discourses on U.S.

imperialism in Asia, Jim Crow–era segregation, and the 1960s civil rights and black power movements. These discourses have been variously embraced, resisted, and reinterpreted by Okinawans. The chapter features the personal narratives of individuals who self-consciously viewed their relationships as transgressing established racial boundaries. Their stories illustrate the struggle of military international couples to understand and rework racial ideologies and expectations in Okinawa's postwar society.

Chapter 3 pivots away from discourses on race and U.S. military men to explore corresponding discourses on sexual propriety and class respectability used to police Okinawan women's behavior. Accounts of women who married during the early postwar period differ from those who married after reversion in 1972, reflecting Okinawa's changing economic circumstances and a reworking and reimagining of class. Stories included in the chapter demonstrate the broader and deeply personal impacts of shifting notions of class, made visible through the lenses of gender and intimate relationships. Occupation-era discourses on moral purity and contamination and discourses that prescribe respectable behavior are most meaningful to older women. Postreversion stereotypes, including the popular image of the *amejo* (a woman who consumes American men), reveal changing formulations of class related to processes of political and economic integration and marginalization within Japan. In response to negative imagery and stereotypes, Okinawan military wives exercise agency through redirecting negative imagery onto various racial and class Others, including mainland Japanese women and Filipinas. This approach, however, often reproduces the very discourses that marginalize military international couples and their children.

Chapter 4 examines the complex procedures known as the "marriage package." During the early 2000s, marriage package procedures were required by U.S. Marine Corps headquarters in Washington as the only legitimate means for marines and navy corpsmen to legalize a marriage in Japan. The process has been streamlined in recent years. Nevertheless it remains an instructive and relevant ethnographic example for understanding the nature of U.S. military and Japanese and U.S. government regulation of intimate relationships. The analysis focuses on institutional representations of marriage and family found in official documents and the mandatory premarital seminar, and how those were received, resisted, or reformulated by service members and their spouses. I examine the impact of institutional discourses on service members' expressions of military affinity and affiliation, and the voices of Okinawan spouses as they articulated subject positions markedly different from their feminist counterparts in the antibase movement. Against the backdrop of Okinawa's postwar political and economic marginalization, the marriage package aimed to recast social and political inequalities inherent in the U.S. military presence in less threatening idioms of gender, marriage, and family. The effectiveness of the marriage package in structuring such notions lay in its focus on the most intimate and personal details of service members' behaviors and relationships. Yet even the military's considerable leverage in imposing official notions of the intimate and private, personal, and professional responsibility had limits, which are explored in detail in this chapter.

Chapter 5 examines strategies that military-Okinawan couples employ to navigate life across the fencelines and achieve acceptance for themselves and their children. Active-duty couples living in central Okinawa, especially young Okinawan women who make use of military family services such as the Camp Foster International Spouse Program, may successfully integrate into the U.S. military community. However, military resources tend to cluster on the mid-island bases, where multiyear accompanied tours and family housing are available. For unmarried couples, retired personnel, and those who have left the military, such resources may be more difficult to procure. Couples in northern Okinawa, without access to or living far from the mid-island bases, tend to rely more on Okinawan family and community organizations for support. By strategically invoking normative discourses on family and community and taking advantage of the actual flexibility of Okinawan family and community models, many couples successfully manipulate these tenets of Okinawan culture and tap resources across the fencelines. The stories in this chapter illustrate how couples struggle to balance commitments to the military, extended family, and local community, conform to American and Okinawan cultural expectations, and contend with challenges to their relationship from both sides of the fences. This sort of maneuvering affects long-term chances for intimate relationships, as well as popular attitudes toward military dating and marriage, biracial children, and broader formulations of Okinawan and U.S. military community. As several stories demonstrate, persons engaging in intimate relationships across military fencelines have the capacity to influence U.S. military–host community relationships and politics in even the most contentious locales.

The conclusion summarizes arguments concerning the shifting and negotiated nature of military fencelines in Okinawa. Due to the ongoing antibase movement, intimate everyday effects of the U.S. military presence, including military international sex, marriage, and family, attract popular scrutiny and become subject to military and community surveillance and regulation. The adeptness with which military couples circumvent official definitions and control by crossing military fencelines reveals the limits of state institutional power and U.S. military empire.

INTERNATIONAL MARRIAGE IN JAPAN'S PERIPHERY

Popularly referred to as the "Gateway to Yanbaru," Nago City (population 62,868) is an administrative unit encompassing a number of towns and villages separated by sugarcane and pineapple fields and large stretches of mountainous subtropical forest scattered between the east and west coasts of Okinawa's main island. It connects to Naha and other cities to the south by two commercial highways that hug the coastlines and the Okinawa Expressway, a more direct high-speed toll road completed in 1975. Nago town, the administrative seat of Nago City, overlooks Nago Bay on the west coast of the island and has been an important market town and commercial hub since the fourteenth century. Today, Highway 58 is the town's central artery, lined with grocery stores and fast-food restaurants, large franchises selling books and music, and the ever-present convenience store. In contrast, the streets of the old town center contain the occasional bar or "snack," family-owned household goods and soba shops, and more than a few vacant storefronts. While fishing, agriculture, and animal husbandry continue to be important, Nago is also home to the Orion Brewing Company, a cement manufacturing plant, a number of sugar refineries, a regional hospital, an agricultural college, and Meio University. In other words, Nago's primary identity is not that of a "base town."

In 1996, however, the Japanese government announced plans to build a new U.S. Marine Corps helicopter base in the Henoko district, a small settlement on the Pacific coast, across the mountains from central Nago. Henoko has hosted U.S. Marine Corps Camp Schwab and the Henoko Ordnance Ammunition Depot since 1957, when the community (then part of Kushi village) became the first municipality in Okinawa to voluntarily lease lands to the U.S. military for base construction. During the Vietnam era, the hilltop neighborhood adjacent to the base was transformed into a thriving entertainment district featuring restaurants, camera stores, pawnshops, bars, and brothels. Entering this neighborhood in the early 2000s, one was struck by the ghostly remnants of occupation-era prosperity. A large rust-stained sign reading "*Yōkoso Henoko shakōgai e*" ("Welcome to the Henoko entertainment quarter") and "WEL COME BAR St." was followed by rows of concrete buildings bearing faded lettering proclaiming the names of bars, tailors, and pizzerias, long abandoned or transformed into private homes.

Since 1996, this out-of-the-way corner of Okinawa has become the frontline of the struggle to contain and ultimately oust the U.S. military presence from the prefecture. As such, it is a mecca for activists and protesters from Okinawa Prefecture, mainland Japan, and around the world, who come to support the local opposition by manning the protest tent that stands on the beach next to Henoko's fishing port, and participating in ocean-based kayak protests and sit-ins outside the gates of Camp Schwab. The prevalence of outsiders in the movement rankles some Henoko residents who have close economic and personal ties to the base. Hank and Mutsuko Megason have lived in the hilltop neighborhood next to Camp Schwab since 1982. After retiring from the Marine Corps, Hank took a civilian position at Camp Schwab, and the couple built a three-story house on land owned by Mutsuko's mother. In recent years, the two have played an important role in Henoko's probase community network, made up of small business owners, construction and transportation workers, cashiers, and other wage earners (Inoue 2007). Mutsuko has held leadership positions in local women's organizations at various levels, while Hank volunteers as an interpreter for community events and organizations aimed at bringing together Okinawan residents and U.S. troops.[1] Hank and Mutsuko are not the only U.S. military-Okinawan couple residing in Henoko. Stew Brown lives with his wife, also Okinawan, across the bridge in a neighborhood bordering Kushi district. After fulfilling his enlistment and leaving the Marine Corps, Stew worked a series of odd construction jobs and then signed on for a temporary gig at the Toyota plant in mainland Japan. After returning to Okinawa, he ran the kitchen at a factory that produced *shima-dōfu* (island tofu) for a few months. When we met in October 2001, he was captaining charter boats for Marine Corps Community Services out of Camp Schwab. Hosing off a fleet of rental kayaks, Stew claimed to have little knowledge of or contact with antibase protestors in Henoko and expressed little interest in the tense political situation. Quickly dismissing my questions, he suggested that concerns and divisions within the Okinawan community were only incidental to his own life. Hank and Mutsuko, on the other hand, interacted frequently with business leaders and politicians in Henoko and Nago and were themselves involved in local base-related politics.

Entrance to former entertainment district, Henoko. Photo by the author.

Military fencelines structure the lives of these couples and others living in Nago City and throughout Okinawa. The communities they live in, whether remote mountain villages or congested urban zones surrounding the mid-island bases, are crisscrossed by physical barbed wire fences, along with symbolic fencelines, sites of negotiation and struggle involving gender, race, class, and nation. Okinawa's fence-lines are a product of shifting local, national, and international history and politics alongside everyday economic transactions, social interactions, and cultural beliefs developed within the contexts of Japanese colonialism, war, postwar U.S. occupa-tion, and continuing militarization. Although Stew Brown imagined himself to be largely unaffected by base-related community politics and sentiments, his lifestyle was entirely contingent upon the U.S. military presence and terms of the status of

Former entertainment district, Henoko. Photo by the author.

forces agreement, which structured his residency, career opportunities, and social networks. Furthermore, as a white American man and former member of the U.S. military married to a local woman, he stood for a particular kind of politically privileged yet economically and socially marginal person in the eyes of many Nago residents. Even Hank Megason repeatedly referred to "those guys" who live in Okinawa but never try to outgrow their dependence on the bases, learn the language, or integrate into Okinawan family and community networks.

This chapter sketches the broad contours of military international intimacy in Nago City and across Okinawa in relation to military fencelines and changing community norms, especially regarding marriage, family, and community. Since the nineteenth century, Okinawan families and communities have changed dramatically due to government modernization and assimilation programs, outmigration and growth of the Okinawan diaspora, war and confiscation of land by the U.S. military, and integration into the global economy. Opportunities for intimacy, ideas concerning appropriate romantic partners, residence and household membership, and responsibilities for childcare, eldercare, and care of the family altar have shifted accordingly. In connection with this history, marriages to individuals from different villages, Okinawa's outer islands, and mainland Japan have been frowned upon. But since 1945, marriages involving U.S. military personnel have sparked strong community opposition due to their symbolic association with colonialism, foreign occupation, and continuing marginalization within Japan. The chapter discusses military international marriage in relation to other types of "marrying out" in Okinawa, as well as international marriage in mainland Japan. I argue that community perceptions of military international marriage are best understood in relation to symbolic fencelines—some associated with the U.S. military presence and others based on prewar and wartime experiences of Japanese colonialism and the Ryūkyū Kingdom—that shape distinctions among "insiders" and "outsiders" and notions of appropriate marriage partners. Examining the narrative strategies Okinawans employ when speaking of military international relationships and other forms of "marrying out," the analysis reveals the many creative ways in which couples assert the legitimacy of their relationships and challenge social norms.

International Marriage in Okinawa versus Mainland Japan

In 2015, the rate of international marriage throughout Japan was 3.3 percent (20,976 of 635,156 total marriages). In Tokyo, one in twenty marriages was a mixed union; in Osaka, the number was one in twenty-five (Japanese Ministry of Health, Labour and Welfare 2016). Although international marriages make up a small fraction of overall marriages, they have increased significantly during the past half century. In 1965, there were only 4,156 international marriages, but the number rose steadily until peaking at 44,701 in 2006 (Nippon.com 2015).[2] As early as the 1970s, municipal governments in rural mainland Japan began recruiting brides from other Asian nations (such as China, Korea, and the Philippines) in an effort to alleviate a shortage of eligible single women caused by the outflow of young Japanese women to larger cities (Asakura 2002).[3] Although the number of international marriages has declined in recent years, the media continues to feature stories about the lives of international couples, feeding popular interest.[4]

In Japanese, the phrase *kokusai-kekkon* (international marriage) refers to conjugal relationships between Japanese persons and persons from foreign countries.[5] Despite media claims that *kokusai-kekkon* is contributing to the formation of a new multiethnic Japan (Curtin 2002a; *Japan Times* 2002), scholars have argued that in Japan discourses on international marriage, like those associated with internationalization (*kokusaika*),[6] "reinscribe notions of Japanese ethnic and cultural homogeneity by marking nationality as the primary index of difference" (Faier 2009, 3; see also Befu 1983). That is, they reinforce the conceptual division of the world's people into two major categories: Japanese and foreigners. In Okinawa, however, the phrase *kokusai-kekkon* carries additional meanings. Compared to other Japanese prefectures, Okinawa reports consistently high rates of international marriage, although not as high as urban centers like Tokyo and Osaka. Moreover, while more than 70 percent of international marriages nationwide are between Japanese men and foreign women, in Okinawa nearly 80 percent involve Japanese women with foreign men. In 2015, a typical year, a stunning 86.8 percent of foreign grooms in Okinawa were American, with most affiliated with the U.S. military (Japanese Ministry of Health, Labour and Welfare 2016).[7] What is more, in addition to marriages with citizens of foreign countries, the phrase *kokusai-kekkon* is also used to refer to marriages between Okinawans and persons from mainland Japan, a dramatic illustration of perceptions of historical variance and racial/ethnic difference from mainlanders.

To illustrate, in 2002 I was invited to give a talk on international marriage at the monthly tea time of a Nago City housewives group. I had been living in Nago for nearly eight months and already knew several members of the group, including the mayor's wife, a past president of the Nago City Women's Association, the wife of the director of the Nago City International House, and Mutsuko Megason, introduced above. These middle-class women were well known throughout the northern region based on their marriages to prominent men and their own volunteer activities. Over tea and snacks, they conducted a brief business meeting and then invited me to speak. After my presentation, the group leader asked Shirota-san, a housewife from nearby Motobu, to comment on her own experiences as a *naichi no kata* (person from mainland Japan; polite) married to an Okinawan man. The phrase *naichi no kata* is a holdover from the Japanese colonial period (1879–1945), when the imperial government maintained an administrative and social distinction between Japanese citizens from the *naichi* (inner territories) and imperial subjects from the *gaichi* (outer territories or colonies). Although Okinawa was technically classified as part of the *naichi*—that is, its governance did not fall under the Bureau of Colonial Affairs (Christy 1993)—Okinawans tended to be excluded from the term *naichi* in popular usage (Morris-Suzuki 1998). As Shirota-san's example illustrates, many Okinawans continue to recognize this distinction, and discussions of *kokusai-kekkon* are convenient opportunities for pointing out mainlanders' continuing outsider status and lack of cultural competence in Okinawa. Shirota-san, who had met her husband while on vacation in Okinawa twenty-five years earlier, admitted that Okinawan language and customs associated with caring for the household altar and family tomb were difficult to master. Her husband was a *chōnan* (eldest son), and this meant that as his wife she would inherit responsibility for carrying out family rituals and organizing family gatherings. Referred to as *yamatunchu-yome* (Yamato, or mainland Japanese, brides) in Okinawan dialect, mainland Japanese women who marry Okinawan men are considered foreigners of sorts, and their marriages are therefore viewed as examples of *kokusai-kekkon* (Ishizuki 2001; Ueno 2001). In mainland Japanese discourses, generally speaking, foreigners embody notions of *soto* (outside) in contrast to Japan's *uchi* (inside).[8] In Japanese print advertising, for example, images of racially diverse foreign Others figure importantly in the process through which a homogenous Japanese national self is constructed (Creighton 1997). More specifically, the racial and cultural diversity of imagined foreign Others constitutes a projection of Japanese heterogeneity onto the outside world, thereby preserving the illusion of racial and ethnic homogeneity *within* Japan (Creighton 1997). Okinawan approaches to *kokusai-kekkon*, however, inclusive of marriages of Okinawans to mainland Japanese, undermine this tenet of Japanese national ideology, supporting instead a noncompliant formulation of Okinawan identity based on regional cultural distinctiveness and a history of Japanese colonialism and suppression of Okinawan language and culture.

Military international marriages in Okinawa also complicate Japanese notions of *kokusai-kekkon* because they contradict the typical gendered pattern of international unions. Nationwide, more than 70 percent of international marriages involve Japanese men with foreign women. This pattern is even more pronounced for certain nationalities. In 2015, for example, more than 95 percent of marriages between Japanese and citizens of the Philippines were between Japanese men and Filipina women. The pattern is reversed in marriages where the non-Japanese partner is from North America, western Europe, or Australia. In 2015, 85 percent of marriages to Americans and 84 percent of marriages to U.K. citizens involved Japanese women marrying foreign men. Until recently, much of the scholarship on international marriage in Japan has focused on just such cases, examining the appeal that Western lifestyles, and especially Western men, have for Japanese women (Cornyetz 1994; Russell 1998; Kelsky 2001).[9] Karen Kelsky's analysis of Japanese women's eroticized discourses on Western men, in which the foreign is sought out and incorporated in a process of self-transformation, has been influential among those interested in women's agency. Sex with foreign men, Kelsky argues, has the potential to free Japanese women from the confines of traditional Japanese gender roles (Kelsky 2001). Women's participation in such discourses— popularly tagged with the Japanese term *akogare*, translated variously as "longing," "desire," or "idealization" of the West—thus constitutes an act of resistance against Japanese patriarchal norms. The space of the foreign, Kelsky writes, "offers those women inclined to use it . . . the means to radically challenge persistent gender ideologies that make authentic Japanese womanhood (and the stability of the Japanese nation) contingent on women's continued subordination to Japanese men and 'traditional' gender roles" (Kelsky 2001, 3). However, as Kelsky points out, Japanese women's celebration of white Western male sexuality simultaneously plays into colonialist narratives that position the "Orient" as inferior to the West. Situated within global relations of power, Japanese women's desire for the West is already constituted through hegemonic discourses that posit the West, imagined as both male and white, as *the* object of desire.[10] Kelsky describes numerous encounters with Japanese women married to white Western men who objected to her research, demanding, "How can you claim that race has anything to do with my relationship? I love X because he is X, not because he is white!" (Kelsky 2001, 145–146). She concludes that discourses of love and romance function in this instance to disarm potential scrutiny of the gender, racial, and sexual politics of Japanese women's internationalism. Thus even women who self-consciously inhabit border zones characterized by multiple languages and cultures participate, intentionally or not, in discourses that police national, racial, and class boundaries. As Kelsky and others argue, mainland Japanese women's discourses on romantic liaisons with Western men primarily concern gender inequalities *within* Japanese society. The symbolic power of the foreigner is invoked, but there is no real attempt to bridge national-cultural divides. Black men in particular are denied any meaningful subjectivity (Russell 1998).

This literature suggests that mainland Japanese discourses on international sex and marriage continue to circumscribe Japanese national and racial identity and difference, but relationships between Okinawan women and U.S. military men do not replicate these same discursive patterns. In Okinawa, assertions of regional cultural distinctiveness and a history of colonialism and marginalization within the Japanese nation-state complicate the simple Japanese/foreigner dualism found in mainland discourses, profoundly reconfiguring the racial, national, and cultural ideologies that this dichotomy anchors. Teasing out the various strands of Okinawan discourses on military international intimacy and other forms of "marrying out," including how they articulate with historically constructed fencelines, requires knowledge of Okinawan history and the multilayered and shifting categories of insider and outsider that such discourses draw on in Okinawa today.

Okinawa: A History of Marginalization and Difference

Today, Okinawa is the poorest prefecture in Japan, with an average per capita income that is just 76 percent of the national average (Japanese Ministry of Health, Labour and Welfare 2014b) and an unemployment rate of 5.1 percent, compared to the national rate of 3.4 percent (Japanese Ministry of Internal Affairs and

Communication 2015). Okinawa is also the prefecture with the highest birth rate, the highest divorce rate, the lowest rate of industrial production, and the lowest scores on national achievement tests (Japanese Ministry of Internal Affairs and Communication 2016). However, for many Okinawans, the most egregious indicator of Okinawan marginalization is the continuing presence within the prefecture of 70.6 percent of the U.S. military bases in Japan (Mie 2016). Historically, Okinawan marginalization has been framed as a matter of local racial/ethnic difference that jostles problematically alongside a national ideology proclaiming Japanese racial and cultural homogeneity. The "Okinawan problem" first emerged during the late nineteenth century as part of the projects of Japanese colonialism, nation-building, and modernity.

The Ryūkyū archipelago was first consolidated into a unified kingdom in 1429 by King Shō Hashi of Chūzan (Middle Mountain), the most powerful of three major Ryukyuan principalities during the Sanzan (Three Mountains) period (1314–1429).[11] Maintaining a tributary relationship with Ming China initiated in 1372, Ryūkyū trading vessels traveled to China, Korea, Japan, and Southeast Asia, while a distinctive court culture developed at home. In the early seventeenth century, the Japanese shogun Tokugawa Ieyasu consolidated power in Japan and, although he had no legitimate claim to Ryūkyū, placed the islands under the control of the Shimazu clan, rulers of Japan's Satsuma feudal domain. When the Ryukyuan king, Shō Nei, failed to demonstrate proper submission, Ieyasu authorized Shimazu leaders to send a military expedition to force compliance. On May 6, 1609, Satsuma troops seized Shuri Castle. Shō Nei was taken to Kagoshima, where he was forced to formally surrender and declare allegiance to the Shimazu. For the next two and a half centuries, Satsuma imposed heavy taxes and directed from behind the scenes Ryūkyū's ongoing tribute trade with China. With the restoration of Japanese imperial rule in 1868, the new Meiji government claimed Ryūkyū as a protectorate of Japan and its residents as Japanese subjects. In 1872, the kingdom was reconfigured as Ryūkyū *han* (feudal domain), well after Japan's other domains were disbanded and reorganized as prefectures, suggesting the reluctance of the Meiji government to deal with Ryukyuans on equal footing with other Japanese. In 1875, however, in response to Ryūkyū's persistence in maintaining diplomatic ties with China, administrative oversight of the domain was transferred from the Foreign Ministry to the Home Ministry, and on March 11, 1879, the kingdom was politically dismantled and incorporated into the Japanese state as Okinawa Prefecture. The last Ryukyuan king, Shō Tai, abdicated upon orders of Tokyo and relocated to mainland Japan where he was given the title of *kōshaku* (marquess), a second-tier noble in Japan's *kazoku* peerage system. The capital was moved from Shuri to Naha, and mainland Japanese elites were appointed to oversee the new prefectural government.

Ryukyuan aristocrats continued to petition China's Qing government to intercede until Japan's military defeat of China in 1895. Tokyo responded with an aggressive assimilation plan designed to reorient Okinawans away from China and toward Japan. Political-economic reforms—including the privatization of communal property (1898–1903), the extension of national conscription laws (1898), the establishment of universal education (1890), and the holding of prefectural and national assembly elections (1909 and 1912, respectively)—were coupled with a campaign to reform the Okinawan character. "Supposed heavy alcohol consumption, walking barefoot, Ryukyuan women's clothing, a preponderance of dialects . . . , 'lazy men and overworked women', and Okinawan music were all taken together as the image of the 'loose Okinawan lifestyle' and visible signs of backwardness" (Christy 1993, 613). Okinawans were encouraged to abandon Ryukyuan kimono and hairstyles for mainland dress, and change the pronunciation of their names to mainland variants. Formal education in Japanese language was an integral component of the government's assimilation efforts, and students caught speaking Ryukyuan languages at school were punished.[12] Linda Angst (2001) has noted the gendered consequences of the assimilation program. While many village leaders supported mandatory schooling and urged parents to send their children to classes, few took issue with the common practice of assigning infant-care responsibilities to young daughters. Angst's interviewees recalled walking to school with infant siblings strapped to their backs and being made to sit outside when the infant fussed. It was also common for girls to drop out of school to do farm work or work in the homes of wealthier families. The belief that education was primarily intended for boys resulted in the steady integration of Okinawan men as modernizing subjects of imperial Japan, while women continued to be relegated to the realm of the traditional, backward, and premodern (Angst 2001; Barske 2013).

Japanese and Okinawan ethnological and philological studies further grounded Okinawa within Japan's cultural sphere by claiming a common origin for Japanese and Okinawan languages and culture. Okinawan folklorist Iha Fuyū—recognized today as the founder of Okinawan studies—was a leading proponent of the theory of common Japanese-Ryukyuan ancestry (Tomiyama 1998; Beillevaire 1999; Barske 2013). Mainland folklorists Yanagita Kunio and Yanagi Sōetsu searched for clues regarding archaic Japanese culture in the beliefs and behaviors of Okinawans (Harootunian 1998). Although these scholars viewed Okinawa as "a valuable 'missing link,' as the cultural repository of a nation threatened by the encroachments of modernity" (Molasky 1999, 193), their research was appropriated to serve imperialist ends. Viewed through the lens of social Darwinism, Okinawans were recast as premodern survivals from an earlier stage of Japan's evolution, in need of guidance to achieve proper development.[13]

Meanwhile, mainland discourses on Okinawan racial difference suggested that Okinawans were not Japanese at all and should instead be grouped with Taiwanese, Koreans, and other colonized peoples. Racialized descriptions of Okinawans, some derogatory and others nostalgic, contained references to Okinawans' shorter stature, darker skin, fuller chest, and rounder eyes. Imperial racial ideologies were evident in the so-called Human Pavilion incident (*jinruikan jiken*) at the 1903 Domestic Industrial Exhibition in Osaka, where two Okinawan women were displayed alongside Ainu and other ethnic minorities from Japan and Asia. The display provoked angry protests from Okinawan residents of Osaka and journalists for the newspaper *Ryūkyū Shimpō* in Okinawa, eventually leading to withdrawal of the Okinawans from the exhibit (Christy 1993; Rabson 1996; Ziomek 2014). Viewed retrospectively, the Human Pavilion incident has been analyzed as an illustration of Japanese orientalism, an attempt to establish Japan as civilized through the display of supposedly primitive others. Scholars focusing on Okinawan protest against the Human Pavilion point out that protestors objected to their own inclusion in the exhibit but not to the exhibit itself. As Steve Rabson (1996) explains, "It was not colonialism in itself that they objected to, but the idea of being placed in the same category as those who were not 'true Japanese.'"

In 1921, prices for Okinawa's principal cash crop, sugar—an industry developed at the urging of Japanese officials—plummeted. The sudden drop in prices hurt farmers first, eventually leading to the closure of businesses and the failure of banks. Unable to collect taxes, the Okinawa prefectural government went bankrupt (Tsunami et al. 2001, 27). The effects of the collapse were exacerbated by Japanese government policies that left Okinawan sugar producers exposed to the market after the government invested instead in the development of sugar plantations in Japan's newest colony, Taiwan (Rabson 2003). Many Okinawans avoided starvation by eating the seeds and trunk fibers of the cycad palm, which had to be specially prepared to avoid food poisoning. Hundreds of thousands migrated to Osaka and other Japanese cities, Japan's overseas territories, and Hawaii, North America, and South America. In mainland Japan, where migrants sought employment in factories and textile mills, they faced widespread discrimination, including denial of lodging and employment (Christy 1993; Rabson 1996, 2003). Pressures to assimilate caused many to abandon Okinawan languages, religious observances, and diet. Many Okinawan elites were complicit in the government's efforts to "Japanize" the population during this period (Christy 1993; Rabson 1996; Tomiyama 1998). Journalist Ōta Chōfu, for example, insisted that "We must even sneeze as the Japanese do" in order to be accepted as the equals of mainland Japanese (Rabson 1996). However, members of the upper classes suffered severe hardship alongside other Okinawans during the Pacific War.

In the months leading up to the U.S. invasion of Okinawa, the Japanese military mobilized thousands of civilians to build airfields and other fortifications and to participate alongside Japanese soldiers in combat. Beginning in the second half of 1943, male students from the Okinawa Normal School, the top boys' secondary school, were organized into the *tekketsu kinnōtai* (Imperial Blood and Iron Student Corps). Female students from Okinawa Women's Normal School and First Prefectural Girls High School were trained as nurses and assigned to medical units of nearby army field hospitals (Martin 1984; Angst 1997). In late 1944, all males ages seventeen to forty-five were conscripted for the local Defense Corps, and in January 1945, the Japanese army mobilized all secondary school students in the prefecture as soldiers or paramilitary personnel (Tsunami et al. 2001, 52–53). Approximately seventy thousand civilians evacuated to Kyushu or Taiwan, and thousands more took refuge in the mountainous northern region of the island, especially after the Allied aerial bombardment of Naha on October 10, 1944, which killed one thousand residents and left fifty thousand homeless (Molasky 1999). Others left their homes and traveled southward, taking refuge in family tombs or seaside caves. Mutsuko Megason's mother fled north from her home in Kadena with Mutsuko's older brother, who was just three years old. Mutsuko was born on April 10, 1945, in a cave where her mother and brother had taken shelter in the Haneji area north of Nago. American forces landed at the Hagushi beaches on the west coast of Okinawa's main island on April 1, 1945. The battle, referred to as a "typhoon of steel," dragged on for three months, wreaking catastrophic devastation that altered the landscape and killed more than 200,000 people, including more than 120,000 Okinawans (Ota 1984; Tsunami et al. 2001, 81). As they advanced northward and southward, the Americans placed Okinawans into resettlement camps, roughly forty of which were established for civilians, with separate facilities for POWs. Michael Molasky has written about the everyday intimacy that developed between Okinawans and U.S. servicemen in the camps. "Unlike the vast majority of postwar Japanese, whose principal contact with American soldiers had been restricted to public spaces, those on the island of Okinawa virtually lived with the American occupiers until their release from the camps. They ate Spam, biscuits, dried ice cream, and other food products contained in 'K-rations,' and they drank powdered milk, smoked Lucky Strikes, and wore HBTs (herringbone twill jackets distributed to those who had no clothes). Children attended school in Quonset huts, which eventually replaced 'blue-sky classrooms' of the early occupation days" (1999, 19). Following the suicide of Japanese military commander Ushijima on June 23, military resistance ceased. Although some residents left the camps and returned home in late 1945, extensive devastation of houses and farmland forced most to remain until March 1947, when restrictions prohibiting the free movement of civilians about the island were lifted.

Okinawan memory narratives emphasize the extreme poverty and suffering of local people during the early years of the occupation. Most of the arable farmland had been razed, and Okinawans lived off of food and clothing rations distributed by the U.S. military. Bedding, school supplies, athletic equipment, shoes, medicine, and even goats and pigs were donated by Okinawan emigrant groups abroad. Images of pots and kettles made from melted down airplane wreckage and tempura fried in motor oil are pervasive in accounts of the time. While still living in the camps, many Okinawans went to work for the U.S. military building roads and unloading freight. Paid positions came to include cooks, laundry workers, drivers, maids, and security guards. Wages for this kind of work were high in comparison to skilled labor and white-collar positions in the civilian sector, and schoolteachers and other trained professionals often opted to take such jobs with the military rather than low-paying professional positions outside the bases. While the occupation of mainland Japan lasted from August 1945 until April 1952, the U.S. military administered Okinawa for twenty-seven years, until May 15, 1972. In 1947, a series of secret negotiations were held in Tokyo, in which Emperor Hirohito indicated to SCAP officials that he was willing to have Okinawa remain under U.S. military authority in exchange for an early end to the occupation of mainland Japan. Okinawans expressed outrage at Japan's "betrayal" when the San Francisco Treaty was signed in 1951, ending the occupation of Japan and placing Okinawa under U.S. military control indefinitely.

Approaches to governing Okinawa evolved in response to changing U.S. military objectives. On May 31, 1945, before American troops landed on the main island, Proclamation No. 1 was issued in the name of Admiral Chester W. Nimitz, commander of the U.S. Pacific Fleet. The proclamation formally nullified Tokyo's authority over the Nansei Shoto (Southwest Islands, including Okinawa), providing the legal basis for the subsequent military occupation. A further document, Operational Directive No. 7, outlined commanders' duties in the areas of government, health and welfare, labor, commerce and industry, finance, transportation, and construction (Fisch 1988). The operational directive, which authorized commanders to "'demand and enforce from the inhabitants . . . such obedience as may be necessary' not only for war purposes and the maintenance of law and order, but also for proper administration of the area 'under circumstances of hostile occupation'" (Fisch 1988, 21), set the tone for the successive military commands that governed the islands. Although the U.S. military government depended on Okinawan officials to implement its policies, decisions were often made unilaterally by military governors whose first priority was to develop

Okinawa as a strategic outpost for the United States. On December 15, 1950, as a strategy for quelling local unrest over accelerating land appropriations, the Joint Chiefs of Staff established the SCAP-like United States Civil Administration of the Ryukyu Islands (USCAR). On April 1, 1952, an indigenous Government of the Ryukyus (GRI) was established. On the surface, USCAR appeared to exercise power more obliquely than the preceding military government. However, as Japanese historian Eiji Takemae has argued, "In reality, little had changed. Like its predecessor, USCAR was controlled from Washington and staffed entirely by Americans. The Military Governor of the Ryukyu Islands, for instance, became Governor of the Ryukyu Islands, but that position continued to be held by the Far East Commander in Tokyo (MacArthur)" (2003, 513). The GRI, whose chief executive was appointed by USCAR until 1960, was charged with implementing the proclamations, ordinances, and directives of USCAR. In 1957, the Office of High Commissioner was created to streamline interactions between USCAR and the United States Army. Filled by a three-star general appointed by the U.S. Secretary of Defense, the High Commissioner wore "three hats," serving as the highest official in charge of the occupation, the representative in the Ryūkyūs of the commander in chief of U.S. forces in the Pacific, and commander of the U.S. Army, Ryukyu Islands (Tsunami et al. 2001, 116).

Unlike GHQ in Tokyo, U.S. officials in Okinawa demonstrated less concern with social and political reform than with the strategic potential of the islands. A series of ordinances in 1952–1953 gave the U.S. military the right to seize privately owned land for base construction, and the military proceeded to confiscate land at gunpoint in what became known as the "bulldozer and bayonet" era (Higa 1963; Yoshikawa 1996). Community meetings and demonstrations were held throughout Okinawa, and by mid-1956, a broad coalition of citizens emerged to protest USCAR's land policies (Arasaki 1986; Tanji 2006). In 1957, however, the community of Henoko in present-day Nago City negotiated the first municipal land lease contract, offering its unused fields for military use. Henoko leaders hoped to bring economic benefits, including electricity and running water, to local residents (Yoshikawa 1996; Inoue 2004, 2007). Other communities soon followed suit.

Throughout Okinawa, the large-scale appropriation of village agricultural lands for military use and the presence of young American soldiers fueled the rise of a new economy catering to U.S. personnel and their families. After release from the resettlement camps, many now-homeless Okinawan families stayed on to work outside the gates of the new bases. They were joined by others from the poor and largely agricultural northern region and outer islands of Okinawa, who flocked to the growing base towns for work. Over the next thirty years, these areas developed into thriving cities dependent upon massive base-related service economies. Koza City (now Okinawa City), in particular, emerged as a symbol of Okinawa as a military base island. Located just outside of Kadena Air Base's Gate 2, Koza was the only township in Okinawa or Japan whose name was officially written in the *katakana* syllabary, connoting its foreign flavor. City streets were lined with shops, restaurants, bars, and brothels catering to a military clientele.[14] Feminist scholars have emphasized the degree to which women's sexual labor drove the Okinawan economy during this period (Sturdevant and Stolzfus 1993). According to the Legal Affairs Bureau of the Government of the Ryukyu Islands, the number of registered female prostitutes was 7,362 in 1969, and annual income from the sale of sexual labor exceeded even revenue generated by the sugarcane industry (Sturdevant and Stolzfus 1993, 251–252).

During the late 1960s, local opposition to land seizures and other effects of foreign occupation became so disruptive that the United States was forced to recognize that continuing American administration of the Ryukyus was no longer advantageous. In November 1969, the U.S. and Japanese governments jointly declared that reversion to Japanese sovereignty would occur in 1972 and that efforts would be made to alter the density of U.S. military bases in Okinawa to bring it in line with mainland Japan (*hondo-nami*). By reversion day, May 15, 1972, however, little had been done to reduce the military presence in Okinawa. Consumer prices rose 14.5 percent during the month following reversion (Arasaki 2000, 83). Political parties, labor unions, and businesses were integrated into their mainland Japanese counterpart organizations, and Okinawan schools were once again subsumed under the Japanese Ministry of Education. Reversion was deemed complete when the direction of traffic switched from the right lane (as in the United States) to the left lane (as in Japan) on July 30, 1978. One of the first major acts of the Japanese government concerning Okinawa was to sign a ten-year, one-trillion-yen promotion and development plan aimed at bringing Okinawa's economy up to the national level. The plan has been thrice renewed, each time increasing the budget, so that over the past forty years, a total of seven trillion yen has flowed into Okinawa in the form of government funds slated for infrastructural development (Cabinet Office, Government of Japan 2014). Government-funded public works projects have included the expressway from Naha to Nago, a new airport terminal in Naha, a series of dams in the northern region, and improved port facilities in several Okinawan cities. Degradation of the natural environment has resulted as riverbeds were concreted over to improve flow, forests were clear-cut for logging or agricultural purposes, and areas of the sea were reclaimed to make way for urban development. Moreover, the flow of easy money from Tokyo has led to new forms of economic dependency.

In recent decades, efforts have been made to develop Okinawa as a resort destination for Japanese tourists. Initially based on war-memorial pilgrimages, since the 1980s Okinawan tourism has been largely associated with luxury beach resorts. Tourists are lured by white sand beaches, stunning coral reefs—which have suffered from devastating bleaching events in recent years—and the promise of island hospitality. American-style restaurants and shopping areas and the "hybrid" leisure culture of Koza and other base towns are also major attractions. Since reversion, economic dependence on the U.S. military bases has decreased from 15.5 percent of gross prefectural revenue in 1972 to just over 5 percent in 2008 (Okinawa Prefectural Government n.d.). However, U.S. military facilities still occupy nearly 15 percent of the main island. In the central region, houses and shops crowd together around the perimeters of the bases, utilizing all available space, while inside the fences, wide avenues, grassy fields, and forested nooks predominate. Accidents involving military personnel and machinery continue to fuel antibase sentiment. In 1995, three U.S. servicemen abducted and raped a twelve-year-old girl from Kin. The rape almost immediately crystallized as a symbol of Okinawan marginalization under Japanese government administration and the continuing U.S. military presence. Eighty-five thousand people participated in the ensuing citizens' rally to demand the complete withdrawal of U.S. forces from the prefecture. Since 1997, the proposed new U.S. Marine Corps base in Henoko has sparked intense local debate and an ongoing legal battle pitting various local and prefectural political actors against the Japanese government in Tokyo.

Claims to a distinctive Okinawan identity, place, and past have been highly politicized and contested, in part because they challenge notions of a homogenous Japanese identity (Weiner 1997; Lie 2001; Hein and Selden 2003). The Japanese state has dealt with the problem of Okinawan difference by encouraging total assimilation to Japanese culture, and many Okinawans have embraced "Japanese-ness" precisely because, as Laura Hein and Mark Selden point out, Japanese society has not been organized in a way that "simultaneously honors cultural difference and full citizenship" (2003, 2). Access to political power and economic success remain, for the most part, contingent upon Tokyo's approval. For this reason, despite the public enunciation of a distinctive Okinawan identity, local politicians have often chosen strategies for development that result in the increasing absorption of Okinawa into the Japanese nation-state (McCormack 1999). In an optimistic statement, Hein and Selden have suggested that "Okinawans are making significant headway in carving out space for a 'hyphenated identity' by reimagining their cultural and political heritage as Okinawans, as Japanese, and as Asians" (2003, 28). However, the broad acceptance of such an identity would necessarily entail a redefinition of Japanese-ness itself.

Marriage, Family, and Fencelines

Okinawan history offers important clues regarding contemporary fencelines, including their construction and consequence. Notably, Okinawa's symbolic fencelines are not simply a product of postwar U.S. military occupation and American bases. Differences and inequalities between U.S. military personnel and Okinawans intersect with other distinctions based on geography, status, wealth, and language/ethnicity relating to Japanese and Ryukyuan social and political hierarchies. In the current moment, these various ideological distinctions articulate with one another in ways that support militarization. Japanese officials manipulate indigenous status and wealth differences, for example, to garner support for the U.S. military presence. Rather than pore over much-publicized political arguments regarding the bases, I explore the personal and intimate impacts of this tangled social formation through a discussion of the politics of sex, marriage, and family, which navigate the same set of intersecting distinctions. Taking this tack reveals the kinds of emotional intensities, interpersonal conflicts, and ideological contradictions that arise from the U.S. presence, as well as the strategies individuals employ to overcome such contradictions within their own lives. The complex nature of military fencelines is especially evident in discourses on military marriage and other unsanctioned forms of "marrying out," which highlight and redraw the lines of difference.

Marriage to U.S. military personnel may be the most conspicuous form of "marrying out" in Okinawa, but it is not the most common. Even today, marriages between individuals from different clans and villages, between members of the former Shuri gentry and commoners, and between islanders and persons from mainland Japan all figure prominently in personal narratives, friendly conversations, and gossip. In his influential critique of American kinship, David Schneider (1980) argued that scholarly kinship analyses mistakenly assumed the universality of Western notions of genealogy as a biologically grounded phenomenon. Following Schneider's critique, feminist anthropologists advocated for more contextualized analyses that explored the mutual imbrications of kinship, gender, and sexuality in specific kinship ideologies, and how these worked to naturalize power and inequality (Collier and Yanigasako 1987; Strathern 1992; Yanagisako and Delaney 1995; Franklin and McKinnon 2002). Applying this critique to Okinawan family and kinship studies, it is evident that since the late nineteenth century, analyses published by Okinawan, Japanese, and American ethnologists and ethnographers have played a role in naturalizing Okinawan difference and inequality vis-à-vis mainland Japan. This is true of studies published during the Japanese colonial and U.S. occupation eras, as well as more recent analyses aimed at explaining Okinawa's higher birth rate, divorce rate, and other perceived social problems (for example, Nishioka 1994). The majority of these studies utilize received terminologies of descent and alliance and impose etic genealogical grids like those critiqued by Schneider. Nonetheless, when analyzed alongside Okinawan history, it is possible to identify shifts in Okinawan marriage and family ideologies and practices over time. After briefly presenting the tenets of Okinawan kinship described in these studies, I discuss the more nuanced set of relationships in several of the families I knew.

Village histories and ethnographies have emphasized ancestor worship and provisions for succession and inheritance as the key drivers of Okinawan marriage and family norms and practices.[15] Okinawan kinship has been described as a dual system with immediate household and close relatives by blood or marriage on one level and the larger *munchū* (clan) on another.[16] A pattern of male primogeniture has been considered typical (Glacken 1955; Lebra 1966). Historians trace this pattern to the imposition of the Meiji Civil Code and the Japanese family registration system in Okinawa in 1903. Under this system, the bulk of family land and other property was inherited by a single designated successor, preferably the eldest son, although other children were often willed smaller plots or other property.[17] Prior to the incorporation of Okinawa as a Japanese prefecture (1879), village forest and agricultural land had been held communally, and a successor's inheritance was limited to the family house and lot.[18] Scholars have further speculated that the unilineal pattern of succession documented during the U.S. occupation was underlain by an indigenous ambilineal system (Wacker 2000, discussed in Kreiner 2000).[19]

Occupation-era ethnographers claimed that in the past younger sons and daughters had left their natal households upon marriage, younger sons to establish new branch houses and daughters to join their husbands' houses (Lebra 1966). By the 1950s, however, Glacken found that a loose system of neolocal residence within the husband's village prevailed. "If the family registers are accurate, the great majority of men were born in the village in which they now live. In the social structure of village life, it is the men who provide the continuity; the women are more likely to be strangers. Most husbands may point to their fathers and grandfathers who live or have lived in the village; fewer wives can do the same" (Glacken 1955, 217).[20] In the countryside, young men and women generally chose their own marriage partners (Glacken 1955; Maretzki and Maretzki 1966), although arranged marriages were preferred among the former gentry (Lebra 1966, 195). Social pressure was applied to encourage village endogamy, the choosing of a spouse from among one's fellow villagers.

> When a girl was discovered carrying on a love affair with a man from
> another village, she was subjected to verbal chastisement and often

physical punishment by the village. If the couple were caught together, the male was usually given a beating. Frequently the girl and sometimes the male were placed astride a board or log and paraded about the village by members of the *wakamung-gumi* (young men's association). Usually, the girl and her parents were afterwards subjected to a public scolding before a village meeting. Marriage with an outsider was permitted only on payment of a large fine (*tima*) in liquor or money to all unmarried men and youth of the village .... Obviously, exogamous marriage was not easily condoned, and old informants attest that it was rather infrequent in the past (Lebra 1966, 130).

The practice of village endogamy is encoded in Okinawan oral tradition in the lyrics of a folk song inscribed on the *ishikubiri*, a stone monument that sits along an ancient forest road connecting the villages of Inoha and Izumi on the Motobu Peninsula. The song honors two lovers who were prohibited from marrying because they were from different villages. According to the story, the two walked along the road in secrecy each night, the young man lamenting: "Despite this road being harsh and hilly, I wish that it would never end" (Ehman 2007, 154).

Historically, the preference for village endogamy was likely related to a legal prohibition against the internal migration of commoners during the latter part of the Ryūkyū Kingdom (1429–1879) and reactions against in-migrating outsiders once the prohibition was lifted. In the late nineteenth century, political and economic changes associated with the *ryūkyū shobun* (Ryūkyū dispensation—that is, the formal dissolution of the Ryūkyū Kingdom and incorporation into the Japanese nation-state) resulted in extensive out-migration of *shizoku* (former gentry) from the capital of Shuri into the countryside. Relieved of their administrative functions, Ryukyuan aristocrats left Shuri in search of employment, many taking up posts in village offices, and others becoming fishermen, farmers, or craftsmen in the village centers.[21] Displacement of villagers occurred again during the early twentieth century due to the collapse of the sugar market, and on an unprecedented scale during the Battle of Okinawa. After the fighting subsided, individuals and whole families left their hometowns in search of wage-paying jobs in areas surrounding the new military bases. Over a relatively brief period, then, Okinawan villages became composed of individuals and families with diverse backgrounds and different perspectives on who constituted a "true" villager, much less an appropriate marriage partner.

Since the occupation era, discourses on marriage and family have thus intersected with ideas about class difference and native village, creating a subtle hierarchy of "appropriate" marriage partners. Occupation-era ethnographies noted an important distinction between families that belonged to the former gentry and other villagers. Maretzki and Maretzki (1966) reported that "Shuri people" in the northern village of Taira still maintained their distinctive traditions during the 1950s. They noted their noble descent in the village registry, and "intermarriage with commoners was discouraged" (Maretzki and Maretzki 1966, 7; see also Kerr 1958; Lebra 1966).[22] Nearly forty years later, an elderly acquaintance who grew up in a "Shuri family" in Higashi village, recalled that, when he was a child, his mother had continually reminded him of his family's noble lineage in order to elicit good behavior "appropriate to his station." Another participant, Nakasone Yasuhiro, remembered the stories his mother used to tell when he was a child, stories about her girlhood in Izumi. "She told me that as a kid, she was often reminded of her family's Shuri origin by her grandmother. Whenever she spoke in *hōgen* [dialect] or behaved badly, her grandmother would tell her that a Shuri person should not talk or behave that way."

Alongside class distinctions based on hereditary status, many Okinawans recognize differences based on island of origin, especially when referring to persons originally from the outer islands of Okinawa, such as Miyako or Yaeyama. Yasuhiro told me the following story about his father, who was born on the small island of Hatoma in the Yaeyama group. Yasuhiro's father met his mother while he was attending college on Okinawa's main island. After graduating, they entered the teaching profession and were both assigned to public schools in northern Okinawa. Upon learning that she was pregnant, the two decided to get married. When she took him to visit her family for the first time, her mother became upset that she had brought home a man from Yaeyama and turned her back to him for the entire length of his visit. She later invoked the phrase *"Yaeyama hijuru"* (cold Yaeyamans) to discourage her daughter from the relationship. This hostility gradually subsided after the couple married and had children. Yasuhiro mused, however, "I think my father sometimes still feels like an outsider in Yanbaru, but less now than before. He does not speak the local dialects and doesn't have much of a local network beyond my mother's family and work-related people. And of course, he likes Yaeyama music better than Yanbaru music."

Similarly, Hideki Yoshikawa (1996) has written that in Kin, the foremost social division has been between native villagers and so-called *kiryūmin* (drifters, out-of-towners), including people who came from Shuri and, later, from Okinawa's outer islands during the period of base construction and the Vietnam War (see Inoue 2004, 2007 for discussion of a parallel distinction in Henoko). My research suggests that similar distinctions developed in base towns throughout Okinawa. For example, Asato Katsuko, an office worker on Kadena Air Base, left Miyako Island for the main island of Okinawa with her mother and brother during the early 1950s. Katsuko's mother opened an inn for fishermen in the Tomari Port area, but she had trouble making ends meet due to a lack of local connections.

Just before Katsuko graduated from elementary school, the family moved to Koza, where businesses in U.S.-approved "liberty" areas were booming. Hoping to tap into the flow of American dollars, Katsuko's mother opened a restaurant (*ryōtei*) that served alcohol and employed hostesses to pour drinks for American customers. Again, "the business didn't do well because we were from off-island, and my mother didn't know many people. Especially in Koza, if you were from Miyako or somewhere else off-island, people hesitated to socialize with you. If you were in business, and you knew a lot of people, then they would try to help you by sending you business. But my mother didn't know that many people, and because of that, her business did not do well." By the time Katsuko finished junior high school, her mother's business had failed completely, and she was forced to quit school and go to work in order to pay off her mother's debts. She took a job as a bartender in a club for U.S. servicemen located on B.C. Street, outside of Kadena Air Base. For women like Katsuko, the distinction between native villagers and those who came from other parts of Okinawa impacted their lives significantly—shaping their attitudes, the opportunities available to them, and their decisions to marry American military men. Katsuko dated American GIs she met at work, and in 1965, she became pregnant. Two years later, she met and married Ray Horner, an enlisted U.S. airman from Pennsylvania. Analyzed alongside village histories and ethnographies, stories like Katsuko's suggest that in towns hosting U.S. military bases, "outsider" Okinawans associated (and *were associated*) with American GIs. Overlapping notions of "outsider-ness" thus linked "non-native" Okinawans to U.S. military personnel.

Today, the Shuri/commoner and Okinawa/outer island distinctions continue to hold meaning for elderly persons, many of whom recall a time when marriages between these groups were rare. More important for younger people are class distinctions based on education and salary that cross-cut older distinctions based on hereditary status and family origin. For example, social worker Hirata Masayo told journalist Ruth Ann Keyso that she married a U.S. serviceman in part because her educational background discouraged Okinawan men from approaching her.

> I think it was the initial excitement of having an American suitor that appealed to me. You see, I wasn't used to men approaching me. Okinawan men are reluctant to approach a woman if they think they don't have a chance of marrying her. I don't know about the States, but here on the island a man considers a woman's class before asking her out on a date. Then usually two people of the same social standing marry one another. Well, a lot of men were apprehensive about asking me out because they knew that I'd been to a good college on the mainland and was

planning to attend graduate school in the States. Not many people back then had the opportunity to do those sorts of things . . . . What I didn't realize for a long time was that to the Americans I was nothing but an ordinary girl. To them my achievements meant nothing. They didn't care if I had good grades or went to a top university (quoted in Keyso 2000, 71, 74).

Considering these stories, it is clear that in Okinawa, "marrying out" is neither a singular nor a stable concept. Military marriages appear to be an important point of reference, but place of origin, privilege of the former gentry, and educational experience all overlap with and reinforce local distinctions between insiders and outsiders.

Marriages between Okinawans and persons from mainland Japan have been subject to similar constraints. In the seventeenth century, court regents wove romantic tales about marriages between Okinawans and mainlanders, possibly as a way to legitimate Japanese rule in the archipelago. During the Japanese colonial period (1879–1945), however, marriages between Okinawans and Japanese administrators were apparently rare. McCune writes, "Okinawans were looked down upon by the Japanese, who considered them inferiors, only a step or two above the outcast Eta class in Japan because they too raised pigs and ate pork" (1975, 56).[23] During the U.S. occupation, travel between Okinawa and mainland Japan was restricted, and opportunities for young Okinawans and mainland Japanese to develop intimate relationships were limited. In the postreversion era, however, opportunities have increased dramatically. In a recent study of *yamatunchu yome* (mainland Japanese brides) living in suburban Naha, Kaorie Ishizuki (2001) argues that acceptance of a mainland bride depends on the position of the son she has married (first son, second son, third son, and so on). Although women who married first sons complained about the time-consuming responsibilities associated with caring for relatives, their position within the extended family was guaranteed (*ittei no ichi*). Women who married second and third sons, on the other hand, had fewer opportunities to interact with their husbands' relatives and therefore tended to remain distant and even to feel deliberately excluded. One woman told Ishizuki, "At first, I too thought that it would be nice to feel at home [with my husband's family], but I finally gave up. Even when I tried very hard, they complained, and I felt offended. But it was always the same complaints. No matter what I did, I was always going to be the '*naichā yome*'" (Ishizuki 2001, 2, translation mine).[24] A second woman objected to the way she was continually reminded that as a *yamatunchu*, she could not be expected to know anything about Okinawan traditions and customs—this despite her thirty-five-year marriage to an Okinawan eldest son and thirteen years of residence in the prefecture.

These stories regarding exogamous marriages—including marriages to foreigners (for example, U.S. military personnel) but also to persons from mainland Japan, the outlying islands of Okinawa, and separate villages, along with marriages that cross historical and modern class boundaries—suggest some rather important points about Okinawa's fencelines. Each of these forms of exogamy rests upon a categorical opposition between a specified group of outsiders and an implied group of insiders. Who constitutes the Them and who constitutes the Us, of course, depends on which form of exogamy the narrator is referencing. Personal histories suggest that these varied groups of insiders and outsiders overlap and become associated with one another. In Katsuko Horner's narrative, for example, her family's status as immigrants from Okinawa's outer islands, former commoners, and newcomers to Koza shaped the family's business opportunities and Katsuko's educational, work, and marriage opportunities. The family moved to Koza, where such forms of difference reinforced one another. Indeed, Okinawa's base towns (such as Koza, Kin, and Henoko) were places where outsider Okinawans and outsider Americans actively sought business contacts and intimate relationships with one another. This insight complicates popular and scholarly representations of military international marriage. Military international relationships in Okinawa do not evoke a clear-cut Japanese/foreigner dichotomy (as Kelsky and others have argued for *kokusai-kekkon* in mainland Japan) nor even a singular U.S. military/Okinawan opposition. Rather, stories of military international intimacy reveal that Okinawa's military fencelines have developed in relation to other distinctions, themselves historically constituted by the policies and practices of the Ryūkyū Kingdom, Japanese colonial administration, and contemporary Japanese government. Regarding the latter, in Okinawa, marriages to mainland Japanese persons also appear to be indirectly associated with military fencelines. At the meeting of the Nago housewives group mentioned above, Shirota-san was called upon to share her experiences as a mainland woman married to an Okinawan man immediately following my presentation on military international marriage. The term *kokusai-kekkon*, of course, applies to marriages to both groups of outsiders, but a deeper perceptual linkage between U.S. military personnel and mainland Japanese persons, the two most prominent groups of "foreigners" in Okinawa, appears to hold as well. Such an association is daily reinforced by Tokyo's alliance with the U.S. government in all matters concerning the bases—for example, in media reports of mainland Japanese policemen brought in to control Okinawan antibase protestors. In other words, the Japanese government's historical role in bringing the U.S. military to the prefecture and collusion in maintaining the U.S. presence and associated fencelines is highlighted not only in political discourses directly related to the base issue but even in seemingly unrelated talk about "marrying out." Across a wide range of stories about *kokusai-kekkon* and "marrying out," different forms of exogamy are inter-discursively linked to one another, producing a single relatively cohesive semantic domain.[25] That domain is premised on the recognition that Okinawan lives, including the most personal and intimate of emotions and experiences, have been thoroughly militarized.

Love at First Sight and Other Fate-Filled Meetings

Further evidence of the links between military international marriage and other exogamous relationships can be found in the common themes and narrative devices that appear in stories of "marrying out" and other unsanctioned relationships. Okinawan women and U.S. military men who are intimately involved with one another commonly speak about family reactions to their relationships, cultural and language differences, and contrasting expectations related to running households and raising children. The difficulties of navigating multiple state bureaucracies and the frequent moves and separations associated with military lifestyles are also important topics. Here, I consider a set of common tropes and narrative devices employed in such accounts. In the face of difficulties and public disapproval, many participants emphasized the love that they felt for one another and from which they drew strength. In a curiously uniform way, many participants—both American military men and Okinawan women—shared stories that involved "love at first sight" and other fate-filled first meetings.

Ralph Dickson, a retired U.S. naval officer living in Nakijin described the moment when he first caught sight of his future wife at a nightclub in Kin. His use of the present tense transported us both, speaker and listener, back to that moment in 1967. "She was the most beautiful woman I ever saw. Just everything about her was beautiful. You want to talk to her, but you're afraid to talk to her. You get a bad case of 'Should I or shouldn't I?' You ask somebody about her, and they say, 'That one, she doesn't go out with anybody. She does her job, and she does what has to be done, but she doesn't date Okinawans or Japanese or Americans. She doesn't date, period.'" Another retired marine who met his future wife in a restaurant during the Vietnam era described a similar scene: "I was twenty years old, and it was love at first sight. It wasn't like, 'I want to meet that girl,' or 'I want to date her.' It was—I fell completely hard. 'That's the girl I want to marry.' I mean, it was that fast. It just hit me. I didn't know if she was married. I didn't know if she was dating somebody . . . . You know on television when they zoom in on one person and everybody else just kind of fades into the background? That's the way it was. As far as I was concerned, everybody else just vanished from the room.

I was engulfed in her beauty." Such stories were told by younger active-duty servicemen as well. Josh Eisner, a young enlisted marine assigned to Futenma Air Station, shared the following experience: "I pretty much knew when I first saw her, when she first smiled at me, that I was a goner. I never expected a thunderbolt. I had thought that I would be one of those guys who would just find some lady who liked me okay and get married. And then she turned around and smiled at me. Boom! Thunderbolt." Well-rehearsed stories involving love at first sight are a common element of American personal histories. As part of a larger corpus of life stories, love at first sight narratives locate the act of finding a romantic partner outside of the narrator's control, dramatizing the value that Americans place on surrendering personal initiative—so important in other areas of American life, such as in professional activities—in order to demonstrate commitment within intimate relationships (McCollum 2002; see also Linde 1993). The American servicemen whom I interviewed claimed that they had not chosen love. It (or rather, some overwhelming sense of beauty or attraction) had chosen them.

Compare the following excerpts from interviews with Okinawan women. Katsuko Horner recalled, "The first night we met, I noticed that his eyes were the most beautiful eyes I had ever seen. To this day, my husband and I believe that it was love at first sight. I cannot explain what it was that I was feeling, but I was thinking, 'Wow, maybe this is it!'" Katsuko's comment "My husband and I believe that it was love at first sight" suggests that her story may have been originally crafted with input from her husband. Katsuko's husband, Ray, shared the following narrative: "Meeting Katsuko was one of those things of fate. It was Valentine's Day, as a matter of fact. Katsuko had a delightful sense of humor and wasn't trying to hustle me for drinks because she was a *real* person. Okinawa in the late sixties—you got tired of people saying, 'Hey, GI, buy me a drink.' But she wasn't one of them. If you'd have asked me when I was out flying earlier that day, 'Do you believe in love at first sight?' I would have said, 'No, absolutely not.' But I was definitely smitten." Other women's narratives were not as obviously adapted to their husband's stories. Two Okinawan military wives in their forties who were ardent Christians made references to "God's will" when explaining how they first met their husbands.

The most unique use of the love at first sight trope, however, came from my interview with thirty-nine-year-old Hiroko Wolf. Hiroko was working in the travel office on Kadena Air Base in 1985 when she met her future husband, Marshall. He had no memory of this first meeting, but Hiroko remembered it vividly. "The first time I saw him was when I was working on base with his ex-wife. I had this feeling that I had met him before, in a past life or something. *Hontō da yo!* [It's true!] I told my coworker Mari—I said, 'I think he is the one, but he's married. How can this be?' Then I quit that job and started working for a Japanese airline, and I didn't see him again for more than a year." The following year, Marshall and his first wife filed for divorce. Shortly after, he began dating one of Hiroko's friends, who introduced him to Hiroko for the second time.

> MARSHALL: My girlfriend said, "Hey, I have a friend who wants to meet an American guy. Do you have any friends? Maybe we can double date."
>
> HIROKO: When I saw him, I thought, "What happened to his wife?" He said they were separated, and I thought, "This is my big chance!" But he was already dating my friend. Then, nine months later, I saw him a *third* time at the O-Club [Officers' Club]. And I thought, "That's right! I knew it!"
>
> MARSHALL: When I saw her the third time, I thought, "Okay, this can't be a coincidence. I guess we are supposed to get together."
>
> HIROKO: And then we found out I have three wisdom teeth. The fourth one never came in. I have only three. And he has five!

Hiroko's assertion that Marshall was born with one of her wisdom teeth reinforced Marshall's feeling that they were "supposed to get together," yet also drew on ideas about past lives and destiny that did not conform to mainstream American cultural scripts. They did, however, serve the similar purpose of legitimizing the relationship while drawing attention away from elements of Hiroko's biography that might draw criticism in Okinawa—such as asking friends to introduce her to American guys or frequenting the Officers' Club.

It is tempting to view Okinawan women's stories as appropriations of the American cultural scripts that their husbands and other members of the U.S. military community employ when talking about romantic relationships. Alternately, one might view these narratives as examples of Anthony Giddens's (1992) transformation of intimacy under conditions of modernity. Giddens has argued that the trope of romantic love and associated ideal of companionate marriage are part of a much larger cultural transformation: the development of the modern individual self. That is, the transformation of kinship away from relationships of social obligation and toward "pure relationships," governed by individual desire, pleasure, choice, and satisfaction, is an element of human progress toward more democratic private and public relationships. Within this context, narratives of romantic love serve as a means for tying ideals of freedom and choice to projects of self-realization (Giddens 1992, 40). Following Giddens, albeit judiciously, anthropologists have documented the global spread of romantic love and the companionate marriage ideal, asking why local peoples have embraced emotional intimacy as the source of ties that bind and how such notions relate to changing gender ideologies (see, for example, Wardlow and Hirsch 2006). Taking such an approach, the contact zones within and around U.S. military bases might be understood as places where modern ideas (initially developed in the West) confront traditional models (assumedly dominant in Okinawa), in which marriage is managed by families, women continue to have low status compared to men, and so on. However, this characterization of traditional marriage does not appear to fit contemporary or historical Okinawan marriage and family norms, except perhaps for members of the former gentry class.

Tropes of romantic love and love at first sight have commonly appeared within Okinawan oral and literary tradition, especially in stories about unsanctioned exogamous relationships.[26] Examples include the song about intervillage romance inscribed on the *ishikubiri* and the tale of Minamoto no Tametomo appearing in the *Chūzan Seikan* (1650), the first official history of the Ryūkyū Kingdom. According to the *Seikan*, Tametomo (1139–1170), a legendary Japanese warrior from the powerful Minamoto family, shipwrecked on Okinawa, married the daughter of a local chieftain, and fathered the first king of Okinawa. According to the legend, Tametomo left his wife and son in Okinawa and returned to Japan to challenge the Taira clan but was killed while away. In true romantic fashion, his wife moved into a cave at Machinatu (Makiminato). For years, she walked the cliffs above the harbor and watched the ocean, waiting for his return. To this day, local people maintain a shrine at the location to honor her love and loyalty.[27] A third example comes from the novels of Shuri aristocrat Heshikiya Chōbin (1700–1734). Heshikiya's protagonists include a Japanese samurai and a Ryukyuan *aji* (nobleman) who both fall deeply in love with prostitutes. Confronted with the impossibility of realizing relationships that would be deemed acceptable in their respective societies, both commit suicide in their grief. Drawing on the interpretations of scholars of Ryukyuan literature, Gregory Smits discusses these stories as a critique of Ryūkyū society under government minister Sai On's influence, in which rigid ethical duties and obligations prohibited individuals from pursuing and fulfilling their desires (1999, 119–125). The message is that "love is a great equalizer, dissolving distinctions in social status—between prostitute and *aji*, for example" (121). Finally, Davinder Bhowmik (2008) examines questions of identity in Ikemiyagi Sekihō's (1883–1951) "Officer Okuma," published in 1922. Ikemiyagi's title character is a young man from a "special hamlet" on the outskirts of Naha, likely the Kume district, a once-privileged village of Chinese immigrants and scholars. Following Satsuma's invasion of Ryūkyū in 1609, Kume villagers' fortunes declined, falling to unprecedented lows after Japan defeated China in 1895. Okuma studies hard and passes the examination required for entry into the police department. There he puts distance between himself and his community, while his new colleagues, appointees from mainland Japan, view him as a foreigner and maintain a cool distance, arousing intense feelings of inferiority. He assuages his loneliness in Tsuji, Naha's red-light district, spending his off-duty hours with a prostitute named Kamarū. The two fall in love but have no chance of a life together as Okuma cannot afford to pay off her debts. The full significance of Okuma's constrained position is brought home when he bravely captures a thief, only to find that the criminal is Kamarū's older brother. This leaves him feeling trapped like a wild animal. Initially parallel to Heshikiya's portrayal of love as a release from social duty, Ikemiyagi ultimately suggests that love is but a temporary solution to the problem of Okinawan marginalization.

Thus romantic love is not a new concept in Okinawa. It has been a common theme in stories about intimate relationships that violate social norms since at least the seventeenth century. Likewise, I heard countless stories of individuals who married across social boundaries—including regional, national, racial, and class boundaries—for love. In addition to being tales of self-actualization, such stories may be understood as attempts to reframe exogamous relationships as morally pure or spiritually ordained and therefore socially legitimate. In other words, narratives of romance and love at first sight are also strategic. "Concepts of emotion [including love]," Catherine Lutz has argued, "can be viewed as serving complex communicative, moral, and cultural purposes rather than simply as labels for internal states whose nature or essence is presumed to be universal . . . . Talk about emotions is simultaneously talk about society—about power and politics, about kinship and marriage, about normality and deviance" (1988, 5–6). In the case of intimate relationships between Okinawans and U.S. military personnel, talk about love redirects attention away from the larger context of the U.S. military presence and toward individuals' subjective experiences of intimacy, while simultaneously absolving them of any wrongdoing. Talk about love thus creates discursive spaces for reconsidering military international relationships as socially legitimate and worthy of respect. Moreover, the love at first sight trope and references to destiny or fate create new linkages between military international intimacy and other forms of "marrying out." When military marriages are perceived, interpreted, and talked about in the same way as other exogamous relationships, military fencelines may be normalized as just another form of social difference, not unlike that which distinguishes Okinawans who grew up on different islands or in different villages. The leveling of political and economic inequalities that occurs as a result of this strategy, with foreign military power recast as an everyday social difference rather than a consequence of military violence and political coercion, contributes to the ongoing militarization of Okinawan social life. As Lutz has written with respect to U.S. military empire, current forms of American imperialism involve "a constellation of state and state-structured private projects successfully aiming to exert wide-ranging control . . . over the practices and resources of areas beyond the state's borders" (2006, 594). This includes, among other things, "a complex set of social relationships entailing culturally constructed emotions, ambivalences, and ambiguities" (595). The narratives of love and romance related here suggest possibilities for creative self-fashioning as couples assert the legitimacy of their relationships and challenge existing social boundaries, but there are also potential drawbacks to this strategy because it serves to normalize military fencelines.

Okinawa's symbolic fencelines extend out from base towns like Koza, Kin, and Henoko, articulating with indigenous social distinctions and dividing people along lines of gender, island and village of origin, historical class, wealth, and education. For each of the participants in this research, understanding an individual's personal and family background provided important information concerning the complex kinds of fencelines that shaped their opportunities and community reactions and that they themselves were engaged in navigating and negotiating. Unfortunately, I did not talk with Stew Brown long enough to learn much of this back story and especially not his wife's. Hank and Mutsuko Megason, on the other hand, provided quite a lot of information about how Mutsuko's family, and consequently the couple themselves, fit into the Henoko community. Mutsuko's family were "Shuri people," members of the former gentry class, and although they were newcomers, having moved to Henoko from Kadena in 1958 to work at newly built Camp Schwab, they were able to purchase land in the hilltop neighborhood outside the main gate. Financial resources and their family name (recognizable as that of an important Shuri family), enabled them to establish a foothold among the landowning families in the area. Although they were never able to fully integrate into the tightly knit social networks of these native kin groups (see Inoue 2007), they were able to claim community membership in a way that was deemed legitimate, eventually emerging as vocal supporters of the military base in solidarity with other "newcomer" business owners and wage earners.

Okinawa's ambiguous position—"at the geographic and ideological margins of Japan, yet at the center of the United States-Japan strategic relationship" (Yonetani 2003, 244)—introduces new and important variables into the study of international marriage in Japan and the study of U.S. military impact on surrounding communities. In Okinawa, sustained social displacement and shifting positionality in relation to Japan and the United States have shaped opportunities for intimacy, notions of appropriate marriage partners, and residence and household membership. Consequently, local understandings of international marriage and other forms of "marrying out," which draw on shifting distinctions between various historically constituted groups of insiders and outsiders, fail to call forth the absolute and diametrically opposed notions of Japanese and foreigner found in discussions of *kokusai-kekkon* in mainland Japan. Indeed, Okinawans also use the term *kokusai-kekkon* to refer to marriages between Okinawans and mainland Japanese, challenging notions of Japanese homogeneity and Japan's exercise of power within Okinawa. In addition, U.S. military husbands, who make up the vast majority of foreign spouses in Okinawa, comprise a unique kind of foreigner. Within such a context, military international marriages have the potential to subvert military fencelines and mitigate some of the more blatant power inequalities in Okinawan society. Their ability to do so depends on individuals' histories, decisions, and strategies, explored further in the following chapters.

RACE, MEMORY, AND MILITARY MEN'S SEXUALITY

I have listened to the personal stories of women who continue to live with the physical and emotional trauma resulting from military sexual violence they suffered during Okinawa's postwar upheaval, when many women had no choice as the family breadwinner but to work in the GI clubs and bars that sprang up around the U.S. military bases. I personally witnessed the soldiers returning from the Vietnam frontlines to take out their pent-up rage and terror on innocent Okinawan women and girls. Analysis shows that the effect of the military's training of young recruits in killing and violence turns them into war machines. The learned violence spills over into their off-duty time, robbing community women and girls of their security and human rights.

—Speech made by Takazato Suzuyo, former member of the Naha City Assembly and co-chair of Okinawa Women Act Against Military Violence (OWAAMV) (quoted in Francis 1999, 198)

The problem is mostly with the marines, and it has to do with the way they are trained. They come to Okinawa to do intensive jungle warfare training. They are sent up to the Northern Training Area, they are given a mission, and they are set loose in the woods by themselves for three months at a time. They're shooting blanks up there, but after a few days of sleep deprivation and a lack of food, it's awfully easy to forget that it's just a training game. One day last year, my wife and I took the kids for a drive to explore the northern area. Suddenly a group of marines appeared alongside the car. They were filthy. They looked like a bunch of wild men. Well, you take a bunch of guys that have lived like that for three months, and you get them back to camp, and you give them the weekend off and send them out into town to the bars in Chatan and Naha and expect them to act normal. It's not going to happen.

—Interview with Terrance Carter, former U.S. airman

American military men—camouflage-clad, faces painted with swirling green and brown, weapons gripped tightly—are a common sight in Okinawa. Canvas-topped trucks and Humvees plug along the island's highways, transporting equipment and troops between the far-flung U.S. Marine Corps bases and train-ing areas. Armed MPs stand at attention at the gated entrances to U.S. installa-tions and patrol off-base recreation areas on weekends. The weapons, the face paint, and the pumped-up physiques combine to transform these foreigners into a frightening reminder of war and military occupation, fueling perceptions of U.S. military personnel as trained killers—often inexperienced in war, perhaps moti-vated by a paycheck rather than patriotism, sometimes generous and gentle, occasionally violent, unpredictable and therefore dangerous. It is popularly assumed that U.S. military training transforms young American GIs, teaching them to de-value human life and predisposing them to commit violent crimes and engage in skewed relations with local civilians.[1] In Okinawa, American service members of-ten have great difficulty convincing local people to look beyond these stereo-types. Many GIs do form lasting friendships with Okinawans. But as a group, U.S. military personnel are deemed polluted by the blood on their collective hands.

Even women like sixty-three-year-old Miyagi Satoko, who readily boasted about her own long and happy marriage to an American serviceman, tended to fall back on such stereotypes when considering individuals other than her hus-band. I was enjoying a friendly lunch in Miyagi-san's sunroom one afternoon when she asked about a mutual friend, a retired American naval officer who had married a woman from northern Okinawa and lived there for the past forty years. I reported what I thought was good news, that our friend had recently been asked to teach English part time in the local elementary schools. I was taken aback when Miyagi-san reacted with a mixture of shock and disgust, upset because "soldiers use dirty language" not suitable for the elementary school classroom. Surprised, I recalled that not two weeks earlier, Miyagi-san had enthusiastically explained to me that her own excellent English language skills were due to the tireless ef-forts of her now-deceased husband (an enlisted marine), who had continually cor-rected her pronunciation and grammar. Before this incident with Miyagi-san, I had not fully understood that familiarity and friendship with individual U.S. ser-vice members does little to diminish the power of existing stereotypes, includ-ing those that depict American military personnel as morally repugnant and dangerous.

The U.S. military occupies vast stretches of land in Okinawa. Barbed wire fences posted with signs reading "U.S. Government Property: Keep Out" consti-tute a daily reminder of war and the long U.S. military occupation. These mem-ories, along with periodic crimes and accidents perpetrated by Americans, play an important role in facilitating the circulation of negative stereotypes.[2] Within such memory discourses, images of American soldiers as invaders, liberators, oc-cupiers, and oppressors are closely associated with images of Okinawan women victimized through either sexual or structural violence, the latter including employment as bar hostesses or sex workers. These images from Okinawa's collective past, along with memories of personal experiences under U.S. military government, are appropriated by public officials and activists as a basis for mass protest against the U.S. military presence. They are also cited in private contexts by friends and family members to dissuade Okinawan women from becoming romantically involved with U.S. military men.

Chapters 2 and 3 explore the impact of Okinawan memories of war and occupation on popular stereotypes of American men, Okinawan women, and military international intimacy. Racialized historical imagery is frequently used to police the boundaries that separate Americans, Okinawans, and mainland Japanese. It also constitutes a key discursive site where contemporary understandings of race, class, and sexuality—key elements of Okinawa's symbolic fencelines—are negotiated and reproduced. This chapter explores Okinawan discourses on race and military men's sexuality, with a focus on how Japanese and American colonial discourses have shaped local understandings of racial difference. During the prewar period, Okinawans were gradually incorporated into Japanese imperial hierarchies of race, ethnicity, and nation to claim a somewhat ambiguous membership in the Japanese *minzoku* (race, ethnic group, nation). Imperial rhetoric drew on a repertoire of racial ideas and images that structurally positioned Okinawans and other Asians—indeed, at times all "colored peoples"—alongside the Japanese in unified opposition to Europeans and Americans. During the postwar occupation, U.S. military and civilian personnel introduced into Okinawa American discourses on Manifest Destiny and U.S. imperialism, Jim Crow-era segregation, and the 1960s civil rights and black power movements. These discourses have been variously embraced, resisted, and reinterpreted by Okinawans within the context of their own experiences. This chapter features the personal narratives of individuals who self-consciously viewed their relationships as transgressing racial categories. Their stories illustrate the struggle of military international couples to understand and rework the complex tangle of racial ideologies and expectations in Okinawa's postwar society. Chapter 3 pivots away from discourses on race and U.S. military men to explore corresponding discourses on Okinawan women's respectability and class identity. Throughout, the analysis examines the production and negotiation of symbolic fencelines associated with gender, race, and class difference. The presence of such fencelines, along with their fluid nature, is evident in strategic deployments of self and Other, and personal and social identity by state institutions, local citizens' groups, and international couples themselves.

Three Narratives of Race and Sex in Contemporary Okinawa

Iha Mayumi

Iha Mayumi, age thirty-four, had been married for just two months when I met her at the busy Mr. Donut restaurant in Chatan in central Okinawa. I had contacted Mayumi to request an interview after receiving her name and phone number from another participant. We had no previous relationship, so I was surprised by her eagerness and candor, especially in such a public setting. I quickly set up the tape recorder, coffee cups clinking in the background, as Mayumi explained that she was presently in a long-distance marriage. Mayumi's husband Isaac, a Marine Corps lance corporal ten years her junior, had received orders soon after their wedding to report to his next duty station at Twentynine Palms, California. He expected to return to Okinawa for a second tour within a year, and Mayumi had decided to stay behind in Okinawa so that she would not lose her job behind the counter at an on-base fast-food restaurant. The two had first met on the volleyball court during a weekend pickup game at the Camp Foster athletic complex. They were both avid volleyball players, and their friendship had developed based on this common interest. Early on, Mayumi had told her mother about her new boyfriend, including the fact that he was originally from Jamaica and had dark skin. Her mother suggested that it might be better to keep this a secret from her father. Soon after, however, the couple met Mayumi's father unexpectedly as they were strolling hand-in-hand along an outdoor shopping arcade in Naha. Her father greeted them coldly, glaring at Mayumi and refusing to shake Isaac's hand. A period of strained family relationships followed, with Mayumi's father blaming her mother for the deception. When the couple announced their plan to get married, Mayumi's mother was somehow able to persuade her father to consent.

I asked Mayumi why her father had been unhappy with her relationship. She explained:

> My father was strongly against the idea of me marrying a black man. He has an old-fashioned way of thinking. You see, his younger sister married a black man several decades ago, and at that time, it seems, black men had a very bad image here in Okinawa. My father, who was the *chōnan* [eldest son], opposed the marriage, and I have the impression that the situation became sort of violent [*bōryoku mitai na kanji de*]. "I won't allow you to go to America at all, much less marry a black man!" That kind of thing. But my aunt went ahead and married him anyway and left for the United States. That's why I didn't want to tell

my father about Isaac. But you know, my aunt is still married and is very happy. My father is just plain stubborn. If Isaac had been white, he would have been more supportive. But because he was black, my father experienced a great shock. He is simply prejudiced.

Considering the pervasiveness of negative stereotypes of U.S. military men, regardless of racial background, I was surprised that Mayumi had attributed her father's disapproval solely to Isaac's skin color. By most accounts, the U.S. military desegregated earlier and more successfully than other sectors of U.S. society. Racial discrimination was officially abolished in 1948, with the signing of Executive Order 9981. Military boot camps, schools, hospitals, and base housing were desegregated during the early 1950s, and the last of the all-black units was abolished in 1954. While segregated off-base entertainment districts persisted during the Vietnam War, Okinawans had been exposed to a mostly integrated U.S. military presence in on- and off-base settings for decades by the time Mayumi and Isaac (and perhaps even Mayumi's aunt and her husband) began dating. I began to consider how widespread such racial attitudes were and why they had endured. Did African American military husbands typically experience less acceptance than other foreign spouses? And how were their children treated by Okinawan family and neighbors?

Terrance Carter

Terrance Carter first came to Okinawa with the U.S. Air Force in the early 1980s. Having grown up in a midsize town in western North Carolina, he joined the military with the specific purpose of getting assigned to Japan. He hoped to meet a successful Japanese businessman who would teach him how to run a business Japanese-style. Japan's bubble economy was at its peak, and Terrance had recently graduated from college. "There were no jobs in the U.S., and Japan was on top of the world." With this plan in mind, Terrance declined the Air Force's offer to send him to officer candidate school in favor of a general enlistment so that he would not have to spend more than four years in the service. He secured an assignment to Kadena Air Base in Okinawa, completed his enlistment, and then separated from the military.

Having developed an appreciation for Okinawa's natural beauty, culture, and people, Terrance was determined to stay. He began working for Eagle Technologies, an American-owned construction company whose primary client was the U.S. military. His future wife, Miyuki, was employed as the company's office manager. Miyuki came from a well-to-do Okinawan family that owned considerable land in Urasoe City. She had studied in the United States for a year and later graduated with a degree in English from Okinawa Christian University. She spoke English fluently. The two developed a close friendship and eventually began dating. In 1993, they decided to marry, but Miyuki's father refused to meet Terrance. Terrance explained, "My father-in-law told my wife that he didn't like black guys. I said okay, I can accept that . . . I grew up in the South where *a lot* of people didn't like black guys." Miyuki's father threatened to write her out of his will if she married Terrance, but she ignored his wishes, declining an inheritance of considerable value. Terrance had still not met his father-in-law when we interviewed in 2002, although he was certain that the two must have crossed paths many times at funerals and other family events during the previous eight years. "You see, my father-in-law was born in the neighborhood where he lives now. He is seventy years old, and he has lived in that neighborhood his entire life. I think he's afraid that his friends would not accept me, or look down on him for his daughter marrying outside of her race."

I asked Terrance if he thought that his father-in-law would have reacted similarly if his daughter had married a white U.S. military man. He told me no, the man had flatly told her that he didn't approve of Terrance because he was black. Terrance offered an explanation that drew on Okinawa's occupation-era past: "After World War II, the black soldiers came in and were in charge of Okinawa, and maybe something happened at that time." During the Battle of Okinawa, he explained, it was white soldiers who took the island during combat, but once the territory was secured, an all-black infantry unit from Kentucky (presumably, the segregated Twenty-Fourth Infantry) was brought in to garrison. He continued, "Those men were placed in a position of power over Okinawans, and they did some pretty terrible things." Pointing to a string of crimes that involved African American GIs—including the rape of a twelve-year-old girl in 1995 and a young Okinawan woman in Chatan the previous summer—Terrance blamed Okinawan racial attitudes on a small group of African American servicemen and their criminal behavior. I asked whether he thought that the adoption of American racial attitudes might also factor into local racism. He agreed, "I'm sure that is also true. My wife's mother had at one time been a maid on base in the officers' quarters, from the mid-sixties through the seventies, when there were no black officers." He then noted that the military had changed and listed a number of high-ranking African American generals who had been assigned to Okinawa.

Aside from the conflict with his wife's father and a relatively distant relationship with her mother, Terrance claimed that he himself had not experienced racial prejudice or discrimination in Okinawa. As an employee of Eagle Technologies and an active member of the American Chamber of Commerce, his business connections included other prominent members of the U.S. expatriate community and their Japanese employees and subcontractors. As a member of his wife's family, he attended weekend camping trips and family events of all sorts. His children were enrolled in Japanese schools and spoke Japanese as their first language. They were welcomed and loved "just like any other grandchild" by his wife's family, even by his father-in-law. Race was not an issue, Terrance told me emphatically, aside from his own relationship with his father-in-law and perhaps among certain strategizing antibase politicians and left-leaning journalists.

Iha Mayumi's and Terrance Carter's stories illustrate the prominence of racial thinking in Okinawan interpretations of the occupation-era past and how that past is invoked to explain contemporary attitudes. Notably, both individuals referred to a generic racialized past to explain contemporary racial attitudes. The story of Mayumi's aunt was narrated as justification for her father's opposition to her relationship with Isaac, but other than the comment "At that time, it seems, black men had a very bad image here in Okinawa," no specific reasons for his feelings were articulated. Terrance also alluded to the past but was not able to pinpoint a precise incident that might have sparked his father-in-law's dislike of black men. This kind of nonspecific narrative explanation is a common way of justifying negative attitudes toward U.S. military men, especially African American servicemen. American racial understandings and prejudices, held by white personnel and embedded in U.S. military policy, have certainly influenced Okinawan views. So too have Japanese systems of racial classification introduced during the late nineteenth century. Nevertheless, examining narrative data from informal conversations and formal interviews, the relatively constant wording and structure of such racialized memories is striking.

On a weekend in June, while taking time off to explore Okinawa's nearby islands, I encountered a different sort of racialized memory narrative, a more specific account of occupation-era violence and victimization. The narrator's open and even self-righteous discussion of the taboos surrounding such stories led me to reconsider the stories and explanations given by Mayumi, Terrance, and others.

The Katsuyama Cave Incident

I met Inafuku Setsuko unexpectedly at a popular snorkeling spot on Zamami Island. Inafuku, an Okinawan tour guide employed on Kadena Air Base, was in Zamami with a group of American military families who had signed up for the excursion at the on-base tour office. She asked about my research and then told me that her parents had forbidden her to date Americans when she was younger, especially African Americans. As if to explain this, she proceeded to tell me about her involvement in a case involving African American soldiers and wartime sexual violence. In 1998, the bones of three U.S. marines were discovered in a hillside cave in the Katsuyama district of Nago City. The three were identified through

dental records as members of the segregated Thirty-Seventh Marine Depot Unit
(Sims 2000a). Soon after the discovery, local newspapers—and later *Stars and
Stripes* and the *New York Times*—featured stories that quoted elderly members
of the mountain community who recalled the circumstances surrounding the
marines' deaths. Residents claimed that after the United States had won the battle,
three black marines (one "as large as a sumo wrestler") came into the village every
weekend and abducted local women, taking them into the hills and raping them.
The violence occurred repeatedly until one day, with the help of two armed Japanese soldiers who were holding out in the nearby mountains, the villagers am-
bushed and shot several marines whom they believed to be the rapists and beat
them to death. They dumped the bodies in a hillside cave and vowed never to
speak of the incident to outsiders. The cave became known to local residents as
kurombō gama (Cave of the Negroes).[3]

Inafuku told me that she had been contacted about the incident by an elderly
man from Katsuyama in the spring of 1997. He had sought her help because she
worked for the military and had been involved in recovering the remains of American and Japanese soldiers in the past. When she began inquiring about the three
marines and looking for the cave, however, both the military and the villagers discouraged her search. Inafuku was indignant that she had been branded a trou-
blemaker by both sides. After several months of searching, she and the man found
the cave and notified local police. She concluded her story matter-of-factly: "You
know, that is why so many Okinawans are afraid of black men."

According to the *New York Times*, the discovery of bones in Katsuyama dredged
up powerful local resentment about violent crimes committed by U.S. military
personnel in the early years of the occupation (Sims 2000a). Women's advocates
claim that as many as ten thousand Okinawan women were raped by U.S. occupation personnel in the immediate aftermath of the war, but most did not report
the crimes out of shame or fear.[4] Tacitly acknowledging the magnitude of the
problem, U.S. military leaders cooperated with local officials during the 1950s to
create specially designated bar districts where U.S. personnel could interact with
Okinawan women employed as bargirls and prostitutes, while protecting other
residents (see chapter 3). Sexual violence against women who worked in these
entertainment districts attracted little public attention or sympathy, revealing
deep-seated gender and class prejudices in Okinawan society (Angst 2001; Tanji
2006).[5]

The reluctance of U.S. military officials and residents of Katsuyama to assist
Inafuku's investigation of the Katsuyama incident five decades later, when most
persons with firsthand knowledge of the incident had long since died, suggests
that powerful taboos continue to govern talk about postwar sexual violence in
Okinawa. For the U.S. military and U.S. and Japanese governments, the public

relations goal of protecting the already-shaky relationship between the bases and local communities guides official responses and positions. For Okinawans, the shame associated with sexual victimization—experienced not only by the female victims, but also by many Okinawan men who interpret the rapes as an affront to Okinawan masculinity—prescribes silence.[6] The international media's most pressing concern, on the other hand, seems to have been timeliness. *Stars and Stripes* and the *New York Times* broke the Katsuyama story days before the 2000 G8 summit opened in Nago, to the chagrin of government officials. Once it appeared in print, the story became a tool for articulating Okinawan subjectivity and racial attitudes toward American military men.

Narrative, Identity, and Racialized Memories in Okinawa

The story of the Katsuyama cave incident is part of a well-known corpus of popular stories and more tangible physical monuments and memorials that evoke the horrors of the Battle of Okinawa and the personal and collective sacrifices associated with U.S. military occupation. Hundreds of war memorials dot the countryside, especially in the vicinity of Mabuni Hill in southern Okinawa, where thousands died. Peace museums and war and peace tours aim to educate schoolchildren and visitors about the specifics of the battle. Postwar literature and theatrical and dance performances express and comment upon the traumatic and ongoing effects of war, displacement, and dispossession (Nelson 2008; Ikeda 2014). Personal testimonials, displayed at the Prefectural Peace Memorial Museum and narrated on television every June 23, Okinawan Memorial Day, also contribute to the repertoire of public memory. It has been argued that Okinawans have a higher historical awareness (*rekishi ninshiki*) than mainland Japanese (Figal 1997, 755). Historian Ishihara Masaie has asserted that since the 1970s, "the collection of oral histories has become a philosophical and cultural movement in Okinawa" (Ishihara 2001, 97). Prior to reversion, personal recollection of wartime experiences was mostly conducted in private, in the presence of no one outside of the immediate family. "For the first twenty-five years after the war it was virtually impossible to record the testimonies of the survivors of the battle. Due to the incredible horror, cruelty, and shame they experienced, most people could not bring themselves to talk about it" (Ishihara 2001, 89).[7] Following reversion, however, personal narratives of the battle became a powerful ideological resource for Okinawan identity formation and identity politics (Tanji 2006). Ishihara argues that this is due to the continuing presence of the large U.S. military bases, which powerfully shape contemporary Okinawan historical consciousness. "The mere existence of the military bases serves as a daily reminder of the searing experiences of the war. Add to that the twenty-seven years of undemocratic American military occupation and the seemingly endless series of base-related problems and incidences, such as crimes, fatal accidents, water and noise pollution, live-fire exercises, the discovery of unexploded bombs in residential areas during the construction of houses, and numerous other problems" (2001, 97). Historian Yakabi Osamu claims that Okinawan memory is distinctive because "'the battlefield,' 'the occupation,' and 'the rehabilitation' are experienced as a simultaneous and multilayered process." He adds, "Whereas the [U.S.] colonizer comprehends these three events to happen one after another as if they form a linear chronological trajectory" (quoted and translated in Kina 2016, 195). Echoing this idea, former governor Ōta Masahide stated with reference to the contemporary antibase movement, "The war is far from over in Okinawa. Then why prepare for more wars?" (Ota and Norimatsu 2010).

Personal narratives, including testimonials by Okinawan war survivors, play an important role in local identity formation. Anthropologists and historians have explored how individuals and groups "use rememberings in the construction of narratives about an historically integrated self" and as a compass for future action (Angst 2001; see also Young 1994; Antze and Lambek 1996). Linguistic anthropologists, more specifically, focus on the ways in which participants employ narratives within social interaction, as well as the semiotic processes that connect stories of personal experience to the shared memories of the group (Ricoeur 1991; Linde 1993; Ochs and Capps 2001; Bucholtz and Hall 2005). The latter approach rests upon the premise that identity, and indeed culture itself, is produced within interaction (Bucholtz and Hall 2005).[8] In postreversion Okinawa, publically shared stories of the Battle of Okinawa and U.S. occupation have come to symbolize or allegorize the experiences of all Okinawans. By pointing to well-known examples, either through direct reference or indirectly via word choice, invocation of a particular spatial setting, or personal judgment, an individual may associate himself or herself with a particular socially recognized stance or identity, even while avoiding open discussion of his or her own painful past experiences. The vague explanations that Mayumi and Terrance received and then reiterated to account for their family members' negative attitudes toward black GIs likely resulted from this narrative strategy. There was no need for Mayumi's father or Terrance's father-in-law to spell out specific reasons for their racial attitudes when they could expect to be understood by simply alluding to experiences that were "shared by all."

Publicly shared narratives of war and occupation also function as a set of scripts that illustrate behaviors that conform to or violate popular codes of behavior and morality.[9] Recited by parents and grandparents, memories of war and occupation

Kazuo Kunishi, *Crossing the Ordinary and the Extraordinary*. © K. Kunishi

continually emerge as evidence for why Okinawan women should not date or marry American military men. Interviewees frequently mentioned that members of their families had been killed or otherwise victimized by American soldiers to explain why parents had opposed their marriages. The specifics of these past events, however, remained vague. Rather, stereotypical images of U.S. military men as invaders, liberators, occupiers, and oppressors, grounded in well-known stories of war and occupation, served as easily recognized mnemonic "signposts" (Fentress and Wickham 1992), signaling the victimization of Okinawans by Americans more generally, along with the undesirability of intimate relationships with U.S. military men. For younger generations, the indexical as-

semblages that link the warnings of parents and loved ones to the broader repertoire of Okinawan memory are not always clear. Whether due to the growing
gulf of years separating today's youth from the wartime and postwar generations, or to the contested nature of public memory itself (Yonetani 2003), the
connections that older Okinawans take for granted are often not obvious to those
with no direct experience of war. Without instant access to the narrative content of
Okinawan public memory, well known to older Okinawans through repeated ex-
posure over the decades, younger Okinawans and many American military
personnel, like Mayumi and Terrance, tend to perceive the warnings of family
members as a reflection of ungrounded racial prejudice. For this reason, the dwin-
dling number of Okinawan war survivors has been of great concern to the dispa-
rate groups that make up today's peace movement, leading to what Julia Yonetani
has described as "a sense of a prevailing crisis of memory of the war" (2003, 200).

Japanese imperial ideologies concerning racial and ethnic superiority over
whites, blacks, and other Asians—propagated throughout the Japanese empire
during the late nineteenth and early twentieth centuries—also contribute to
Okinawan perceptions of U.S. military men. Yasuhiro Okada (2011) has argued
that such discourses, alongside encounters with the Jim Crow U.S. Army, contributed to prejudice against African American garrison troops in mainland Japan.
Such ideologies also took hold in Okinawa, where they were reinterpreted and
transformed in response to encounters with American invaders and occupation
personnel. The following discussion explores Okinawan racial thinking in relation to Japanese imperial ideologies. Although elements of this history may not
be familiar to younger residents of the prefecture, their effects are evident in the
testimonies of those who survived the war, and they contribute to how that group
responds to military international intimacy.

Race in Japanese Imperial Discourses

It has been argued that ideas of race and racism, in the present-day senses of the
terms, did not exist in Japan before the nineteenth century (Morris-Suzuki 1998;
Russell 2007). Until the late eighteenth century, most Japanese views of lands and
peoples outside of the archipelago were influenced by China. The Chinese *hua-yi*
model of humanity organized the world into a series of concentric circles, with
China (called *hua*) representing the civilized center, surrounded by strange and
exotic foreigners (called *yi*), marked by their unrefined customs and values. Within
the Chinese model, strangeness or barbarism increased as one moved outward
from the center—that is, from China's "middle kingdom" outward to Mongolia
in the north, Korea and Japan to the east, India and Java to the south, then Arabia,

Europe, Africa, and eventually, to lands inhabited by giants, dwarfs, people with multiple heads, and so forth. Imported into Japan by scholars of the Chinese classics, the *hua-yi* model (pronounced *ka-i* in Japanese) was adapted over time so that by the end of the eighteenth century, Japan rather than China came to occupy the center. Tessa Morris-Suzuki (1998) traces this transition, noting the important role of peripheral peoples like Ainu and Ryukyuans in representing the boundaries of the Japanese and helping solidify their position as the civilized center of humankind.

Beginning in the early seventeenth century, after Satsuma invaded Ryūkyū (1609), elaborate tribute missions were organized in which Ryukyuan princes and other government envoys, merchants, and craftsmen traveled to Kagoshima and then over land to Edo to demonstrate their respect and submission to the Tokugawa shogun. Satsuma carefully managed impressions of Ryūkyū as an exotic foreign land and itself as the only Japanese feudal domain powerful enough to command a foreign kingdom. Ryūkyū envoys were instructed "to carry long swords, dress in brocade, and bring with them 'Chinese-style' weaponry" (Morris-Suzuki 1998, 19). Ryukyuans were further identified by their unique hairstyles, women's hand tattoos, and their bone-washing funerary practices. Morris-Suzuki argues that Japanese thinkers of the period tended to view such differences as cultural, consisting mainly of outer appearances and etiquette, rather than as immutable racial differences. Thus in theory, it was possible for Ryukyuans, Ainu, and other exotic peoples to *become* Japanese by tying up their hair in the Japanese fashion, learning to speak Japanese, and adopting other Japanese customs. This kind of assimilation was encouraged during the Meiji period (1868–1912), as Japan embarked on its own Western-style modernization program.

Within the *ka-i* framework, Europeans and others living outside of Japan's orbit, while also recognized for their strange beliefs and behaviors, tended to be characterized in terms of their physical differences from Japanese.[10] European traders from Portugal and Spain, referred to as *nanbanjin* (southern barbarians), appeared in Japanese writings, paintings, and maps with large, rounded eyes, pointed noses, and red hair. Abundant facial and body hair were observed, leading to associations with animals and poor hygiene, and the development of an overall link between hairiness and barbarian status (Gottlieb 2006).[11] After 1641, Dutch merchants became the only Westerners permitted to maintain trade and shipping in Japan via Deshima, an artificial island in Nagasaki Bay. Dutchmen were described as tall with slender legs, sallow skin, and sparkling green eyes. They were observed to eat meat (which caused them to stink), drink alcohol, smoke tobacco, and spend entire nights having sex. Not surprisingly, they tended to be short-lived, with almost no one reaching the age of seventy or eighty (Keene 1969;

Leupp 2003; Vos 2014). Over time, the term *orandajin* (Hollander) acquired a more general meaning and came to refer to all white Europeans.[12]

Japanese descriptions of Africans and Southeast Asians who arrived on European ships noted their darker skin color but tended not to interpret physical features as indicative of racial superiority or inferiority. Malays, Indonesians, East Indians, and Africans accompanied Europeans as sailors, interpreters, artisans, servants, and slaves. Japanese observers commented on the mistreatment of Africans, in particular, by Europeans. Physician Hirokawa Kai, for example, wrote that "the *kurobō* [blacks] possess a fine character. They perform backbreaking and dangerous tasks for their masters without complaint . . . . I cannot fathom the ways of the red-hairs [the Dutch in Nagasaki], who work and lash [their slaves] as if they were beasts and who kill the young and the strong who resist and throw their bodies into the sea" (quoted in Russell 2007, 26). On the basis of comments like these, John Russell has argued that Japanese views of Africans were generally favorable before European racial ideologies and prejudices took hold. During the seventeenth and eighteenth centuries, the *ka-i* explanatory framework, which positioned Japan at the civilized center of the world, came under increasing pressure as Western scientific texts, from astronomy to medicine, filtered into Japan via the Dutch trading post in Nagasaki.

During the same period, Western ships also landed periodically on islands in the Ryūkyū chain. Initially, Shuri government officials expressed little concern over these sporadic encounters, greeting the foreigners in the same way they did passengers of all foreign vessels, granting assistance as requested while remaining vigilant. Following the Satsuma invasion, the government's main concern was negotiating Ryūkyū's precarious relationships with Satsuma, the Tokugawa *bakufu*, and imperial China (Smits 1999).[13] Ryūkyū officials and intellectuals clearly viewed Japan and China as their most noteworthy Others. During the 1840s, however, the number of European landings in Ryūkyū increased dramatically, with local officials reporting to the government an average of four encounters with French, British, and American ships each year (Hellyer 2010, 152). Notable European visits included the 1846 arrival of the British ship *Starling*, carrying the Protestant missionary Bernard Jean Bettelheim. The Bettelheim family disembarked from the ship under cover of night and set up residence in Naha's Gokoku-ji temple, which they continued to occupy for the next seven years against the wishes of local officials. American naval officer Matthew Calbraith Perry also called at Naha in 1853 and 1854 on his way to and from Edo. During his second visit, Perry hosted a banquet for local administrators with a blackface minstrel show as entertainment, demonstrating American attitudes toward and ridicule of blacks. The British defeat of China in the First Opium War (1839–1842) alarmed officials in Ryūkyū and Japan, and in response, the *bakufu* issued an edict requiring Japanese domains to repel European ships that appeared in their waters, using force if necessary. Without the means to fend off foreign ships, Shuri officials were pressured by Perry to sign the Lew Chew Compact (July 11, 1854), a treaty outlining conditions of future friendship and commerce between Ryūkyū and the United States. The compact permitted unlimited visitation and residence by Americans in Ryūkyū and mandated that American criminal suspects be turned over to U.S. authorities, foreshadowing later agreements such as the postreversion status of forces agreement (Rabson 2016). Perry's success in opening Japan and Ryūkyū to American trade and ending the Tokugawa seclusion policy contributed to the eventual collapse of the shogunate and the restoration of Japanese imperial rule in 1868.

In the whirlwind years following the Meiji Restoration, Japanese politicians and intellectuals initiated sweeping changes throughout Japan's territories to strengthen social and economic institutions and counter the foreign threat. Within decades, they had created a highly centralized government, a constitution and elected parliament, a well-developed transport and communication system, an educated population, a rapidly growing industrial sector, and a powerful army and navy. They had also established control over borders and annexed neighboring lands: Ezo (renamed Hokkaido, 1869), the Kuril Islands (1875), the Ogasawara Islands (1876), Ryūkyū (renamed Okinawa, 1879), Taiwan (1895), and Korea (1910). During this period of rapid modernization and imperialist expansion, notions of Japanese culture (*bunka*) and civilization (*bunmei*) were reformulated incorporating European ideas, leading to revised ideas concerning Okinawans and other peripheral peoples, and Japan's position vis-à-vis the West. Notably, Meiji intellectuals reconceived the spatialized model of difference that underlay the older *ka-i* framework in terms of a chronological stagelike progression from barbaric traditional societies to civilized modern ones (Morris-Suzuki 1998). Western racial classifications, embedded in the writings of European philosophers and sociologists, were adopted along with this stage theory of social progress. In *Outline of a Theory of Civilization* (1875), scholar and statesman Fukuzawa Yukichi (1834–1901) divided human societies into three developmental stages: barbarism (represented by Africa), semi-civilization (represented by Asia), and civilization (represented by the West). In his bestseller *World Geography* (1869), Fukuzawa sorted the world's peoples into five color-coded and hierarchically arranged racial categories—white, yellow, red, black, and brown—using civilizational advancement as evidence of racial superiority.[14] Within this framework, Japan trailed Europe in the development of modern civilization, but it appeared comfortably advanced alongside neighboring Ainu and Ryukyuan peoples. Intrigued by this model, Japanese ethnologists Torii Ryūzō (1870–1953) and Yanagita Kunio

(1875–1962) conducted research in Japan's periphery to document disappearing folk practices and search for links with Japan. Yanagita and others maintained that Okinawans and other peripheral peoples represented an earlier stage of human development; they lived as all Japanese peoples had once lived throughout the archipelago. Yanagita argued, for example, that Ryukyuan religion, and especially the spiritual power of women, represented an earlier or original form of Japanese Shinto. In 1906, Okinawan linguist and folklorist Iha Fuyū (1876–1947) published an influential article in the newspaper *Ryūkyū Shimpō* on the historical relationship between the Okinawan and Japanese peoples. Based on comparative linguistic evidence and his reading of ancient historical texts, Iha argued that the two peoples collectively composed a single race that had separated from one another several thousand years ago. Together, the two shared a common ancestor, which distinguished them from the Ainu and Taiwanese "barbarians" (*seiban*) (Matsumura 2015, 119). Iha concluded with a statement celebrating the reunification of the two "siblings" under the emperor system. Iha's theory of shared origins and support for Japanese annexation did not necessarily indicate his agreement with complete assimilation. Rather, his work set the stage for Okinawan intellectuals to demand equality based on the shared relationship, along with rights that were not available to other imperial subjects (Tomiyama 1990; Nelson 2008; Matsumura 2015).

Beginning in 1880, Japanese elementary schools were established throughout Okinawa to carry out the essential work of linguistic assimilation, needed for communicating with Japanese colonial administrators and instilling patriotism. A normal school was established to train teachers, and middle schools were opened to develop a corps of government clerks and interpreters. In 1882, five young men of former aristocratic families were sent to Tokyo to study at government expense.[15] They were followed by a cadre of Okinawans who attended university in mainland Japan, including Iha Fuyū and his brother, Iha Getsujō, a prominent poet (Bhowmik 2008). Tomiyama Ichirō (1998) has stressed the gap between elite Okinawans who eagerly pursued education and supported Japanization and conservative non-elites, particularly in the countryside, who quietly resisted by neglecting to pay taxes or send their children to school, employing local religious specialists rather than medical doctors, singing Okinawan folk songs, and speaking Ryukyuan languages. By 1902, however, the rate of elementary school attendance had reached 99.3 percent (Bhowmik 2008, 21). Elementary school geography textbooks, many directly modeled on Fukuzawa's *World Geography*, were a primary means through which the stage-theory of social progress and Western racial hierarchies were disseminated to school-aged children throughout Okinawa (Takezawa 2015).

The Japanese concepts of *minzoku* (variously translated as race, ethnicity, or nation) and *jinshu* (biological race), both imported from the West and enthusiastically adopted by Meiji-era Japanese, require additional explanation. Whereas Western imperialists depended heavily on concepts of race and racial difference—that is, the classification of human beings into putatively fixed categories based on shared physical characteristics or ancestry—to justify the social and political inequalities of colonialism (Stoler 1989, 2002), Japanese imperial expansion required a different conceptual apparatus. Some ardent nationalists declared the Japanese to be a racially homogenous group descended from the gods via the imperial bloodline. Others embraced scientific studies showing that the archipelago was settled by varied peoples from the continent and Southeast Asia; the Japanese were therefore racially mixed.[16] Still others dodged the question of race altogether, emphasizing instead the cultural unity of all Asian peoples as a justification for pan-Asian political aspirations. As Morris-Suzuki (1998) points out, the term *minzoku* was fraught with ambiguity and contradiction with respect to physical differences, cultural similarities, and relative civilizational advancement, rendering it useful in nationalist discourse. "All three justifications of colonial expansion—the ideas of racial uniqueness, ethnic commonalities, and civilizational advancement—coexisted at different layers within the intellectual world of the 1920s, 1930s, and 1940s, and the use of ambiguous imagery of 'nation' and 'ethnos'—*minzoku*—allowed a continuous slippage backward and forward between different levels of justification" (87).

Whereas the flexible term *minzoku* was used when describing differences and similarities among the peoples of the Japanese empire, *jinshu* was preferred when referring to Westerners and other non-Asian peoples. The latter term's meanings were shaped to a large degree by Meiji intellectuals like Fukuzawa, who used *jinshu* to refer to the five color-coded divisions of humankind. Even so, John Dower (1986) argues that Japanese understandings of race were not so much a system of physical categorization as a set of claims regarding spiritual purity and moral righteousness. That is, while European-like notions of race showed up in a preoccupation with lineage, and especially the shared lineage of the Japanese people, the point was to argue that whereas Westerners were tainted by a quest for wealth and power, the Japanese lineage was uniquely situated to attain "pure heart." Japan's imperial mission for the Greater East-Asian Co-Prosperity Sphere was thus to rid the world of the moral impurities, such as egocentrism (individualism), extravagance (capitalism), and materialism (Marxism), and establish a new world order based on the ideals of harmony and "proper place" (Dower 1986, 226). In wartime propaganda, American soldiers were characterized as *spiritually* unclean, beastlike, and demonic, sometimes represented visually by horns, a tail, or animal hindquarters. They were said to be preoccupied with sex, fixated on creature comforts, and aspiring to world domination. But this had little to do with skin color. Rather, it was Western history and culture that led them to behave like animals.

Their inhumanity was evident in their race-hate, demonstrated by a long history of anti-Japanese prejudice and discrimination, slavery, and the lynching of blacks. Within this rhetoric, African Americans appeared as the oppressed targets of white racism. In fact, Japanese ideologues often expressed solidarity with black Americans as fellow people of color. At the same time, they continued to articulate Meiji-era ideas concerning race and social progress, which positioned blacks as the least developed of the world's peoples (Russell 2007).

These imperial racial discourses circulated widely in prewar and wartime Okinawa and were embraced by Okinawans of all classes. Elites and members of the nascent middle class were heavily indoctrinated through the Japanese education system. Acceptance of modern theories of race and social progress and support of government assimilation policies marked them as already-modernized subjects of the emperor, and thus as the vanguard of Japan's civilizing project. Serving as local government officials and teachers, educated Okinawans helped implement government initiatives and spread imperialist propaganda throughout the islands, including notions of duty and devotion to the emperor and characterizations of the foreign enemy as bestial and demonic. Testimonials of survivors of the Battle of Okinawa illustrate the power of imperial propaganda. From Isa Junko, orphaned during the battle at age fourteen: "From these same [Japanese] troops, we also heard that women who'd been captured in the central areas of the island were being raped by American soldiers and that these Americans were killing children by ripping them apart at the crotch" (Keyso 2000, 6).[17] From Chibana Kamado, survivor of the group suicide at Chibichiri Gama in Yomitan village: "Even in private, we were always talking about it. [The American soldiers] will cut off our ears and our noses, so don't let them capture you, never be taken prisoner . . . . It's better to die than to be treated like that" (Junkerman 2016). From the diary of a sixteen-year-old boy, found by an American soldier shortly after organized Japanese resistance had ended: the boy wrote about joining the local defense forces in order to repulse the invasion of American "devil-beasts" (kichiku) (Rabson 2010, 21). These examples suggest that wartime propaganda, spread through schools, media, and the Japanese military, was extremely effective. Embedded within such ideological messages were concepts of race. Although skin color and other physical characteristics were deemphasized, group origins and bodily practices were considered important. Especially relevant to postwar perceptions of U.S. military personnel, enemy soldiers were believed to be ruled by animal-like desires, lack self-discipline and social discipline, and be devoid of human compassion. Above all, they were associated with rape and killing. During wartime, such stereotypes were mainly applied to white American soldiers, but they also affected perceptions of nonwhites. During the postwar occupation, this imagery was overlaid with American discourses on race and became associated with specific groups of American GIs, namely those marginalized by U.S. racial ideologies embedded in U.S. military institution and occupation government discourses.

Race during the U.S. Occupation

Terrance Carter's narrative draws attention to another important source of racialized memories in Okinawa: official histories of the U.S. occupation, including material drawn from government documents and distilled in military and political histories and school textbooks. U.S. control of the Okinawan government until 1972 has meant that official statistics on crimes committed by American soldiers reflect the perspective of the occupiers rather than the victims. Furthermore, official histories tend to interpret such crimes within the discursive framework of mid-twentieth century race relations in the United States, rather than as a result of wartime violence and the power inequities inherent in foreign military occupation. Postreversion Okinawa has inherited this "history," even as interpretations of the past are refracted through present-day social and political values.

Race, with an emphasis on skin color, has been a primary organizing principle of official policy and popular understandings of U.S. military expansion since the late nineteenth century (Bender and Lipman 2015). Despite a wide array of voices within the military, a consistent set of racial images and tropes have been continuously recycled in official statements and private letters, diaries, and memoirs of American military men. References to the African slave trade, ideas of Manifest Destiny and a mythic American frontier, and an abundance of "Indian country" metaphors appear in accounts of U.S. military interventions in the Philippines in 1898 (Murolo 2011), Haiti from 1915 to 1934 (Renda 2001), Japan during World War II (Dower 1986, 1999), Vietnam during the 1960s and 1970s (Slotkin 1992), and Iraq and the Middle East since 2003 (Silliman 2008). Furthermore, historians have documented the pervasiveness of analogical links between African Americans and Native Americans on the one hand, and Filipinos, Japanese, Vietnamese, and Iraqis on the other. They argue that these links reflect an overall framing of U.S. military conflict as a sustained race war, an ideological framework that desegregation of the military did little to abate. Historian Kimberley Phillips has argued, "Even as African Americans' roles in wars expanded, . . . sustained wars and militarism allowed for the realignment and solidification of racial ideologies in [U.S.] law and culture. Wherever the military appeared, its racial practices followed, and it empowered populations around military bases to police segregation, including in areas where it had not previously existed" (2012, 8).[18] In Okinawa, official histories of the occupation accordingly characterized African

American and Filipino garrison troops in much the same way as U.S. enemies in combat had been characterized during preceding conflicts.

Two major tropes organize images of white U.S. military men in official histories and popular memory: American soldiers as members of an invading army and American soldiers as liberators. As Michael Molasky has pointed out, "Despite the tremendous devastation visited upon Japan's main islands, the American assault was waged from the skies and the enemy was invisible . . . . Few civilian residents of Japan's main islands actually saw U.S. troops in combat, and most never set eyes on an American soldier until he arrived, transformed, as the occupation soldier" (1999, 15). Okinawans, on the other hand, first encountered American GIs as flesh-and-blood combat soldiers—"as the enemy, pointing guns into the caves and ancestral tombs where civilians and soldiers alike had taken refuge" (Molasky 1999). Moreover, since war and occupation were simultaneously ongoing in different locales in Okinawa during the spring and summer of 1945, "the distinction is blurred between those American soldiers who waged war, those who occupied the islands between 1945 and 1972, and the tens of thousands who have been stationed there since reversion" (Molasky 1999).

Alongside these warrior images, the trope of American soldier as liberator is also firmly entrenched in Okinawa, as it is in mainland Japan.[19] The war was over, and the American occupation force behaved in a more humane manner than was initially feared. In Okinawa and mainland Japan, social, political, and economic reforms were enacted, including the granting of women's suffrage. Food and clothing were shipped from the United States and distributed inside refugee camps and ration distribution centers, enhancing the image of the United States as a generous benefactor. One of the most evocative images featured American soldiers offering Hershey's chocolate or chewing gum to crowds of eager children. This stock image resonated for many Okinawans I spoke with. On occasion, perfect strangers approached me to talk about the kindnesses of American GIs during the early months of the occupation, inserting themselves into the clichéd chocolate-and-chewing-gum storyline. On New Year's Eve, at the temple yard in Yabu village, for instance, I met a man who told me that he and his boyhood friends had made a game of chasing U.S. military jeeps as they rumbled along the unpaved road that ran through the village. The soldiers were frightening with their large guns, but they threw chewing gum and candy to the boys, who scrambled after the sweets and then dashed away to the safety of the trees. "We were so very hungry," he recollected with a sad smile.

As Molasky argues, the liberator trope communicates mixed moral messages. In occupation-era literature, "images of the friendly occupation soldier are often coupled with a sense of humiliation and envy at his overwhelming material and physical endowment. The occupation soldier is not only remembered as big and strong but as possessing an endless supply of material wealth—including the basics of food, clothing, and shelter, which were in short supply for several years following Japan's defeat" (1999, 9). As Molasky glibly points out, the soldier in the chocolate-and-chewing-gum image was invariably white (1999, 71). No segregated African American infantry units directly participated in the invasion, although several army and Marine Corps divisions had segregated port and amphibious truck companies attached. The segregated Twenty-Fourth Infantry arrived in late August 1945 to help garrison the island when the Tenth Army redeployed to Korea. Contrary to popular images of white soldiers, images of African American garrison soldiers emphasized physical difference, along with instances of violent behavior and, most prominently, rape (Molasky 1999).

The U.S. Army's importation of Philippine Scouts to garrison Okinawa when the segregated African American units departed reinforced the perceptual equivalence between African Americans and Filipinos.[20] Filipino men living in Okinawa today—including active-duty U.S. servicemen, DoD civilians, and those who reside in Okinawa independently—are impacted as much as African American men by the discursive intersections of skin color, occupation-era violence, and moral prescriptions. Several women related to me that their parents would not be happy with either an African American or a Filipino son-in-law.[21] Histories written by U.S. Army historians further illustrate the equivalence. U.S. military histories claim that sexual violence during the early occupation was perpetrated by a handful of "undisciplined" servicemen, mostly enlisted men from the all-black and Filipino garrison units. For example, army historian Arnold G. Fisch (1988) blamed the army's segregation policies for the frequency of violent crimes committed by black soldiers, yet deflected criticism away from military leadership onto "poorly trained" and "substandard" African American soldiers themselves. "Bound by the Army's racial policy, field commanders were forced to concentrate large numbers of black troops, who neither by aptitude nor training belonged in the service, into the small number of black units where their impact overwhelmed the able black soldiers whose abilities and ambitions were most often overshadowed . . . . The reputation for crime and misconduct earned by black units in the Ryukyus, therefore, could be traced to the substandard character of these units formed by the Army's racial policies" (83). Fisch's explanation echoes official military discourse on desegregation during the Korean War.[22] The argument that segregation concentrated poorly trained soldiers into a limited number of all-black units is integral to the military's own internal critique of segregation in the ranks (Mershon and Schlossman 1998). In Okinawa, this line of argumentation reinforced racist assumptions that African Americans were unreliable soldiers who were more inclined to commit violent crime—in short, that their essential inferiority was exacerbated by the military's segregationist policies.

The departure of all-black segregated units from Okinawa in 1946–1947 did not coincide with a decrease in the number of crimes involving U.S. military personnel.[23] Once the segregated units left, however, accusations were transferred to the Philippine Scouts who rotated in to replace them. Fisch wrote, "One week after the 44th Infantry (Philippine Scouts) arrived, the Okinawan civil police commissioner reported to military government officials that the regiment's commanding officer had insulted uniformed Okinawan police officers and that the 44th Infantry was 'extremely undisciplined. Police members and inhabitants alike feel anger toward these Filipinos trespassing into civilian areas at all times.' It was a lament that would often be repeated as the Filipinos replaced the black servicemen in the islanders' perceptions as their principal tormentors" (Fisch 1988, 85). The American director of public safety claimed that crime statistics for the Philippine Scouts were worse than those for the black troops they replaced, characterizing the deployment of the Scouts to Okinawa as "the biggest mistake the Army made in the Ryukyus" (86). Fisch again blamed Filipino soldiers themselves for the violence. "If this behavior was unjustifiable, it was to some extent understandable. Many of the Filipino servicemen had experienced, or at least witnessed, atrocities committed by the Japanese in the Philippines during the war. It proved difficult for some of these men to curb their resentment toward Japanese citizens, a resentment that often translated into violence against the docile and cooperative Okinawans. This vindictive behavior also served to instill resentment among the local citizens toward all the occupying services" (85).

Official histories, such as Fisch's, blame black and Filipino soldiers categorically for the thousands of violent crimes committed by U.S. service members against Okinawans. Although different reasoning is used to explain their violent tendencies—for African Americans, the military's segregation policies which concentrated "substandard" soldiers into a small number of units, and for Filipinos, "understandable" vengeful feelings against the Japanese—ultimately in both cases, the tendency to commit violent crime is understood to be a group characteristic. Fisch's interpretations reflect racial ideologies typical of Western colonialist discourse. Feminists and others have discussed a systematic relationship between military training, war, and unsanctioned violence, including rape, regardless of soldiers' color, creed, or nationality (Littlewood 1997; Enloe 2000). But in occupation-era Okinawa, the U.S. military's control over the state, including how it responded to and compiled statistics on violent crimes, has guaranteed that incidences of military violence would be remembered as part of a larger story about race, defined increasingly as skin color and other visible physical traits. The predominant images are of dark-skinned soldiers committing crimes while white commanders attempted in vain to control their unruly subordinates. These are the images that Terrance Carter seems to have drawn from when explaining his father-in-law's dislike of African Americans.[24] The Katsuyama cave incident and other stories thus reinforce popular racial ideologies that denigrate African American servicemen, even as Mayumi, Terrance, and others argue that such stories misrepresent the majority of African American military men who have served in Okinawa.

Intersections of Race, Gender, and Sexuality

Of concern to military-Okinawan couples today, both official histories and personal memories tend to focus on military men's sexuality. Stories and other representations of occupation-era rapes are an example. Stereotypical images of sexual entertainment in segregated bar districts also link popular notions of military sexuality to understandings of racial difference. Beginning in 1949, the Government of the Ryukyu Islands created official bar districts in Koza, Naha, Maebaru, and elsewhere, reversing an earlier (March 1947) all-out ban on military-oriented prostitution (Takushi 2000, 127). In 1953, the government again expressed its tacit approval of military prostitution by instituting the infamous A-sign system, in which restaurants, bars, and cabarets that met official standards for hygiene were conspicuously posted with a sign bearing a large "A" and the words "Military Approved." During the occupation, incoming service members learned about these officially recognized entertainment districts and the A-sign system immediately upon arrival in Okinawa. Segregated recreation zones were pointed out on maps as "safe liberty areas" for white and black soldiers by the officers running orientation briefings (Dickson interview). In Koza, white airmen were encouraged to visit the commercial and residential area located outside of Kadena Air Base known as the Ville. Black soldiers, on the other hand, were consigned to the Teruya neighborhood, known as Four Corners or the Bush.[25] Ralph Dickson, who was first assigned to Okinawa during the mid-1950s, related the following story about his experiences as a white sailor in the Teruya area:

> I worked in the laboratory. I worked in preventative medicine on what used to be called the VD tracer.[26] When a person got a venereal disease, you were supposed to get the name of the place where the contact was and then go tell that person that they may have been exposed and that they needed to get tested. Well, the first one I got, I went down into the Bush, not knowing that I wasn't supposed to go there. And you meet some pretty shady men, some pretty mean-looking black dudes, down there. And they want to know what you're doing down there, white boy. And you tell them, and then they take you to meet the boss-man [an

African American soldier], and he says, you know you're not welcome here. Thank you for coming, I'll take this off of your hands, and don't come back here anymore. I took him at his advice, and if I got any more that said they were exposed there, I didn't take the papers. I didn't go.

Rumors circulated about GIs who were killed for venturing outside of their own racial territory, and Okinawan women were warned that they should confine their relationships with Americans to either black men or white men. Moving from one race to another was not tolerated.[27]

Racial Discourses Deployed by Okinawan Women

Today, Okinawan women involved in intimate relationships with American military men continue to be racialized based on the skin color of their romantic and sexual partners, along with their preferences in music, dress, hairstyles, and other visible trappings of American culture. An analysis of women's comments regarding race reveals how they utilize race as a framework for understanding intimate interactions and relationships. As with Iha Mayumi and Terrance Carter, elements of the memory and historical discourses discussed in preceding sections inform their narratives.

Chieko Pierce was born and raised in northern Okinawa. Like many of her classmates, she married a local boy at a young age and had two children, but she was not able to reconcile her desire for financial independence and equality with the expectations of her husband. After the two separated, she lived for a time with another man, also Okinawan, and gave birth to a third child. When we met in 2001, she was in her mid-forties and single, recently divorced (although she had not yet told her friends and neighbors) from a third man, this time an American. Her youngest son was in high school and still living at home. She had become a successful businesswoman and was well liked in the community, but she worked long hours and had little time and few prospects in her hometown for developing a stable and fulfilling intimate relationship. She hid her loneliness behind a veneer of ready laughter and good humor for the sake of her son and her business.

For years, Chieko had worked in cosmetics sales, visiting customers in their homes to sell products, teach application techniques, and give shoulder and neck massages. In 1991, she rented space downtown and opened a salon, which quickly attracted a loyal clientele. The long hours she spent at the salon led to the breakup of her second relationship.

After my younger son's father and I broke up, I decided that I would never date or marry an Okinawan or Japanese man again. Okinawan guys' thinking is very old-fashioned. They look down on their wives. They want to be boss. I have always wanted a relationship that was fair, one in which we could share the housework, and I could work outside the home. But neither my first husband nor the second man I lived with wanted that kind of lifestyle. They wanted me to be at home all the time, so I worked all day outside the home and then came home and worked all evening there. I became interested in meeting an American man. I had heard so much about gender equality in America and about how strong American women were, and I wanted that style.

Chieko met the enlisted U.S. airman who would become her second husband at a reggae concert. They exchanged telephone numbers and began to meet regularly, going out for dinner, attending concerts, and taking salsa lessons together. Chieko's children accepted the man because their mother was happy, but her family, neighbors, and clients were not as welcoming because he was African American. Chieko's equation of race with skin color stands out.

Many people in my hometown, especially children, are afraid of black men. White people resemble Japanese persons in skin color, but black people are different. In my hometown, there are no black people. A few younger women have married black men, but they live in the United States. If I had married a white man, they would not have been surprised at all, but because he was black, they said bad things about me. My father, especially, is very old-fashioned. I explained to my family that my husband was a good person. "It doesn't matter if you are black, white, or yellow. It's just skin color. Inside, we are all the same." Little by little, they understood and accepted him.

Chieko had been reluctant to marry the airman at first. "He was so uptight and serious, whereas I am wild [wairudo], so I was concerned that our personalities were not well-matched." He was persistent, and she eventually agreed to marry based on her desire for a relationship of equals. She was pleased with his attitude toward her business. He didn't complain when she worked late. He helped prepare dinner and clean the apartment. "He liked to clean. He used to tell me, 'Clean house, clean person!'" But she was bothered by subtle cultural differences in the way they approached relationships with others. "My husband thought that we should always be socializing together as a couple. But in Okinawa, husbands and wives go out separately. Especially if they have children, somebody has to stay at home with the kids. Well, I have a business, and I have to give back to customers who regularly come to my shop, so I often visit their shops and restaurants. My husband didn't understand when I wanted to go out with my girlfriends and he wasn't invited. It's fine to go out together occasionally, but my friends were starting to complain." Chieko also expressed annoyance with her husband's increasing interest in her friends' class backgrounds. "I have many friends, both low-level people and high-level people. I introduced him to the mayor, and he liked him. But he looked down on my other friends. He told me over and over, 'You have to be classy!' What does that mean, classy? I don't have to be classy. In fact, I have a business. I have to be nice to people who come into my shop. I cannot say, 'You are low-level. I cannot be friends with you.' I told him that I could choose my own friends, thank you."

With minor annoyances like these beginning to accumulate, Chieko lost her composure when her husband decided to extend his enlistment an additional year instead of retiring in three months, as planned. He announced that he would leave Okinawa for a yearlong tour of duty in North Carolina. Chieko could accompany him if she wished.

> He said, "I'll come back in one year." One year? Why do you need to go back to the U.S. for just one year? Is the little bit of extra retirement money that important to you? I could not leave. My son had just entered junior high school. If he had been little, then maybe I could have taken him to America, and he would have picked up English quickly. But not as a junior high school student. We were also planning to build a house, a large house with American-style decoration. No tatami floors for him. I had already bought the land, gotten permission to build, and hired a contractor. After he left, I called him and told him that he needed to take some responsibility and help pay for the house, but he said that he did not have any extra money to send to me.

Furious, Chieko visited the legal office at Kadena Air Base for assistance with collecting the house payments. Air force lawyers contacted her husband's command, and soon a check arrived, but it was only for half the amount she had requested. "After that, I did not trust him anymore. I did not want him to come back to Okinawa. I wanted a divorce." She consulted with a civilian lawyer, who drew up divorce papers and obtained the necessary signatures. She had the papers in her possession when we first met, but she had not yet submitted them to the municipal office. "I haven't told my parents and many of my friends that I have gotten divorced again. If I take the papers to the village office, then everyone will know. It will be bad for my business. I married a black man, and I worked very hard to convince people that he was a good person, that they should accept him. If they knew that we were divorced, it would be no good. People in this town, they become happy looking at other people's sadness." She planned to register the divorce after her son graduated from high school and moved away. At that time, she hoped to move as well, preferably to the United States. In the meantime, she told me, if she met a nice American man who asked her to return to the States with him, she might consider marrying again.

> So now I have had bad experiences with both Okinawan and American men. But if I have the chance to marry again, then it will definitely be to another American, not an Okinawan or Japanese guy. After you've been with a foreign man, you can never go back. Japanese men don't like strong women, and Okinawan men are even more old-fashioned than Japanese men. They don't help out with the housework. They don't take care of the children. And as for sex, most of them treat their wives like tools, instruments [*dōgu mitai na kankaku de*] for their own pleasure. Foreign men, on the other hand, treat women well. They cherish their wives and value their feelings. They care about their partner's satisfaction.

Looking forward to a future in America, Chieko expanded her business to include tattoos (*tatū*). Several evenings a week, she closed the salon and drove across the island to Camp Schwab to decorate the shoulders, backs, and biceps of young American enlisted men, taking advantage of every opportunity to practice English and save money to follow her dream. It was a senior enlisted marine who first introduced me to Chieko. The two had struck up a friendship after meeting at the Enlisted Club at Camp Schwab. Chieko often hosted parties for the marines in his unit at her spacious American-style house. Through her military contacts, she had also met other Okinawan women who worked on base and socialized with Americans. Many had dated, married, and divorced American servicemen. The women eagerly shared their experiences with one another late at night, after the Americans had left and returned to base.

One night as we washed dishes and cleaned up, Chieko, Harumi Olsen, age thirty-two, and I discussed how race had affected their relationships. Both women had previously been married to American servicemen, Chieko to the black airman described above and Harumi to a white marine stationed at Camp Foster. Chieko initiated the discussion, stating that she had noticed that black and white servicemen don't get along very well. "They are civil to one another, act friendly, but they don't seem to have much to say to one another." Harumi, who had dated several African American servicemen after her failed marriage, added that black men were very proud and that this showed a strong sense of identity but also made communication difficult.

> Black men, their hearts don't open up to you. You can't get in. There's some kind of barrier. White men have open hearts, but with black men, something isn't right. It's like . . . they're half Japanese! What I mean is,

with black men and Japanese men, it feels like they are continually creating walls. You think that they've been having fun hanging out with you,
but there's that other side.

She offered an example: "Say you've just attended a party together. A white man
might say 'Wow, that party was really fun. I had a good time.' But a black man
would probably not say anything at all." The two women agreed that white servicemen were more open, talkative, and more expressive of their feelings. Sometimes, they talked *too* much. But Chieko confessed she found that style easier
because there was no mistaking what her partner was thinking.

When I interviewed Harumi again several weeks later, I asked her to talk
more about how racial difference had affected her relationships with American
men. She insisted that while married to a white serviceman, she had not noticed
any major differences between herself and her husband. While dating black
men, on the other hand, "*jinshu no chigai kanjita* [I sensed that we were racially
different]." Seeking to clarify, I asked if she was referring to culturally different
values or lifestyle differences. "Not *bunka* [culture]," she replied. "*Seikatsu mo
daijōbu da kedo, jinshu wa* ... [Living together was fine too, but race ...]."
Harumi seemed to suggest that racial difference—which she, like many young
Okinawan women, equated with black men in particular—was irreducible to
specific ways of talking, thinking, or doing. It simply *was* in the purest possible
sense.

Harumi's and Chieko's comments on intimacy and sex with American men
recall the scholarship of John Russell, who has written extensively on popular
representations of racial difference in Japan. Literary examples analyzed by Russell include Yamada Eimi's novella *Bedtime Eyes* (1985), which tells the story of
Kim, a nightclub singer who falls in love with an African American deserter from
the U.S. Navy called Spoon. Developing themes of sexual liberation, drug addiction, and violence, *Bedtime Eyes* was lauded by critics as a controversial and path-
breaking early example of Japanese women's writing that evoked images of foreign
men to challenge conservative Japanese social and behavioral norms. Russell
(1998) has argued, however, that such literature amounts to little more than an
apolitical celebration of black sexuality and style. While the bodies of black men
are seen, appreciated, and consumed, no meaningful subjectivity is attributed to
them. Black men remain silent (if not mute) instruments of Japanese women's
emerging body awareness. Japanese women's discourse on African American men,
Russell argues, "lacks any clear subversive direction or intent, since it reifies difference as racial, uncritically accepts American racial imagery, rejects meaningful dialogue with blacks, and confirms rather than problematizes Japanese
identity" (119).

Harumi's comments regarding the racial difference of her African American lovers (which was not reducible to specific ways of talking, thinking, or doing) seem to play directly into the discourses on interracial sex critiqued by Russell. Yet Harumi's words also recall the nonspecific sense of difference that motivated Terrance Carter's father-in-law to refuse to meet his African American son-in-law and Iha Mayumi's father to oppose her relationship with Isaac, the Jamaican marine. In this context too, the racial difference of African American GIs cannot be easily measured or neatly summed up with list of discreet features; it simply *is*. Harumi's and Chieko's comments clearly have additional local significance and represent more than a simple celebration of black sexuality and style per Russell's critique. While Okinawan military wives and girlfriends often speak of their own self-transformation through relationships with American men, it isn't always clear what or whom they are resisting. Are traditional Japanese or Okinawan gender and sexual norms their primary target? Or are their words and actions directed against the social limitations and closed thinking of small-town Okinawa? How has the militarization of Okinawan society and the erection of symbolic fence-lines contributed to the difficulties they encounter, including the marginalization of those who reside in remote, economically depressed communities with limited opportunities? Reconsidered within this context, the racial difference of American military men, and especially African American men, acquires additional meaning as a metaphor for militarization itself and the alienation that it engenders, including the inability to understand or resolve continuing social and economic difficulties, or to connect with family, friends, and neighbors in meaningful ways.

Ultimately, the racial boundaries separating African Americans and other American military men from Okinawans are reinscribed in everyday discursive practices, including the comments of women like Chieko and Harumi who engage in intimate international relationships. Okinawan women who develop intimate relationships with U.S. military men may strategically attach positive or negative valence to existing popular racial categories as they attempt to fit into local Okinawan communities, but they rarely challenge the categories themselves.

Silences within Okinawan Racial Memories and Classificatory Schemes

Popular accounts of interracial sex and dating in Okinawa are generally silent with regard to the presence of non-Filipino Asian American military personnel. This is curious given that Japanese American and Okinawan American soldiers have frequently been assigned to positions that involve extensive interfacing with

local community officials and citizens, such as public relations or community specialist positions.[28] Moreover, the vast majority of military marriages registered in
Okinawa during the late 1940s were between Okinawan women and Japanese
American servicemen. During the thirty-day period from July 23 to August 21,
1947, fifty-three of the sixty-three U.S. personnel applying to marry Okinawan
women were Japanese American (Takushi 2000, 117).[29] One might assume that
perceived racial similarity has rendered such relationships invisible in popular discourse. My interviews, however, suggest that these silences follow instead from
the anomalous position of Asian Americans within popular Okinawan understandings of racial difference.

Tatsuko Lee, age fifty-one, recently widowed when we first met, was quite un-
sure of her husband's true identity even after twenty-three years of marriage.
Tatsuko was confused from the moment she first laid eyes on him, and she was
still frustrated by the inconsistencies she perceived in her husband's life. In the
early 1970s, Tatsuko, twenty-four years old at the time, had interviewed for a position at an American-owned company that sold pots, pans, and other kitchen
wares. After passing a written and spoken English test with the company president, she was asked to return for a second interview with the company manager.

> So again, I put on my nice clothes, nice shoes, everything. I came to the
> office and was sitting reading a magazine that they had on the coffee table
> when I heard somebody in the back talking in English. In a beautiful,
> low voice. And not just any English, but *good* English, educated English.
> I couldn't help but turn around and take a look. Who is that? Because I
> had met the company president the day before, and he was nothing, he
> was just an American. Compared to his English, this English was *very
> good*. I turned around, and it was an Oriental guy! He looked very old,
> wearing glasses, like a typical Japanese man. "Wow! An Oriental guy talk-
> ing like that!" I said to myself, "He must have studied very well some-
> where in the States." The president called me over and said, "Miss
> Oshiro, here's our manager." I said, "How do you do?" He said, "How do
> *you* do?" completely naturally. Then he said, "Would you come into my
> office?" So I followed him. And then he said, "You speak good English."
> "Sir," I said, "you speak good English too." He laughed and said, "I'm
> American."

Tatsuko's story, which began with this simple case of missed expectations, became
more and more confused as she explained that her husband was fluent in English,
Japanese, and Russian, while he claimed German ancestry. (Tatsuko expressed
doubt about this last claim: "Yes, Germans have blue eyes like he did, but they
aren't known for long legs and long arms like he had. I think he must have had

some Russian blood as well." On the information sheet she filled out for me, she listed her husband's racial/ethnic background as one-half Japanese, one-quarter American, and one-quarter Russian.) During the twenty-three years they were together, he never produced a U.S. passport and eventually admitted that he was "stateless." Thus they never married legally, and their two sons held only Japanese citizenship. He was connected in some way to the U.S. military, but Tatsuko confessed, it was unclear exactly how he was connected. They did not have access to the military bases, for example. "Maybe he was CIA," she shrugged disgustedly, still visibly upset with the ambiguity she had been forced to live with. "I don't even know how old he really was," she complained. He had told her that he was in his fifties when they first met, but after he died, his son by a previous marriage said that his father was actually ninety-four. While Tatsuko's story would be considered bizarre by most accounts, her comments about her husband's nationality, physical appearance, ancestry, and language abilities reflect an expectation that these elements should line up consistently (as in nation = race = language). Tatsuko's husband's identity complicated all components of this schematic equation.

Kaoru Kaneshiro, age thirty-seven, who worked for the U.S. government in Okinawa, also spoke of the contradictions that confused Okinawans when they met her husband, a completely bilingual Japanese American man who was born in Okinawa and raised there as a member of the American military community. Kaoru emphasized that while her husband looked Japanese, "inside" he was American.

> The Japanese, most of them are very modest. They don't say things straight. But my husband is very honest, and sometimes the words he chooses when speaking Japanese are a little bit strong. I remember thinking, "*Heee*, why did he say that?" Maybe if he looked like a regular—I was going to say a regular American [chuckle]. But if he looked American, not Japanese, I wouldn't have been surprised at what he said or how he treated us. But because he looked Japanese, the way he spoke was sometimes confusing. Finally, I realized, he is not Japanese. He is an American citizen. He is American. Once I accepted that, our relationship became much easier.

Unlike Tatsuko, Kaoru delighted in the opportunities for playful subversion opened up by her husband's background.

> My husband talks to my friends in Japanese, and now they know that he is a U.S. citizen. But before, they didn't know. Suddenly, he would talk in English in front of them, and they would go, "Oh, your husband speaks English!" And I would go, "Of course, he is American." And they would be so surprised. Sometimes I like to see my friends surprised. Like the

time my brother-in-law came to visit us from Hawaii. His name is Richard, but he looks Japanese. And every time we went out to dinner, it was "Richard this" and "Richard that." And people were like "Richard is an American name. Where is the American?" Sometimes watching people, how they react, is interesting. You know, I am observing them just as they are observing us.

Kaoru found her husband's ability to disrupt commonly held assumptions concerning race, language, and nationality amusing, an opportunity to return the gaze that others directed at international couples. Together with Tatsuko's story, however, her comments suggest that the reason Japanese Americans do not appear in popular accounts of military transnational intimacy is not because they are perceived as racially and culturally identical to Okinawans, but rather because their looks and language abilities don't mesh with dominant racial categories of U.S. military personnel. Considering the prevalence of marriages between Okinawan women and Japanese American military men, this topic begs further study.

U.S. military men, particularly African American men, represent the racial Other in contemporary Okinawan racial discourses. This has developed from the prefecture's complicated history of Western contact, Japanese colonialism, U.S. occupation, and the history and memory discourses surrounding each. Whereas the term *minzoku* (ethnicity or nation) was used to discuss differences and similarities between mainlanders and subjects of the Japanese empire, including Okinawans, *jinshu* (biological race) was used to distinguish Japanese and Okinawans from Westerners and other non-Asian peoples. Modern theories of race and social progress were embedded in colonial modernization and assimilation programs, and characterizations of American enemy soldiers as bestial and demonic were spread within Japanese imperialist propaganda. U.S. soldiers were portrayed as animal-like, lacking self-discipline and devoid of human compassion, perpetrators of rape and killing. During wartime, such stereotypes were applied to white American soldiers, but they also came to affect perceptions of nonwhite military personnel. During the postwar occupation, this imagery was overlaid with American discourses on race that degraded African American and Filipino soldiers. American racial thinking was embedded in occupation government discourses, from which official histories of the period draw. Elements of these historical discourses, along with allegorical references to occupation-era sexual violence, are invoked by Okinawans to explain their perceptions and attitudes toward U.S. military personnel, including women involved in intimate relationships with U.S. military men.

From the U.S. military perspective, perceptions of racial difference from local people are perpetuated by the physical isolation of personnel assigned to U.S. bases, as well as the physicality of military labor. As a prelude to her analysis of the 1995 rape of an Okinawan girl in Kin village, Linda Angst has linked these characteristics to instances of violent crimes committed by U.S. service members against Okinawans.

> The marines in Kin are physically isolated from the general population, living and working within the barbed wire fences of the camp and removed from the urban centers of life on the island . . . Marines at Camp Hansen are also separated from others through the nature of their work as combat soldiers, labor that is physically and mentally focused on learning to fight. Through their work and their isolation, the attention of many is intensely fixated on their own physicality. As well as being outside the bounds of ordinary Okinawan life, they most profoundly experience their difference from local people in terms of their physical [including racial] difference. All of these factors contribute to producing a situation in which an occupation army of restless young, foreign men who have received little preparation for understanding Okinawan society constitute a clear and present danger to the local community, especially its women and girls (2003, 136–137).

As demonstrated, physical and especially racial difference also figure in Okinawan perceptions of American GIs. Notions of racial difference are embedded within official and popular memory discourses, and they play an important, though not always overt, role in the discursive construction of public morality and Okinawan identity politics. Within discourses on morality and identity, race is the primary mechanism used to distance U.S. military men, their wives, and their children from ordinary Okinawans, as well as to distinguish groups of soldiers from one another. The individuals I interviewed repeatedly invoked the frame of racial difference to clarify popular attitudes toward military international intimacy. Social worker Hirata Masayo reported, for example, that most Okinawan families would readily welcome a Caucasian son-in-law, whereas many would oppose marriage to an African American serviceman. I heard countless stories of young women who had been ostracized from their families for marrying African American military men, and local advocates and scholars have documented widespread prejudice and discrimination against Amerasian children, especially those with African American fathers (Uezato 1998; Koshiro 1999; Murphy-Shigematsu 2001, 2002). However, personal interviews fail to confirm Hirata's impression that *only* African American servicemen and their children experience prejudice and discrimination in Okinawa. My data suggests that the labels black (*kokujin*), white (*hakujin*), and Filipino (*firipinjin*) all tend to be racially construed due to their association with memories of the Battle of Okinawa, the American occupation, and continuing presence of U.S. military bases in the prefecture. Japanese American servicemen appear to occupy a discursive gap, or silence.[30]

Molasky (1999) has noted similar constructs in the literary works of authors from mainland Japan during the U.S. occupation. Since the 1980s, however, mainland images of foreign men, particularly black men, have shifted to commodified cultural forms that primarily index alternative sexuality and style. In Okinawa, the continuing U.S. military presence has meant that occupation-era racial understandings, with American military personnel as their primary referents, remain viable. Mainland Japanese discourses celebrating black style and white internationalism have gained some currency among young Okinawan women, but stereotypical images of white soldiers as invaders and liberators, African American GIs as violent occupation soldiers, and Filipino servicemen as vindictive labor troops continue to structure views of U.S. military men. The deployment of such discourses, including the interpretation and value attached to the racial categories of white, black, and Filipino, varies along generational and political lines. However, the racial categories themselves are rarely subjected to scrutiny, even within the narratives of women who cross fencelines by dating or marrying American military men.

LIVING RESPECTABLY AND NEGOTIATING CLASS

During the spring and summer of 2002, I often visited Satoko Wilson to enjoy a chat in her cheery sunroom before the heat and humidity of the day set in. Satoko-san's property sat high on the mountainside overlooking the crystalline waters of Nakijin Bay and the East China Sea. Her home, designed and built with her American husband in the 1970s, was surrounded by blooming flower and vegetable gardens. We walked among the rows of eggplant, tomatoes, *kabocha* (pumpkin), and *shimana* (a bitter green), talking recipes and cooking techniques while Satoko checked the moisture of the soil and twisted off spent blossoms. Afterwards, we headed into her kitchen to boil water for tea or cook lunch. The house was a hybrid of Okinawan and American tastes with tatami and Western-style carpeted rooms. To the left of the entryway, a sliding door opened into a formal tatami room, minimally decorated with a seasonal hanging scroll and *ikebana* flower arrangement. To the right, a linen *noren* hung at the entrance to the spacious kitchen with ample counter space and a Western-style oven. In the living room, a sofa and two armchairs were arranged around a wooden coffee table. An antique chest of drawers, a family piece her husband had shipped from the United States, stood against the far wall, topped by a framed watercolor of Canada geese in flight.

At sixty-three, Satoko was a child during the Pacific War. Her earliest memories were of playing hide-and-seek with her brother among the ruins of Hokuzan castle, located next door to her father's farm.[1] Her stories suggested a childhood of poverty typical of village Okinawa but not directly touched by the fierce battle raging to the south or the subsequent land seizures and buildup of U.S. military bases. After graduating from high school, Satoko moved to Koza (now Okinawa City) and was hired by an American pharmaceutical company. Sometime later, she was offered a position as a receptionist in the accounting office at Marine Corps Camp McTureous, an on-base position that paid double her salary at the pharmacy. It was there that she met her husband, John. He was smart, generous, and romantic. During their years together, John surprised her with flowers almost daily, drove her to seaside overlooks for sunset, and insisted on doing the dishes. When they later moved to Nakijin, he won the trust and affection of Okinawan neighbors by offering rides to elderly women waiting at the bus stop and by spontaneously inviting friends and neighbors home for dinner. John died unexpectedly in 1984, leaving Satoko to carry on with the upkeep of the house and garden. Not long after, she took a job as translator and regional case manager for an international nonprofit organization dedicated to providing medical care and education to Amerasian children.

Satoko's attitude toward military transnational intimacy was complex and sometimes contradictory due to her class difference from the families she managed as a caseworker. Her own middle-class identity was constructed with reference to a variety of prestige- and wealth-based factors. First, she was a Christian. During early adulthood, she had contributed to family income by helping a local American missionary family, providing translation and interpretation at church events. Her growing faith in the Christian God set her apart from many of her fellow villagers. The translation experience also enabled her to position herself as a white-collar worker when she later sought office jobs in Koza. Next, her marriage to an American military man in the higher enlisted ranks afforded her a lifestyle with all of the markings of middle-class status, including a comparatively large and comfortable house, car ownership, and income from her husband's U.S. military and social security checks. Now, having held numerous professional positions, her social and professional network included prominent Americans in Okinawa and international aid workers abroad. Meanwhile, the families she assisted were among the poorest in the village, with few economic resources and children who were considered racially Other.

From a position of relative class privilege and based on her experiences as a caseworker, Satoko sometimes invoked negative and distancing stereotypes of women who were sexually involved with American soldiers, even while her own marriage suggested other possibilities. Nowadays, she explained, it was common to see young people with *chapatsu* (hair dyed brown) and *kinpatsu* (hair dyed blond) in Tokyo and even central Okinawa. But during the early years of the U.S. occupation, children with light-colored hair were assumed to be half-Okinawan and half-American, illegitimate and fatherless. They were taunted, called "American," and discriminated against. "In the early days, there were many instances where young Okinawan women met GIs, dated or simply had sex with them, got pregnant and gave birth to children without getting married. They deposited the kids with grandma and grandpa, and then left to work in the base towns or in mainland Japan. Commonly, you saw Okinawan grandmothers walking around with small blond children in towns like Motobu and Nakijin. Older folks were ashamed of the children because it was generally assumed that they were conceived by mothers who were involved in prostitution [*yoru no shigoto*, literally 'night work']." Today, she explained, young people tended to view America as a land of big houses and big movie stars, an object of longing and fantasy (*akogare*). But during the occupation, casual sexual encounters between Okinawan women and U.S. military men, especially sexual entertainment and prostitution, cast a shadow over Amerasian children and couples who met and fell in love. Themes of occupation-era hardship, community pressure, unkind gossip, and race and class difference emerged throughout Satoko's narratives, reinforcing her own middle-class respectability.

This chapter continues the discussion of links between Okinawan memories of the U.S. occupation and popular stereotypes of military transnational intimacy, pivoting away from American military men to examine discourses on sexual propriety and class respectability used to police Okinawan women's behavior. Accounts of women who married during the early postwar differ from those who married after reversion in 1972, reflecting Okinawans' changing economic circumstances and a reworking and reimagining of class. Scholars of Okinawan social movements have documented changes in Okinawan notions of class and identity, especially in relation to oppositional politics (Tanji 2006; Inoue 2007). The stories included here demonstrate the broader and deeply personal impacts of shifting notions of class, made visible through the lenses of gender and transnational intimacy. Occupation-era discourses on moral purity and contamination, and corresponding discourses that prescribed respectable behavior are most meaningful to older women of Satoko Wilson's generation. Postreversion stereotypes, including the popular image of the *amejo* (a woman who consumes American men) and accounts of Japanese tourists who travel to Okinawa to have sex with U.S. servicemen, reveal changing formulations of class related to political and economic integration and marginalization within the Japanese nation-state. In response to negative imagery and stereotypes, Okinawan military wives often exercise agency through redirecting negative imagery onto racial and class Others, including mainland Japanese women and Filipina sex workers. This approach, however, reproduces the very discourses that marginalize military international couples and their children.

Occupation-Era Intimacy and the Long Shadow of Military Prostitution

Okinawan women who married American military men during the U.S. occupation (1945–1972) are beleaguered by stereotypes connecting romantic and sexual intimacy with GIs to the sex trade flourishing outside of U.S. bases. Even recently, an elderly participant reported that upon returning to the island from her home in the United States, her taxi driver rudely asked if she had met and married her American husband while working as a bar girl. It is often presumed that women who dated, married, or conceived children with Americans during this period were bar workers or prostitutes.[2] In interviews, older military wives like Satoko Wilson often mentioned these stereotypes and then used a variety of narrative and other discursive strategies to distance themselves from such imagery. Many focused on the fine details of interaction during their initial encounters with their husbands, while studiously avoiding mention of the physical settings in which those encounters took place. They offered lengthy explanations of who introduced them, first impressions, and almost verbatim conversations. Only two women revealed that they had met their husbands while working in bars, both indicating that they were bartenders. Two others reported that they had met their husbands at events sponsored by the United Service Organizations (USO), where they held part-time jobs that involved dancing with young enlisted men. During the occupation, women were recruited for work as dance partners through military and nonmilitary channels, primarily by word of mouth. They boarded buses at the start of the evening that took them onto the base and dropped them off at the USO. There they were expected to talk and dance with GI customers in exchange for a small wage and perhaps a meal.[3]

Junko Brenner explained why she had taken this sort of *baito* (part-time job) and how such work was perceived.

> I was on the Japanese mainland for a couple of years, and when I came back to Okinawa, I did not have a job. My friend asked me to go on base and dance with guys for a couple of hours. It was a part-time job. I needed the money. I knew it wasn't a good job, so I didn't tell my parents what I was doing. If I had told them, they wouldn't have approved. I wanted to take knitting classes, and I already had a machine, but you have to buy yarn. So I went to the Point [the Onna Point Marine Corps base] at night and did the *baito* there, and during the day, I took knitting classes. But that didn't last too long because I met Bill, and then we got married. That was in 1972.

Sitting comfortably on an oversized leather couch in her home, with husband Bill clacking away on the computer in the next room, Junko spoke openly about the USO job. But a second participant, whom I met at an upscale coffee shop in the elegant Renaissance Hotel in Onna Village, was not as forthcoming. She spoke hazily of attending dance parties with her sister. I asked where the parties were held, and she told me that they were on base, at the USO. I asked if she had needed a military escort to enter the base, as is the practice now. She answered that she had ridden onto the base in a military bus. Recalling Junko's interview, I asked the woman if she too had been paid for attending the USO parties. Quickly, she changed the subject and launched into an elaborate description of the first time she met her husband, ignoring my question about remuneration.

In fact, none of the women I interviewed spoke openly of being paid for sex. It is possible that some engaged in prostitution. Others may have been involved in relationships that were not experienced as purely transactional but still involved exchanging sexual companionship and housework for a place to live and spending money.[4] Ultimately, I learned to avoid explicitly distinguishing and sorting entertainment work into categories of prostitution, live-in companion, and other. While military prostitution is an important touchstone for critical scholarship and antibase activism, for Okinawan women who dated, married, or conceived children with American GIs, attempting to pin down and classify their relationships rouses suspicion and concern with the considerable social risks of being associated with military sex work. Such attempts ignore the infinite variety of individual experience and emotional attachments between Okinawan women and American men, and the complex interrelationships between labor, structural (and sometimes physical) violence, care work, and pleasure.

Sexual Purity and Contamination in Japanese and American Empire

Community condemnation of sex with U.S. military men has been based in part on Okinawan conceptions of moral purity and contamination. Generally speaking, sex with American soldiers has been considered morally contaminating behavior. This has much to do with the association of U.S. military men with war. However, the emphasis on racial differences between American GIs and Okinawans also suggests a connection between conceptions of moral purity and notions of racial integrity. Tracing the linkage of these ideas in imperial rhetoric, John Dower has located a source of the relationship within the Japanese written language itself. Two key words in the lexicon of imperial Japanese moral values, *sekishin* (one's true heart) and *sekisei* (sincerity), both contained the character meaning "red" (*seki*), which was in turn associated with blood. The equation of blood with redness, and redness with sincerity, Dower argues, was straightforward in imperial Japan due to the visual richness of the written language (Dower 1986, 210–211). As a key component of wartime rhetoric, the association between pure heart and pure blood contributed to a larger discourse celebrating Japanese racial and cultural uniqueness that was used to marginalize Okinawans as "impure" Japanese. Locally, such ideas may have contributed to condemnation of sexual relations between Okinawan women and American soldiers during the early postwar, as they did in mainland Japan (Koshiro 1999; Molasky 1999).[5]

Following Japan's surrender, in mainland Japan and Okinawa, prostitution was tolerated because it created a barrier between American soldiers and respectable Japanese women. In August 1945, Japanese officials in Tokyo established the Recreation and Amusement Association (RAA) to provide sexual "comfort" for the American occupiers. Volunteers for the RAA were recruited from the ranks of young women who had lost families, homes, or jobs during the war.[6] At the inaugural ceremony of the RAA, held on August 28, 1945, in front of the Imperial Palace, an oath was read aloud to the assembled women. "The time has come, an order has been given, and by virtue of our realm of business we have been assigned the difficult task of comforting the occupation army as part of the urgent national facilities for postwar management. This order is heavy and immense. And success will be extremely difficult . . . . And so we unite and go forward to where our beliefs lead us, and through the sacrifice of several thousand 'Okichis of our era' build a breakwater to hold back the raging waves and defend and nurture the purity of our race" (quoted in Dower 1999, 127).[7] U.S. Army leaders gave official permission for the RAA to operate its facilities under the supervision of U.S. military police and directed the Japanese government to reestablish its venereal disease regulation system, including compulsory examinations and medical treatment. Rather than prohibiting the Japanese state-licensed prostitution system, U.S. occupation authorities used the system to ensure the health of U.S. soldiers (Takeuchi 2010, 85). When occupation authorities ordered the abolition of the RAA in early 1946, declaring it undemocratic and in violation of women's rights, while privately citing the alarming spread of venereal disease among American troops, government-managed brothels were replaced by government-regulated "red zones," special entertainment districts where officially registered sex workers continued to sell their sexual labor under the supervision of health officials and the police. Meanwhile, Japanese women's organizations and Christian groups pushed for the prohibition of prostitution altogether out of a concern for women's safety, putative social and genetic problems of mixed-blood children, and the erosion of sexual mores among Japanese youth (Garon 1997; Koshiro 1999).

Likewise, in Okinawa the creation of special bar and cabaret districts during the late 1940s was developed by local leaders in consultation with U.S. military officials as a multipurpose solution intended to ensure public safety, moral and racial containment, and the health of U.S. soldiers. Social worker Shima Masu recalled the situation as follows:

> At that time, Goeku Village [now part of Koza] had already become the symbol of Okinawa as a military base island [*kichi Okinawa*]. The adjacent villages of Chatan, Kadena, Yomitan, and Misato were under siege by the U.S. military camps. In Goya, Nakasone, and Uechi as well, Americans were everywhere. Black soldiers stood out in particular . . . . Day and night, black soldiers appeared in the Okinawan housing areas, hanging around and calling out names in broken Japanese. Almost daily, it was reported that they had snuck into one of the private homes and violated the women there . . . .
>
> In Koza, there were many women specializing in American soldiers. Most of them rented rooms in private homes, where they brought black men. In many of these homes, middle school and high school students were living as well. This kind of environment could not have been good for the children. Thinking about how these families lived in fear, I could not just stand by and watch . . . . Nearly every day, I met with Mayor Shiroma of Goeku Village and his wife, the vice president of the women's association, and we three worked out a series of measures [intended to eradicate the problem]. For the sake of environmental purification [*kankyō jōka*] and the prevention of youth misconduct, we had to intervene. The first measure consisted of making prostitutes leave the residential areas (quoted in Takushi 2000, 126–127, my translation).[8]

When Goeku Village leaders approached local military officials with their list of special measures, the Americans proposed establishing a special bar zone in the open land just outside the settlement. This plan was accepted by community leaders, and a new recreation district was built. In 1949, the Government of the Ryukyu Islands designated special entertainment zones in Koza, Naha, Maebaru, and elsewhere (Takushi 2000, 127). Takushi reports that Okinawans reacted variously to the concept of special zones, but that the majority of men, and many women too, believed that separate zones would help protect young women of "good" families (128).[9]

In European imperial systems, regulating sexual encounters was a key method for maintaining racial and class distinctions between colonizer and colonized, and between various class segments within each of these groups (Stoler 1989). Likewise, in occupied Japan and Okinawa, regulation of sexual encounters was a strategy adopted by occupation forces and local elites for maintaining the racial and class inequalities that buttressed American power.[10] The recurring trope of military prostitution as a breakwater or barrier between American troops and women from reputable families reveals the extent to which notions of sexual propriety infused Okinawan understandings of class during the occupation. During the late 1940s and 1950s, Okinawans as a group lacked significant legal and economic power relative to American occupiers. In popular political discourse, this led to the formation of a distinct modality of Okinawan identity founded on the idea of a uniformly poor and oppressed people, eventually leading to large-scale collective protests in 1956 and culminating in the so-called reversion movement (Inoue 2007). Yet prewar class distinctions, based upon aristocratic birth and differences in speech, dress, and attributed sexual practices, continued to flourish. During the Japanese colonial period (1879–1945), upwardly mobile Okinawans attempted—many through assimilating to Japanese cultural norms and expectations—to distance themselves from colonial discourses that symbolically associated Okinawa with conniving market women and prostitutes (Christy 1993; Angst 2001). Aspiring members of the middle class focused on women's sexuality as a means for distinguishing themselves from peasants and members of the urban working classes, a strategy which survived into the postwar period. During the postwar occupation, many Okinawans assumed that women who sold their sexual labor to American soldiers came from lower-class backgrounds. They had little education, and their families depended on their income for survival. According to the stereotype, most military sex workers came from the northern countryside and outlying islands of Okinawa, where poverty and a lack of urban sophistication resulted in women with little sense of modesty who were sexually promiscuous to begin with. It was only natural, the stereotype suggested, that these women should turn to prostitution and that they should specialize in servicing the overly sexed American occupiers. For women like Satoko Wilson, who hailed from northern Okinawa, such beliefs added to the discomfort of having their marriages scrutinized and questioned. Notions of sex, race, class, and region thus intertwined in ways that marginalized some Okinawan women more than others.

The trope of prostitution as a barrier demonstrates how fencelines, both physical and figurative, were erected not only by the U.S. military and Japanese and U.S. governments but also by Okinawans to contain undesirable Americans and military culture within the boundaries of installations, as well as to maintain class distinctions among Okinawans themselves. Fence-crossing activities and relationships, including military international marriage and children, were viewed as problematic all around, serving as an uncomfortable reminder of the intermingling of Okinawan and American military people and culture, as well as the extreme class leveling that had taken place as a result of the war. Within this context, images of bargirls and prostitutes were appropriated by Okinawan writers and activists to symbolize the unequal relationship between U.S. occupiers and Okinawans. Metaphors of rape, castration, and impotence were employed to express the pain and powerlessness of Okinawans whose land was appropriated by the U.S. military, and images of military prostitution were employed to demonstrate the morally deleterious effects of U.S. rule (Molasky 1999). Unfortunately, as Linda Angst has observed, the widespread use of such symbolism all too often led to the pain of actual victims being co-opted to further specific political agendas and then forgotten (2003).

For Okinawan women who married American men prior to reversion, the association of military intimacy with prostitution led to divisions between generations of military wives, even after emigrating to the United States. Haruko Benjamin, who met and married her U.S. military husband in 1964, made the following comments about her life in the United States:

> The younger generation of internationally married Okinawan women won't have much to do with the older generation. There is a lot of prejudice against women like me who married Americans early on. They think that we older women must have met our husbands while working in bars or nightclubs. Maybe we were prostitutes. Even though all of these women are Japanese, all internationally married, and all living in the United States, there is still that prejudice. *Nisei* [second-generation Japanese Americans] and *sansei* [third-generation Japanese Americans] are often prejudiced against war brides too. They think that we must have been "bad girls" or that we were desperate for American money.

Haruko's description of the prejudice that younger military wives and Japanese Americans have against "war brides" draws from the body of tropes and images of military international intimacy in Okinawa. In the United States, however, such discourses circulate in tandem with American discourses on young and inexperienced "boy" soldiers stationed far from home, vulnerable to the seductions of unscrupulous bar owners and Asian women trying to reach the United States (Lutz 2001, 136; see also Liu 2003). American stereotypes are amplified by orientalist images of Asian and Asian American women as docile, submissive, and sexually compliant (Johnson 1988; Ma 1996; Liu 2003). American military personnel arrive in Okinawa having been exposed to these ideas, which in turn inform their encounters with Okinawans. In interviews, several American military men discussed how their thinking was initially influenced by such discourses and how that changed as they became increasingly involved with their future Okinawan spouses. One participant provided the following description of his experiences in 1950s Okinawa: "Regarding attitudes, many GIs considered any friendliness by the local girls to just be an attempt to get a ticket to the States. This probably included myself to some extent. It was some time before I came to realize what my future wife had to go through and the *sacrifices* she made for me and our marriage. Her looking for a ticket to the States couldn't have been further from the truth. Her willingness to gamble on me might have been somewhat influenced by a very good friend of hers who had earlier become engaged to an air force serviceman who returned to the States and then came back to marry her."

Finally, even for younger Okinawan military wives who married after 1972, negative stereotypes associating military marriage with occupation-era prostitution informed the perspectives of older parents and loved ones. Participants who grew up during the 1970s and 1980s often reported that family members used sexual imagery and stereotypes to dissuade them from becoming romantically involved with U.S. military men. Images of "fallen women" working in Okinawa's entertainment districts continued to serve as a popularly recognized symbol of sexual impropriety and immoral behavior, made all the more powerful by guilt-inducing appeals to consider how one's actions might reflect upon the family. Having been exposed to images of occupation-era bargirls and prostitutes, women like thirty-three-year-old Noriko Sacca, who dated and married her Marine Corps husband in the late 1990s, concealed their relationships from parents and neighbors. "It was a big no-go for me to date Americans. When my parents were growing up, people thought that all ladies who went out with Americans were bar girls. Tony and I weren't doing anything bad, but a lot of people my parents' age looked at us that way. I was afraid that my parents would be ashamed. I lived in Naha, so I didn't really care what people thought, but my parents would have to face their friends and neighbors in Ogimi Village."

Satoko Wilson and the Strategic Use of Pity

In interviews, older Okinawan military spouses often expressed pity toward occupation-era sex workers rather than condemnation. At the same time, their depictions of poor women, forced to sell sex in order to feed their families, conspicuously demonstrated their own detachment from such scenes. Although sincerely intended, distancing expressions of pity served to remove the speaker from the world of prostitution, elevating her above the stereotypes of lower-class and uneducated women with questionable sexual morality. My discussions with Satoko Wilson are a case in point. In conversations about her experiences as a caseworker at the nonprofit for Amerasian children, Satoko expressed dismay at the way mixed-blood children (*konketsuji*) were treated in Okinawa. Referring obliquely to her own Christian morality, she avowed, "All children are equal in the Lord's eyes, and all need love in order to thrive." However, while Satoko talked openly about her work at the nonprofit and about her marriage to John, she rarely discussed the two topics together. The one exception involves a story that she has recounted to me several times throughout our fifteen-year friendship. The story opens with a description of a particular family she worked with at the nonprofit, defined in explicitly racial terms. In an early iteration, she told me that the family included four children—"two Japanese, one black, and one white"—who were being raised by their grandparents while their mother lived and worked in the vicinity of the U.S. military bases in the south. The children had suffered greatly, Satoko explained, because of their mother's "poor choices," the implication being that the woman worked in the entertainment district because she had lax morals and was not educated enough to understand the consequences of her sexual activities. In a later telling, Satoko related an occasion when one of the children, the one with darker skin, had become ill and needed medical attention. The mother and grandparents refused to take her to the doctor due to their embarrassment and discomfort with being stared at. Satoko and her husband, John, intervened and took the child to the hospital themselves. "But that was even worse! Here we were, a white American man and an Okinawan woman with a black child!" Her face reddened with the memory. The tale ended with Satoko expressing sympathy for the family who had to endure such scrutiny daily. However, the child's racial difference, explicitly mentioned in each telling, underscored Satoko's own separation from the child and the circumstances under which she had been brought into the world.

Satoko's stories about her work at the nonprofit usually included no mention whatsoever of her own marriage and personal life. Her personal history of leaving Nakijin to work in Koza, as well as her intimate relationship with an American military man, ostensibly had no bearing on her views of interracial sex, sexual labor, and Amerasian children. As a Christian and a member of Okinawa's middle class, Satoko's experiences and beliefs were presented as starkly opposed to the morally compromised beliefs and behaviors of her less comfortable clients. By setting up and tenaciously guarding this opposition, she was able to project negative stereotypes away from herself, even as she reinforced the overall truth value of such imagery by representing herself as an authority on the subject, based upon her experiences as a caseworker at the prestigious international organization. Satoko's use of pity to deflect negative stereotypes away from herself was not unusual among the women I interviewed. By participating in wider public discourses on military prostitution, older Okinawan military spouses often ended up reinforcing the racial and class-based stereotypes that marginalize military international couples and their children within Okinawan society.

Changing Images of Military International Intimacy and Marriage

In the decades following reversion to Japanese sovereignty, Okinawan notions of identity and class, along with associated images of military international intimacy and marriage, shifted in response to changing political and economic conditions. The Okinawa Reversion Agreement, signed in Washington, D.C., and Tokyo on June 17, 1971, transferred the administration of Okinawa to Tokyo the following year but also granted privileges and rights to the United States for the continuous and unrestricted use of existing military bases, with Tokyo pledging to pay a significant portion of the operating costs. In an effort to control Okinawan discontent with the arrangement, Tokyo has continuously transferred massive payments of public funds to Okinawa in the name of *hondonami* (catching up with the mainland), a program intended to bolster the local economy but also functioning as compensation for the continuous U.S. military presence. Funding for *hondonami* projects has been channeled into three primary areas: public works (such as construction of roads), tourism, and bases (for example, rent for land occupied by the bases). While critics argue that the program has enriched mainland construction and tourism companies while increasing Okinawa's economic dependence on Tokyo, it is also true that living standards have markedly improved for many Okinawans. Masamichi Inoue's description is especially vivid: "Old images of Okinawa—the lack of electricity and water, walking with bare feet, sweet-potato eating, thatched roof homes with 'unsanitary' toilets, and muddy roads washed away by typhoons, etc.—have been replaced with images of air-conditioned cars, fast food, and concrete homes and roads" (Inoue 2007, 66). In the process, the economic advantages enjoyed by U.S. service members in prereversion Okinawa have disappeared.[11]

With increasing affluence, older formulations of Okinawan identity founded on the idea of a uniformly poor and oppressed people have given way to notions that involve a more confident, diverse, and globally connected citizenry. As the most visible point of reference for prereversion understandings of class difference—the socioeconomic divide separating Americans from Okinawans—has faded, economic divisions *within* Okinawan society have taken on greater meaning. Inoue's (2007) analysis focuses on social and political fragmentation resulting from emerging divisions between municipalities awarded public works projects in exchange for hosting bases and municipalities with no bases, and between landowners who have grown wealthy on government rent money versus wage laborers who continue to depend upon the bases and associated work projects for regular paychecks. The U.S. bases themselves, Inoue argues, have come to be viewed not so much as an oppressor against which all Okinawans would be politically unified, but as a source of income and political bargaining chip that could be appropriated to express Okinawan pride, culture, and distinction from mainland Japan. Indeed, as new economic structures have developed, a more celebratory vision of local culture, centering around nostalgic evocations of the Ryūkyū Kingdom, has emerged, encouraged by mainland Japanese touristic consumption. Inoue suggests that these new forms of local culture may have functioned to deflect critical views of the U.S. military presence onto the depoliticized plane of cultural pride (Inoue 2007).

Ironically, the economic changes affecting postreversion Okinawa have led to a rather different set of shifts with regard to military international intimacy and marriage. Prior to reversion, middle-class Okinawans focused on women's sexual relationships with American men as a means for distinguishing respectable women and families from peasants and working-class women. In the postreversion era, the general rise in living standards has enabled most Okinawan women to leave sex work for employment in the expanding service industry. Dilapidated entertainment districts still catering to U.S. military clientele are now staffed primarily by Filipina women, and many entertainment areas have been altogether repurposed as destinations for mainland Japanese and other Asian tourists. While women's sexuality continues to be a focus of identity construction, divisions between "us" and "them" have been redrawn so that "we" Okinawans, who have moved beyond the kinds of economic struggles that once forced local women into prostitution, are collectively reimagined and repositioned above others (such as Filipinas) whose lifestyles and behaviors now mark the limits of respectability. Familiar stereotypes associating military intimacy with lax morals and prostitution have thus been remapped onto non-Okinawan Others, including mainland Japanese tourists and Filipina entertainers, while understandings of class difference within Okinawan society have shifted subtly and now index a broader range of behaviors and elements of self-presentation.

The *Amejo* Stereotype

Despite economic shifts, Okinawan women continue to date and marry American military men in significant numbers, calling into question assumptions regarding "global hypergamy"—the belief that Asian and other nonwestern women marry European and American men out of a desire to "marry up" into a higher socioeconomic group. Popular discourses on global hypergamy, in which "passive and desperate Asian brides escape poverty and backwardness to a wealthy and advanced West" (Constable 2005, 2), are often invoked by Americans to explain the motivations of international brides, particularly those from formerly colonized regions. However, this belief tends to reflect the self-justifying discourses of colonialism as a mostly benign, even altruistic enterprise, while conveying little about women's actual desires and aspirations. Nonetheless, when viewed solely in terms of perceived economic benefit, it is true that many young Okinawan women today believe that marriage to U.S. military personnel provides certain economic guarantees. Benefits such as subsidized military housing and utilities, schooling, and access to base stores contribute to images of GIs as economically stable and fulfilling husbands. As Ayako Mizumura (2009) points out, even the privilege of being able to travel freely between on- and off-base spaces may be viewed as desirable. In interviews, older Okinawan women related the surprise they experienced upon relocating to the United States and leaving the military, when they lost access to their husbands' COLA, a supplementary cost of living allowance given to service members stationed overseas, along with subsidized groceries, utilities, and leisure activities.

In mainland Japan, the conventional international marriage pattern of Japanese women marrying Western men gradually reversed itself as the Japanese economy grew during the 1970s and 1980s, so that now the overwhelming majority of international marriages are between Japanese men and foreign (mostly Asian) women. This reversal has not occurred in Okinawa. In Okinawa, nearly 80 percent of international marriages still involve Japanese women marrying foreign men, and 86.8 percent of foreign grooms are American (Japanese Ministry of Health, Labour and Welfare 2016). At the same time, popular opposition to the U.S. military presence has continued to simmer, with mass protests flaring up following particularly egregious crimes and accidents. Within this context, the derogatory term *amejo* emerged during the early 1990s. The etymology of the term is debated. While many assume that it should be written アメ女 (with *ame* short for *amerika* and *jo* meaning woman, hence "American-(loving) woman"), others suggest that it is short for *amerika jōgū*, an Okinawan phrase meaning, "women who consume/eat American men" (Yoshikawa 1996; Takushi 2000; Ueno 2001). Applied to young women who engage in intimate relationships with American military men, the term evokes images of short skirts, high heels, and heavy makeup, much like the *pan pan* during the early postwar period (Dower 1999; Molasky 1999). Above all, *amejo* is equated with sexual promiscuity.

Japanese feminist Ueno Chizuko has written a short essay about the *amejo* image, drawing parallels between derogatory stereotypes of women who married American soldiers immediately after the war and negative images of Okinawan women who date and marry Americans today (Ueno 2001). Having conducted on-the-spot interviews with fifty young Okinawan men and women between the ages of twenty and thirty-five, Ueno sketches the *amejo* image with the following quotations:

> "Women who go to on-base nightclubs night after night looking for American men."

"They wear tacky clothes that expose their bodies."

"Women who like sex."

"Women who walk alongside black guys who look like they belong in gangster movies."

"Women who shamefully prefer American men to Japanese partners."

"Women who boast about leading foreigners on."

"Women who long for [*akogareru*] the kind of world portrayed in Yamada Eimi's writings." (Ueno 2001, 172, my translation)[12]

As is clear from these characterizations, the term *amejo* is commonly used to criticize and marginalize women who become sexually involved with American military men, much like occupation-era stereotypes of Okinawan bargirls and sex workers. What is less clear is who uses the term and why. Notably, the term appears to be used most often by Okinawan and Japanese men, as noted by Mizumura (2009, 127–128). For men, who tend to assume that women who appear in public with U.S. servicemen are having sex with the Americans, *amejo* signals a group of women who are no longer considered acceptable intimate partners for themselves. Highlighting a different usage, Chris Ames reported three women in Okinawa's heavily militarized central region who embraced the term, competing in a playful rivalry over who most exhibited the stereotypical characteristics (2007, 333). Ames interpreted this as an instance of resistance and self-empowerment, in which the women reappropriated the pejorative label as a source of pride and distinction, demonstrating the courage to be different. None of my interviewees ventured into this socially risky territory, perhaps out of a desire to maintain already-fragile connections with family and neighbors in the small towns where they grew up and continued to reside in northern Okinawa.

Like those who married U.S. military men before reversion, the young women I interviewed often mentioned negative stereotypes, including the *amejo* image, and then carefully distanced themselves from such discourse. For example, twenty-eight-year-old Akiko Jones told me that she often felt uncomfortable waiting at the gate to Camp Foster for her American fiancé to sign her onto base.

> Before I got married, I had to wait at the gate for my husband, and I saw many young Japanese girls out there waiting too. And—they didn't even look Japanese. They were wearing short pants and low-cut blouses, things that they would never wear downtown. You know, Okinawans have this thing—a woman puts on too much makeup and dresses like that and ends up getting in trouble. Maybe rape or something. And then everyone says, "Americans are bad," and it hurts the relationship between America and Japan. I think that those girls, and the American GIs too, need to think more seriously about their actions. Many of those girls are

just interested in their own emotions. "Please pay attention to me." Then when they get in trouble, they say, "I didn't do anything." But they *did*. Before I got married, when I was waiting at the gate, Japanese drivers would pass by and look at me like I was an *amejo*. They saw me as the same. That made me feel so bad.

Concerned with not being labeled an *amejo* herself, Akiko engaged in a distancing technique similar to those employed by occupation-era military wives. By projecting negative stereotypes onto others—in this case, women who seek U.S. military boyfriends in order to satisfy their own emotional needs and attract attention—Okinawan military spouses avoided derogative labels, even as they reinforced the overall truth-value of such imagery. In Akiko's case, this included voicing a belief that women who associate with U.S. military personnel are somehow less deserving of empathy if they are raped or otherwise victimized by American men. Her words suggest that such women are to blame for damaging the relationship between America and Japan. This sort of victim-blaming is unfortunately common, despite the efforts of consciousness-raising organizations like Okinawan Women Act Against Military Violence (see below).

In the same interview, Akiko, who grew up in Yomitan Village in the shadow of Kadena Air Base, employed another common distancing strategy, commenting with evident disdain that many of the women who frequented on- and off-base clubs were actually from mainland Japan.

When I was in high school, whenever the bus dropped me off on Highway 58, I was approached by girls from mainland Japan. They would ask me, "Where is Sunabe? Where do the American guys go? Where are the American guys?" Things like that. They wanted to meet an American for a summer fling. They saw it as an adventure.

Indeed, stories about mainland Japanese women who travel to Okinawa specifically in order to find American boyfriends are common. Yuki Eisner, twenty-eight, for example, told me that she had heard rumors that certain mainland Japanese travel companies were offering Okinawa sex tours to young single women from Tokyo and other large cities, with American GIs as the sexual bait. Comments of this sort are tied to the larger social and political project of constructing a distinctive Okinawan identity vis-à-vis mainland Japan, and as such, they reflect a community-wide posture of resistance against mainlanders and mainland discourses that cast Okinawans as second-class citizens. More specifically, such statements may be interpreted as a response to mainland Japanese views and sentiments concerning international dating and marriage. Within mainland discourses, American military men are not viewed as particularly desirable dating or marriage partners for young upwardly mobile Japanese women. Quoting Kida Midori's *Women! What Do You Want from America?* (1998), a practical informational guide for women who wish to relocate abroad, Karen Kelsky writes:

> According to Kida, too many Japanese women throw themselves away on men with no resources and no prospects, misled by their own Hollywood-driven *akogare* for "tall blond-haired, blue-eyed Adonises—the kind Japanese females can't resist" (82). Nevertheless, "You've come all the way to America, and it would be a terrific waste if you didn't hook up with the kind of fine man [*ii otoko*] you almost never see in Japan" (80). Kida is unrepentantly materialistic. "Beware of men with no earning power," she begins her discussion; "don't choose the wrong man; make sure you have a solid strategy for finding the right kind" (84). The right kind is emphatically not a military man; Kida devotes a chapter to the stories of women who met and married mainly black Army men on U.S. bases in Japan, only to find themselves stranded in the United States with alcoholic husbands, or abandoned, poverty-stricken, and on welfare. Kida is entirely unsympathetic: "You can make various excuses that they picked the wrong person or had bad luck, but the fact is, it's the fault of their own ignorance [*ninshiki no amasa*]" (97). (2001, 167–168)

Kida's text makes it plain that military marriage—the kind of international marriage that Okinawa is known for—is the poor (indeed, "ignorant") woman's road to international adventure. Although Kida does not mention Okinawa specifically, her patronizing words must surely have sounded familiar to Okinawan readers. Kida's text plays directly into long-standing discourses, inherited from the Japanese colonial period that cast Okinawans as unsophisticated provincials, saddled by social and economic difficulties of their own making.

In response to Kida's unabashed pursuit of sex/love and socioeconomic status together, Okinawan women's disdainful comments about mainland Japanese women who come to Okinawa to find U.S. military boyfriends can be seen as a sort of backtalk. Using a language that measures class according to popular standards of decency, including dress, self-other orientation (that is, selfish versus selfless), and sexual behavior rather than wealth or education, Okinawan women declare tactics like Kida's to be indecent, immoral, "class-less." Echoing the discursive stance adopted by young Okinawan women, social worker Hirata Masayo shared her impression that military dating in Okinawa is qualitatively different from encounters between Japanese women and U.S. military men in mainland Japan: "In Yokosuka [a city in the greater Tokyo area, home port of the U.S. Seventh Fleet], international dating consists mainly of *asobi* [playing around]. Here,

Okinawan girls are more interested in settling down and making a life together [*seikatsu ni mitchaku*]."

Asian Women in Okinawa's Entertainment Districts

Younger women who married after reversion also invoked older occupation-era stereotypes of military prostitution, redirecting them at non-Japanese Others, including entertainment workers from the Philippines and elsewhere. Filipinas began staffing hostess clubs in Japan and Okinawa in the 1970s and increasingly through the 1980s and 1990s until March 2005, when the flow of Filipina entertainers was halted by a bilateral Philippine-Japan agreement to prevent them from being trafficked into Japan's sex industry (Suzuki 2011). During this period, tens of thousands of women entered Japan on entertainer visas and began working at hostess bars and nightclubs, including establishments catering to U.S. military personnel. There they performed a variety of tasks, including sitting with customers, offering light conversation, making drinks, taking food orders, lighting cigarettes, keeping tables clean, singing karaoke, dancing with customers, and sometimes performing dance routines and sexual acts. The living and working conditions of Filipinas in the entertainment district adjacent to Camp Hansen in Kin were described as abysmal by feminist scholars Saundra Pollock Sturdevant and Brenda Stoltzfus, who visited Okinawa in the early 1990s and collected life histories from women working there (1993; see also Yoshikawa 1996).

In Okinawa, contemporary images of Filipina entertainers strongly resemble older stereotypes of occupation-era military prostitutes (poor family background, little education, compromised sexual morality, moral and racial contamination, and so on). In Kin village, for example, Hideki Yoshikawa has documented the following community sentiments.

> The presence of the base [Camp Hansen] is perceived by many townspeople as causing "moral decay" in the town. Moral decay is often associated with the presence of the "sex industry" in the Shinkaichi [bar] section whose main customers are U.S. military personnel. In relatively large bars and clubs of the Shinkaichi section, nude dancing is performed by Filipino "entertainers" and the selling of sexual labor by Filipino women to military personnel is widely suspected by many townspeople . . . . In the late 1980s, the possibility of the spread of AIDS panicked the Shinkaichi section as well as the town as a whole. It was seen as a symbol of the moral decay in the town, especially in relationship to the

suspected sex industry in the Shinkaichi section. It opened up a series of discussions in the town assembly on the sexual practice of military personnel in the town. As a result, the blood donation from U.S. military to the town and Okinawa as a whole was halted and tight control on Filipino women was proposed. However, since the townspeople recognize that people living in Kin themselves run these businesses, they are often reluctant to criticize the presence of the sex industry openly.

Moral decay is also perceived as a clash of different sets of culturally appropriate behaviors existing in the same place, namely those of Okinawans and of Americans [U.S. military personnel]. For example, the behaviors of military personnel jogging with their shirts off and kissing women [Filipino women] on the streets in the Shinkaichi section are not considered culturally appropriate behaviors in Okinawa . . . . These behaviors of military personnel are, however, often considered too foreign to have any direct influence on the townspeople. In contrast, there are certain behaviors of U.S. military personnel which are considered by military personnel as rather normal but are seen by the townspeople to have negative effects on the townspeople. The behaviors of chewing gum while talking or engaging in work or eating while walking are good examples. They are considered to have negatively influenced students of Kin Town to "behave like Americans," causing moral decay among the students (Yoshikawa 1996, 73–74).

Yoshikawa's description of townspeople's concern with the social effects of military prostitution and other "American" behaviors resembles discourses on female "breakwaters" that circulated in Okinawa during the late 1940s and 1950s. Filipina sex workers are today thought to provide a barrier between U.S. servicemen and Okinawans, to the extent that the sexual behaviors of American military personnel (including kissing on the street) are believed to present less of a problem than cultural behaviors (like chewing gum while talking and eating while walking) in terms of contributing to the moral degradation of Kin youth.

In interviews, Okinawan military girlfriends and spouses invoked these popular discourses, which position Filipina bar workers and the sexual contamination they represent outside of Okinawan society altogether, implying by way of contrast that the speakers themselves are conforming to popular definitions of virtue.[13] For example, one evening when I was attending a private party hosted by Chieko Pierce and attended by six Okinawan women (three of whom had previously been married to Americans) and their U.S. marine boyfriends, the group began to discuss an outing they were planning to an off-base club in Kin. In line with the outrageous anything-goes persona she adopted at such parties, Chieko declared that she would like to see the infamous "banana show." The "banana show" is a well-known stage show—I have heard it mentioned by Okinawan men and women and U.S. military men—which involves a woman inserting a banana into her vagina and then squeezing the flesh out into the audience. The men all groaned, and one responded that he had seen that show the first time he had been stationed in Okinawa ten years ago, and he had seen it again recently, and that the same Filipina woman had been performing the show for the past several decades. The women laughed uproariously and comments were made about saggy Filipina *obāchan* (grandmothers) performing tricks with bananas. The conversation eventually turned to other topics. No plans were made to attend the show. Chieko had expressed interest merely to get a reaction out of the crowd that evening. Those attending the party apparently viewed elderly Filipina entertainers as a source of racialized comic relief. Implicitly, these Okinawan women, who might themselves have been labeled *amejo*, seemed to be defining themselves and their own normalcy against the sexual deviancy of Filipina women employed in the military entertainment districts.[14]

Okinawan discourses on Filipina entertainers do not simply recycle stereotypes of occupation-era military prostitution. They also articulate with the racialized discourses of Japanese imperialism. Feminist scholars and activists have traced the material and discursive links between Japanese wartime military prostitution, involving the recruitment or abduction of "comfort women" from Korea, China, and the Philippines to sexually service Japanese soldiers, postwar U.S. military prostitution, sexual tourism by Japanese men in Korea and Southeast Asia, and the present-day trafficking of non-Japanese Asian women to work in Japan's domestic sex industry (see, for example, Hicks 1994; Enloe 2000). Against this backdrop, and within Okinawa's postreversion political economy, the full constellation of imagery associated with occupation-era military prostitution is transferred onto women from regions over which Japan dominates economically, an economic sphere of influence that is a residue of Japan's military empire of the past. Thus, for many Okinawans, a focus on Filipina women's sexuality has enabled a reworking of Okinawan notions of class identity, in which Okinawans are collectively reimagined as superior to Filipina Others whose lifestyles and behaviors now mark the limits of respectability.

Reevaluating Occupation-Era Military Marriage

Finally, Okinawa's shifting economic conditions have contributed to new perspectives on occupation-era military marriage itself. Several persons I spoke with, although rarely military spouses themselves, expressed admiration for the "courageous" women who had married Americans during the occupation, when such relationships were viewed as a transgression of local norms concerning sexual morality and family. Comments of this sort almost always involved a comparison, explicit or implied, between women who married Americans before reversion and those who were doing so now. Translator Nakama Tetsu, for example, who came to Koza from Miyako Island in 1957 to set up a translation business, remarked that women who married U.S. military men forty years ago were truly remarkable compared to those who do so today.[15] "*Erai, naa. Ano yō na kokusai-kekkon, yokatta naa.*" ("That kind of international marriage [the kind that occurred during the early years of the occupation] was truly impressive.") Nakama described the majority of women who married GIs in the 1950s and 1960s as having had "old-style educations" and "old-style values." When they committed to marriage, it was for good. They had no career skills to fall back on, and they had no money of their own. Once they left with their husbands for the United States, they could no longer depend on the support of Okinawan friends and family, and flying back for a visit was unthinkable for all but the wealthiest of individuals. Many women left believing that they would never see their families in Okinawa again. They came to Nakama's office in order to have the required marriage documents translated, many unable to suppress tears. But their resolve was firm. Today, Nakama maintained, travel between Okinawa and the United States is relatively inexpensive. Many women who marry American GIs are well-educated, and they have careers and salaries of their own. Divorce has become a valid option, he reasoned, and therefore women enter into such marriages more easily, often motivated by little more than current fashion.

Nakama's comments represent a reversal of the prejudice against older war brides described earlier in this chapter. The association of military intimacy with morally contaminating lower-class sexuality is displaced onto younger women who are well-educated, have careers and money of their own, and can therefore afford to take marriage less seriously. Compared to these women, occupation-era brides with "old-style educations" and "old-style values" represent the side of moral purity. In fact, within comments like Nakama's, one might argue that class seems to have lost its economic moorings altogether and instead has become a pure signifier of sexual morality and social distinction—as in the adjectives *classy* and *classic*, or the put-down "She has no class." References like these to class, reimagined as social distinction, frequently emerge in postreversion discourses on military-Okinawan intimacy. Denunciations of *amejo* as self-centered young women who shamelessly pursue sex, and even criticisms of "American" behaviors like chewing gum while talking and eating while walking, depend upon such distinctions. Indeed, the collective experience of postreversion economic growth appears to have encouraged Okinawans to abandon socioeconomic difference as a primary source of identity in favor of a more diverse and diffuse set of social-behavioral standards. Nonetheless, women's sexuality remains a focus for generating such distinctions. Focusing analysis on popular discourses on women's sexuality, especially in relation to military intimacy, the resonances between pre-reversion and postreversion stereotypes, as well as the similar strategies that women use to avoid them, suggest that reversion has done little to mitigate the considerable personal and social burdens that Okinawan women shoulder in association with the ongoing U.S. military presence.

Continuations

Satoko Wilson is fully retired now, still living in Nakijin and keeping a garden, although it is reduced in size, and still active in her church. As is common in cases of international marriage, Okinawan friends and neighbors refer to her by her maiden name, Miyagi Satoko, while American acquaintances continue to use Wilson. During a recent visit, she patiently answered my questions regarding her marriage to John and work at the nonprofit organization, helping me fill in gaps and correct misinterpretations. I learned more about her childhood, her experiences with the church, and John's final year of life, spent hospitalized at Camp Lester because Nakijin was simply too far away from doctors and medical resources in case of emergency. Most importantly, Satoko-san wanted me to understand that her previous comments regarding women who worked in occupation-era entertainment districts were not meant spitefully, but rather came from her love and concern for the children they left behind in the villages, children that she had dedicated her life to supporting and caring for. She reminded me about her star pupil, an Amerasian girl who had endured severe poverty and discrimination growing up without a father in northern Okinawa, but who had studied hard, won the national English speech contest, attended high school and university in United States on full scholarship, and gone to work for Goldman Sachs in Tokyo. Tears filled her eyes as she told me about the girl's search for her father in the United States and his eventual recognition of her as his daughter, a gift that had changed her life. Satoko's willingness to continue working with me, and her trust that I would eventually understand her real intentions and her true heart, have helped me understand that the words and experiences of the women discussed in this chapter are not reducible to my analysis. Satoko's expressions of pity were never entirely about buttressing her own middle-class identity. Akiko Jones's assertion that young Japanese women bear responsibility for their own victimization was made as she was attempting to adjust to life in the U.S. military community and may have reflected her own disquiet with recent military crimes. Chieko Pierce, who once joked about Filipina grandmothers performing the banana show in Kin, is now a grandmother herself, working long hours to help support her son, his wife, and their two young children, who live at home with her.

Women who engage in intimate relationships with U.S. military men navigate complex and shifting social and political fields. During the early occupation, memories of war and overwhelming political and economic inequality between U.S. military occupiers and local people shaped perceptions of military intimacy, and stereotypes of dire poverty and prostitution loomed large. In the years following reversion, improved standards of living, alongside continued political marginalization, have led to changes in popular discourses on military intimacy. The meaning of "class" in such discourses seems to have shifted from socioeconomic status to broader conceptions of dress, attitudes, and sexual behavior. Through it all, women's romantic and sexual experiences continue to be symbolically appropriated to police racial divides, perform class distinction, and generate a distinctive Okinawan identity. Women engaging in military intimacy participate in producing these meanings by adopting familiar stereotypes and using them to criticize others, including poor women, older women, younger women, mainland Japanese tourists, and Filipina entertainers.

For Okinawan military spouses and girlfriends, it has been a continuing challenge to develop alternative ways of talking about intimate relationships with U.S. military men. Efforts have been made by a number of community organizations to move beyond existing paradigms. Okinawan Women Act Against Military Violence, a women's peace, human rights, and demilitarization advocacy group, has joined forces with international feminist movements to focus attention on the burdens women shoulder as a result of the U.S. military presence in Okinawa (Akibayashi and Takazato 2009). From incidences of military sexual violence to the elements of sexism and misogyny that infuse military training, women in this group are attempting to reframe government claims surrounding the need for the bases, asking whose "security" the U.S. military is actually protecting. For local people, and especially women and children, the group claims, the military has in fact been a source of insecurity.[16] A second community initiative, the AmerAsian School in Okinawa, was established in 1998. Founded by five mothers who set up a study group on the educational rights of Amerasian children, the school's mission is "to provide a safe non-discriminatory place for AmerAsian children to get a good education and opportunities while improving their self-esteem" (AmerAsian School in Okinawa 2012). The school's bilingual and bicultural curriculum is designed to fill gaps and correct biases that exist in Japan's public education system, which is notoriously difficult to navigate for students who are not native speakers of Japanese or otherwise different from mainstream Japanese students.

For both organizations, an important goal has been to identify structural problems related to the U.S. military presence. Unfortunately, many military spouses and girlfriends do not feel that their experiences and concerns, including widespread popular misunderstanding and discrimination, have been adequately represented by such organizations. They have sought acceptance in both the U.S. military and Okinawan communities using other means, including expertly tapping family and institutional resources on both sides of the fencelines, discussed in detail in chapter 5.

THE MARINE CORPS
MARRIAGE PACKAGE

On the outskirts of Kita-Nakagusuku in traffic-congested central Okinawa, about a ten-minute drive from U.S. Marine Corps Camp Foster and across the street from a small family-owned sugarcane field, there was an apartment building, not particularly notable except for the tenants who occupied one of the fourth-floor flats. The rental contract for the apartment listed Yuki Shimabukuro as sole tenant, but the flat was occupied by Yuki and her American husband, Josh Eisner, a low-ranking enlisted U.S. marine. The small apartment had a cramped kitchen, and the adjoining living room was sparsely furnished with a worn black leather couch and glass-topped coffee table picked up at one of the ubiquitous military yard sales. Despite the heat, humidity, and utter lack of a cross-breeze, the air-conditioning unit sat idle. Yuki explained apologetically that it was too expensive to run during the day. The Eisners spoke about their personal and family backgrounds, Josh's rocky relationship with Yuki's parents, and their carefully considered decision to marry. Throughout the interview, Josh expressed irritation with official Marine Corps rules and regulations. "After I asked her to marry me, I discovered what a pain in the butt it was to *get* married. There was this 'package' that the Marine Corps wanted you to fill out, where eventually, it was like asking the general of First MAW, who I'd never met, for permission to get married. Like the guy could decide for me if I was smart enough to pick the right girl!" Rather than submit to this sort of institutional surveillance, the Eisners had opted to get married "out in town." As a result, Yuki was not "command sponsored"—that is, she had no access to military health care, she could not fly stand-by on military flights, and they did not qualify for the comparatively spacious and air-conditioned base housing.

Countless U.S. military couples in Okinawa, like the Eisners, actively circumvent official U.S. military marriage and family regulations.[1] As a result, they are able, to some degree, to fly under institutional radar. Yet published memoirs, internet blogs, and personal interviews suggest that even for couples who marry "by the book," military marriage and family regulations constitute a much resented symbol of the unrelenting institutional surveillance and control the U.S. military exercises over its own personnel. Marriage and family regulations, along with fraternization and personal conduct orders, are a key means by which the military structures and regulates opportunities for intimacy, as well as interpretations of sex, sentiment, and family. The military exercises this sort of biopolitical governance in and around overseas posts throughout the world, extending the social, economic, and cultural reach of the United States well beyond its territorial borders.

This chapter examines the complex set of procedures known as the "marriage package." When I first lived in Okinawa in 2001–2002, the marriage package was mandated by U.S. Marine Corps headquarters in Washington as the only legitimate means for marines and navy corpsmen to legalize an international marriage in Japan. In recent years, the process has been streamlined for marines assigned to the Okinawa-based III MEF.[2] Nevertheless, it remains an instructive ethnographic example for demonstrating U.S. military and Japanese government approaches to regulating military international marriage. The analysis here focuses on institutional representations of gender, marriage, and family that appeared in marriage package documents, and how those were received, resisted, and reformulated by service members and their spouses. More specifically, I examine how institutional discourses influenced service members' expressions of military affinity and affiliation, while also considering the voices of Okinawan spouses as they articulated subject positions markedly different from their feminist counterparts in the antibase movement.

Marriage package directives specified the need for U.S. military and Japanese government documents substantiating the nationality and family background of the applicants, as well as physical examinations of both prospective spouses. The heart of the process, and the target of the most vociferous complaints, comprised a mandatory two-day premarital seminar and group counseling session led by military chaplains. Seminar content presupposed an American male head of household and institutional gender and racial ideologies. Long-standing stereotypes of foreign brides continually emerged in seminar language. On another level, seminar lectures drew on a model of marital strife as a clash between essentialized males and females. Seminar participants were thus exposed to a military institutional model of the ideal military family wherein men served their country by participating in combat while women served their country by supporting their military husbands. Against the backdrop of Okinawa's postwar political and economic subjugation to the United States and Japan, the seminar recast social and political inequalities inherent in the prolonged U.S. military presence in less threatening idioms of naturalized gender difference, marriage, and family.

The marriage package thus functioned as a convenient tool for restructuring gendered and racialized notions of "cultural citizenship" in Okinawa. The concept of cultural citizenship refers to the ideological process through which individuals become tied to or subjected to the state and state authority along cultural lines, for example as members of a social group deemed deserving of state benefits and protection. The effectiveness of the marriage package in structuring such notions lay in its focus on the most intimate and personal details of service members' behaviors and relationships. Yet even the military's considerable leverage in imposing official notions of gender, marriage, and family, and personal and professional responsibilities had limits. In Okinawa and throughout the global U.S. military community, service members and their spouses *negotiate* cultural citizenship, identity, and intimacy, with implications for the cultural reproduction of U.S. empire.

Cultural Citizenship and U.S. Military Marriage Procedures

Cultural citizenship refers to the interplay between coercive definitions of citizenship emanating from state centers of power and the responses of citizen groups who embrace, challenge, and transform imposed ideologies and policies (Rosaldo 2003). Investigating the changing dynamics of state power and citizenship in southeast Asia, Aihwa Ong has explored cultural citizenship as a process of subjectification, "in the Foucaultian sense of self-making and being made by power relations that produce consent through schemes of surveillance, discipline, control, and administration" (1996, 737). Ong emphasizes the role of state institutions in this process. "Hegemonic ideas about belonging and not belonging in racial and cultural terms often converge in state and nonstate institutional practices through which subjects are shaped in ways that are at once specific and diffused" (738). State institutions play an important role through their involvement in biopolitical modes of governing, which "center on the capacity and potential of individuals and the population as living resources that may be harnessed and managed by governing regimes" (Ong 2006, 6; see also Foucault 1978). In Okinawa and throughout the global U.S. military, official marriage procedures and family regulations serve as a site of biopolitical governance and cultural citizenship processes. In general terms, U.S. military governance works through the bodies of

U.S. military personnel, as well as enemy combatants and occupied civilians. The military employs an elaborate array of bureaucratic regulations and procedures to reinforce a training regimen that produces soldiers who are prepared to commit otherwise intolerable acts and place loyalty to fellow soldiers and one's mission above concerns for their own survival. Regulation of intimate domains, including sex, sentiment, and family, is an important component of military code. Overseas marriage, for example, is governed by location-specific orders, established in accordance with status of forces agreements (SOFAs) and General Orders of conduct.[3]

Cultural notions of national or racial hierarchy and gendered images of the ideal military service member, spouse, and family are embedded in official marriage protocols and practices. In the Marine Corps premarital seminar, institutionalized understandings of what it meant to be an active-duty serviceman romantically involved with an Okinawan woman—including assumptions concerning the primacy of the serviceman's language, family, and career—created a diverse array of unequal subject positions, differentiating seminar participants (servicemen and their prospective Okinawan spouses) along lines of gender, nationality, and race. The resulting hierarchies contributed to a sense of entitlement among service members, who were repeatedly told that their missions were of utmost importance, not only for maintaining the balance of power and supporting American economic interests but also for securing life, liberty, and happiness for Americans and Okinawans alike. Many Okinawans, however, do not see the U.S. military in this light. Members of the group Okinawan Women Act Against Military Violence, for example, assert that the U.S. military presence decreases women's security, putting them at higher risk of sexual violence due to the nature of military training and labor. More broadly, there is widespread popular concern that Okinawa will once again become a military target due to the concentrated presence of U.S. bases. Perhaps unaware of these sentiments, U.S. personnel regularly display their privilege, prerogative, and control in off-base settings. For example, many U.S. service members believe that Okinawans should bear the burden of learning English in order to communicate with Americans and see no need to learn Japanese themselves. Likewise, many demonstrate a lack of cultural knowledge and sensitivity while off base, expecting local merchants and Okinawan neighbors to behave according to American social mores. Moreover, crimes perpetrated by U.S. military personnel against Okinawans often receive inadequate attention and response across all ranks of the military. The premarital seminar and other programs thus reinforce the historically constituted symbolic fencelines that configure Okinawan society, laying the basis for interpersonal misunderstandings, conflict, and sometimes violence between U.S. military personnel and local civilians.

Military institutional "truths" of this sort do not go unchallenged, including among military personnel themselves. The critical stance of the Eisners and others exposes the seams of U.S. military power, built upon shifting hierarchies of rank and branch of service, as well as race, class, nationality, and gender. Ultimately, rigid military training and discipline, along with a flexible approach to dissonance, encourage a range of acceptable and functional notions of citizenship and empire, crucial for the projection of American military power in Okinawa and elsewhere. American empire is buttressed not only by physical coercion but also by a cultural language that is used to naturalize and normalize the U.S. military presence, making it appear unremarkable, inevitable, and legitimate (Lutz 2009, 20–29). More subtly, the negotiation of and even overt resistance to the disciplinary practices of the U.S. military, including oppositional stances adopted by U.S. service members and occupied people, often play a role in reproducing the power dynamics that underpin U.S. empire.

History of Marriage and Family Regulations in Japan

U.S. military leaders have discouraged marriage between military personnel and Okinawan women since the early postwar. Following Japan's surrender on August 15, 1945, U.S. troops were instructed to avoid socializing with members of the former enemy, and formal antifraternization regulations were introduced throughout Japan (Koshiro 1999, 59–62). SCAP Circular No. 7 drew attention to antimiscegenation laws in many U.S. states and U.S. immigration law, stating that no armed forces approval would be granted to American servicemen to marry Japanese women at the U.S. consulate, the only registration recognized by Japan or the United States (Koshiro 1999, 156).[4] In May 1946, SCAP ruled that Americans in Japan must abide by the Japanese civil code to establish the legality of a marriage. Following this order, many U.S. servicemen were legally married to Japanese women by Shinto, Buddhist, or Christian priests, even though they had not received official military approval.[5] U.S. immigration laws, however, barred Japanese persons—defined as those having 50 percent or more Japanese blood—from entering the United States and becoming citizens or permanent residents. Thus American servicemen were not able to take Japanese wives or their children back to the United States. With the exception of a thirty-day reprieve of immigration quotas in June 1947, Japanese brides were not permitted to immigrate to the United States until the McCarran-Walter Act was passed in 1952, allocating to Japan a yearly quota of 185 persons permitted to enter the United States.[6]

During the 1950s and 1960s, marriages between U.S. military personnel and Okinawans continued to be strongly discouraged by both the military and the local Okinawan community. In interviews, former military men spoke of numerous bureaucratic obstacles and mixed responses from commanding officers. Retired airman Ray Horner, nineteen years old when he began dating Asato Katsuko in 1968, reported, "If he (the commanding officer) found out that you were living with somebody, officially he couldn't condone that. But he always asked us to have a map of where we were living on the back of our locator card so that somebody could find us in case of emergency. So it was a kind of tacit approval." Other commanders routinely discouraged such relationships on the grounds that interracial relationships would draw public disapproval in both Okinawa and the United States. George Johnson (who married in 1966 in the Philippines) explained, "The primary argument was 'Son, you're away from home and lonely. This is something we're sure your family is not going to accept. You're letting your testosterone think for you instead of thinking logically.'" Bill Brenner, a retired Marine Corps staff sergeant married in 1972, complained, "The chaplain was talking about how dirty these people are, and this kind of stuff, and how I didn't really want to get married." Thomas Cooper, married in 1968 while recuperating from combat injuries in Vietnam, described a meeting with a gunnery sergeant who tore up his marriage application and threatened, "You'll marry a damn gook over my dead body." Personal and institutional racism against Japanese and Okinawans thus provided the political and cultural context for military regulations concerning marriage between American GIs and Okinawan women. Meanwhile, the sexualized nature of the American occupation led many in the Okinawan community to oppose the marriage of Okinawan women to U.S. military men (see chapter 3).

Responses of U.S. service members and Okinawan spouses to military and community opposition varied. For many U.S. servicemen, narratives of occupation-era dating and marriage highlighted bureaucratic obstacles and unsupportive officers and chaplains, building an overall image of determined and fair-minded selves positioned against an oppressive and racist U.S. military institution. For Okinawan wives, personal narratives carefully constructed the narrators' experiences of love and marriage as distinct from the experiences of occupation-era sex workers. This strategy, however, tended to reinforce popular discourses that marginalized Okinawan-U.S. military couples and their children, illustrating the complexity of processes of subjectification. Notions of cultural citizenship emerging out of institutional and community approaches to military transnational intimacy were thus multifaceted and unpredictable. Even oppositional notions of self and citizenship served to naturalize overarching relations of power.

The Marriage Package: Procedures and Rationale

During 2001–2002, the marriage process for U.S. marines and navy corpsmen serving under Marine Corps commands was detailed in an eleven-page instruction obtained from the Personal Services Center at Camp Foster.[7] The instruction divided the marriage process into three phases. Phase One included the premarital seminar, preparation of necessary documents, and medical examinations. The premarital seminar was mandatory for military members, who had to be excused from duty in order to attend, and was recommended for civilian prospective spouses. Simultaneous interpretation was provided in Japanese for "local-national" prospective spouses. Military members had to produce a passport or birth or naturalization certificate, and Japanese fiancées had to obtain and translate a copy of their family register (*koseki tohon*) from the local municipal office. Also under Phase One, both parties were required to schedule physical examinations and blood tests for HIV/AIDS, tuberculosis, and syphilis. Active-duty service members were able to arrange these at the naval hospital at Camp Lester. Japanese fiancées, however, had to go to the Adventist Medical Center in Gushikawa, the only medical facility in Okinawa approved to do physical examinations for U.S. military marriage and visa purposes. AMC did not accept Japanese national health insurance, and the cost of the exam and tests (approximately $250) had to be paid out of pocket.

After attending the premarital seminar, couples began Phase Two. The active-duty partner was required to submit an Application for Authorization to Marry

---

MARCORBASESJAPAN 1752.1A
04 MAY 2001

MARRIAGE IN JAPAN CHECKLIST

Pre-Marriage

____ Schedule/Attend Personal Services Centers' Premarital Seminar.
____ Obtain documents to substantiate nationality of applicant and prospective spouse.
____ Obtain physical examination (both parties – valid six months only).
____ Obtain family register (Koseki Tohon) with English translation (for Japanese citizens).
____ If under legal age for marriage, obtain written consent of both parents or legal guardian.
____ Submit Application for Authorization to Marry to the LSSS to obtain Affidavit of Competency to Marry.
____ Translate into Japanese the Affidavit of Competency to Marry.
____ Obtain registration of marriage (called Konin Todoke) from City Hall. Two witnesses over the age of 20 of any nationality must sign/witness the Japanese forms.
____ After issuance of Certification of Marriage (marriage certificate), obtain English translation.

Post-Marriage

____ Update Record of Emergency Data (Service Record Page 2) and DEERS/RAPIDS with supporting Consolidated Administration Office. Take all marriage-related paperwork to the office. Obtain new ID card for new spouse.
____ Submit request for Command Sponsorship to CO.
____ File Form I-30 (Petition to Classify Status of Alien Relative for Issuance of Immigrant Visa) within 30 days after date of marriage.
____ File IRS Form W-7 (Application for IRS Individual Taxpayer Identification Number) within 30 days after date of marriage. (Contact LSSS for assistance).
____ When 6-7 months of transfer from duty in Japan, contact the visa office of the American Embassy or Consulate for the purpose of initiating the process for an immigration visa to the United States for the foreign-born spouse (if applicable).

Requirements for the marriage package. Adapted from U.S. Department of Defense, 2001.

to the senior overseas area commander for approval. This application included a statement of financial resources indicating future plans for employment, current bank account balance, property ownership, insurance, and other data showing how he planned to support his fiancée while alive and in case of his death. The couple could not marry until military approval was granted, and they could not begin the immigrant visa application for the Okinawan spouse until they were married. Couples who married in Okinawa reported that it took anywhere from several months to a year or more to receive official approval to marry. After approval was issued, the military member obtained an Affidavit of Competency to Marry from the legal services office at Camp Foster. The affidavit had to be translated into Japanese for another fee and presented to the local Okinawan municipal office, which issued the actual marriage certificate. At the municipal office, the Okinawan spouse filled out the necessary paperwork, and the couple and two witnesses signed the document. They paid yet another fee and submitted this document to the city in exchange for the marriage certificate. The couple was now officially married and facing the even more extensive paperwork process of obtaining a U.S. spouse immigrant visa for the Okinawan spouse.[8]

The military had established the rationale for the marriage package in a joint service instruction, MILPERSMAN 5352–030, which governed marriage in overseas commands. The document stated: "This instruction is intended to make both aliens and U.S. citizens aware of the rights and restrictions imposed by the immigration laws of the United States and to assist in identifying and precluding the creation of military dependents not eligible for immigration into the United States." Built into this statement was an acknowledgment and justification for the overlap between the marriage package and U.S. immigrant visa procedures. Unfortunately, the various tests and checks conducted for the marriage package could not be used again for the visa application. Applicants had to retrace their steps, scheduling the medical examination and gathering all documents and their translations a second time, a considerable financial burden for a couple living on an enlisted service member's salary.[9]

The marriage package was thus designed to prevent a situation in which a foreign spouse was unable to obtain a U.S. immigrant visa, an outcome that could adversely affect the service member's ability to change duty stations when ordered to do so. The MILPERSMAN document went on to make the following statements concerning international marriage: "The restrictions imposed by this instruction are not intended to prevent marriage. These restrictions are for the protection of both aliens and United States citizens from the possible disastrous effects of an impetuous marriage entered into without appreciation of its implications and obligations." The linking of the overseas marriage process to immigration procedure placed foreign brides at the center of concern. This statement rested on the assumption that marriages to such women were often impetuous and entered into without a full understanding of the obligations that marriage entailed. It was unclear whether this clause referred to servicemen who married based on physical attraction and later regretted their marriages or to Okinawan women whose interest in marrying an American the military customarily regarded with suspicion. Nevertheless, statements like this called to mind long-standing stereotypes of crafty Asian women bent on marrying naïve young GIs in order to enter the United States and obtain a green card.[10]

Marriage package procedures were clearly developed with an American male head of household in mind. All marriage paperwork had to be handled by the U.S. military member, the majority of whom were male. The service member picked up the instructions for the marriage package from the Personal Services Center, walked the appropriate forms from office to office to obtain signatures, and then submitted the marriage request to his commander. The service member was the only person authorized to check on the status of the couple's marriage request. Okinawan fiancées had little control over the process. This was due, in part, to the provisions of the SOFA, which consigned military family members to a subordinate legal status while their active-duty spouses or parents were stationed in Japan. For Akiko Jones, twenty-eight, this was a source of great frustration. Her U.S. military fiancé was afraid of making waves and did not want to investigate why they had not yet received marriage approval. As it turned out, the couple's paperwork had been misplaced by the command, having fallen behind someone's desk.

The Premarital Seminar

On a Tuesday afternoon in spring 2002, I sat in the driver's seat of my little 660-cc mini-car, parked outside the gate of Camp Foster with the engine turned off. I had the windows rolled down, and a steady breeze was blowing up from the East China Sea. The drive from Nago had only taken forty minutes, and I was early for my appointment with Chief Tulabut, the Marine Corps warrant officer in charge of the premarital seminar. At exactly 1:00 p.m., the chief pulled up in a white Marine Corps Community Services (MCCS) van. He jumped out, quickstepped over to me, and extended his hand to shake mine. As we stood in line at the guardhouse behind a group of Okinawan construction workers, the chief and I talked about the premarital seminar. He remarked that I had chosen a good month to sit in on the seminar because there were even more Japanese fiancées attending than usual. Also, a civilian employee of MCCS who was married to a "foreign-national" had volunteered to speak to the participants about his own ex-

perience in an international marriage during the lunch hour. After the ritual of
signing me onto base, I climbed back into my car and followed the chief along
the wide avenues of Camp Foster, passing a strip mall with a Taco Bell and Dom-
ino's Pizza, long rows of khaki-colored buildings surrounded by well-watered
grass fields and exercise areas, and units of camouflage-uniformed marines march-
ing in formation.

Inside the Foster Chapel, the chief presented me with a folder of materials he
had prepared, including the documents governing Marine Corps and navy marriage procedures in Okinawa (MARCORBASESJAPANO 1752.1A and COMNAV-
FORJAPANINST 1752.1P), photocopies of several *Stars and Stripes* articles on
military international marriage, and a copy of the PREP Leader Manual that the
chaplain would be drawing his lectures from that day. "They're in here," the chief
lowered his voice as he opened the door into a large classroom. Twenty-six pairs
of eyes turned away from the chaplain to watch as I made my way to the back of
the room. The chief offered me a chair behind and off to one side of the seminar
participants seated around tables arranged in a large U-shape. The chaplain
quickly regained the attention of the group as he wrote out a list, "Relationship
Trouble Spots: Money, Children, Household Chores," on the portable whiteboard
at the front of the room. The afternoon session was underway.

Following Okinawa's reversion to Japanese sovereignty in 1972, chaplains and
legal officers established an all-island premarital seminar to meet the requirement
for premarital and legal counseling. Premarital coordinator Robert Radansky developed a full-day seminar, whose topics included language-related issues (ESL
and JSL classes), interactions between partners and relations of dependency that
shifted depending on where the couple lived, relationships with parents and in-
laws, moving to the United States, raising children in a bicultural home, and building networks of support. An associated workshop series included segments on
American and Okinawan history and culture, cooking and other homemaking
skills, military medical facilities, spouse employment, money management, legal
issues (including visa procedures, insurance, and taxes), and parenting (Radansky 1987). The seminar and workshop were fully bilingual and included a two-
hour period during which American-American couples were sent into another
room to receive counseling in "Communication and Stress Management" while
the U.S. military-Okinawan couples addressed questions and concerns to a panel
of successfully married couples. The addition of this "Concern Group" panel discussion was intended to "eliminate traces of negativism which characterized
legal and chaplain counseling in the past" (Radansky 1987, 55). An average of
twenty international couples attended the seminar each month. In 1982, this all-
island premarital seminar was integrated into the Family Services program, "where
it would have official status, funding, and continuity and where it could benefit

from routine planning and development" (Radansky 1987, 57). At the time of my observation in 2002, however, the current premarital coordinator was not aware of this history. The frequent rotation of personnel in and out of duty posts had led to a situation in which there was little continuity in the content of the seminar.

In the 1990s, the U.S. Marine Corps systematized its premarital training across installations worldwide and replaced Radansky's seminar with PREP (Prevention and Relationship Enhancement Program), a comprehensive couples' counseling program developed by psychologists at the University of Denver. The PREP Leader Manual described the program as "a research-based approach to teaching couples how to communicate effectively, work as a team to solve problems, manage conflicts without damaging closeness, and preserve and enhance love, commitment, and friendship" (Markman et al. 1999, 6). The specific goals of the program were "(a) the development and guided practice of constructive communication and conflict resolution skills, (b) the clarification and modification of relationship beliefs and expectations, (c) the development of understanding to enhance commitment, (d) the maintenance and enhancement of fun, friendship, and spiritual connection . . . , (e) the creation of an agreed-upon set of ground rules for handling disagreements and conflict . . . , and (f) the development of skills to enhance, understand, and maintain commitment" (Markman et al. 1999, 19). According to the manual, PREP was built on a model of marital failure in which couples began marriage with little experience coping with significant disagreements or conflict. As they spent time together, and the problems of life arose, partners responded to situations according to "their previous experiences within their families of origin, past relationships, and the cultural context," as well as their expectations concerning marriage, gender roles, and family. Over time, "patterns of mismanaged conflict" led to a situation in which partners began to associate one another with pain and frustration rather than with pleasure or support, and a "me versus you" type of thinking took hold. The PREP intervention explored "(unconstructive) patterns of communication, conflict management, dysfunctional beliefs, and understandings and motivations regarding commitment" (Markman et al. 1999, 11–12). The manual provided no specific instruction for counseling cross-cultural or international couples.

The overall structure of the premarital seminar was the same every month. On the first day, the program ran from 8:15 a.m. until 4:30 p.m. and included presentations on the topics of U.S. immigration, U.S. citizenship procedures, financial issues, legal concerns, and on-base social services.[11] These briefs concluded at 2:00 p.m., and the remainder of the first day and all of the second day were devoted to PREP. According to records kept by Chief Tulabut, during the two-year period from January 2000 through December 2001, a total of 387 active-duty servicemen attended the premarital seminar, and 206 (just over 53 percent) indicated that they were marrying Okinawan or Japanese women. At the March 2002 seminar that I observed, fifteen of the seventeen servicemen attending were marrying Okinawan women.

On the days that I observed, the PREP program was led by naval chaplain Patrick Buckman, a Presbyterian minister assigned to Camp Kinser. Chaplain Buckman addressed his audience from the front of the room. He lectured on each topic as it appeared in the PREP manual, writing key terms on a whiteboard: Escalation, Invalidation, Negative Interpretations, Withdrawal, Avoidance, Mind Reading, Character Assassination, Catastrophic Interpretations, Blaming. Late on the first day, the group was given fifteen minutes to practice a PREP communication skill called the Speaker/Listener Technique, in which a piece of paper labeled "the floor" was passed back and forth between two participants in an argument. The person holding "the floor" had the right to explain their position without being interrupted. The listener had to paraphrase the speaker's concerns to the speaker's satisfaction before "the floor" was handed over. They could then take their turn. The chaplain paired up individuals to practice with one another. I was paired up with a young marine named José. We were told to choose a low-level conflict and discuss it using the technique. José suggested that we use a situation in which a wife was angry at her husband for throwing his dirty laundry on the floor. Shy and reserved at first, José soon grew comfortable and started joking with me. At one point in our argument, he smirked and stated that the reason he married me was so that he wouldn't *have* to pick up his dirty laundry. I often encountered this kind of gendered teasing from young servicemen in Okinawa and responded using the Speaker/Listener Technique. The Speaker/Listener Technique was awkward, even for native speakers of English, but the chaplain explained that this served the purpose of slowing down interactions and encouraging better listening when discussions became heated. One of the marines raised his hand and commented that when he and his fiancée became angry, fast and heated conversations were almost never a problem. In order to be understood at all, they had to speak slowly and simply, and they often used a dictionary while working through disagreements. The chaplain conceded that this couple seemed to have worked out a system that might function as well as the Speaker/Listener Technique because the dictionary provided structure, making honest communication safe.

An interpreter had been employed for Japanese native-speakers, and periodically Chaplain Buckman stopped his lecture so that she could explain the points he had covered. Her interpretations were sharply abbreviated, usually limited to a word-for-word translation of the scant material the chaplain had written on the whiteboard. Inadequate translation and lack of accommodation for cultural differences presented significant problems, making it impossible for the Okinawan women to participate on an equal footing with their prospective husbands. Many of the women appeared to be depending on their American fiancés to interpret the chaplain's anecdotes and jokes into language that they could understand. While the American participants laughed and appeared to be enjoying themselves, many of the Okinawan women looked bored. Of the 207 questions and comments made by workshop participants over the course of the two days, Japanese native-speakers spoke out only twice. The first time, an Okinawan fiancée asked the translator for clarification after hearing her two-minute translation of the chaplain's fifteen-minute lecture on the Speaker/Listener Technique, and the second time, the chaplain insisted that "one of our Japanese fiancées" come to the front of the classroom and read the part of Mary in a dialogue that illustrated negative communication patterns. "Well, which of our Japanese fiancées does pretty well with English? [Soft giggling. No one volunteers.] Oh, God, I hope *some* of you do. *Any* of them? Who can read English? Can she read English? Can you read English? Can you read English? [The third woman nods yes.] Come on up, please."

Some of the topics that Chaplain Buckman covered did not come from the PREP Leader Manual. The additional lectures mainly concerned differences between men and women and between individuals from different cultural backgrounds. For example, early on the first day, the chaplain concluded his explanation of the goals of the PREP workshop with the following comment:

> We tend to live in a politically correct world where there's some people out there that are bent on creating a unisex. Well, I have good news for you. It ain't ever gonna happen, alright? God created male and female, and as far as I can see, there's always going to be males, and there's always going to be females. And we may need to share the same uniform. We may absolutely deserve equal pay for equal work. But males think like men. Females think like women. And each couple, with one male and one female in it, owe it to themselves to get an education on what the other sex thinks. We're not talking that one is better than the other. We're not talking that one is right as opposed to wrong. But the fact is that men and women filter things, react to things, deal with things, think through things differently. And if we can latch on to that and not deny that that exists, we will have far better relationships.

While the PREP manual stated that men and women tended to adopt different communicative strategies, Chaplain Buckman took this further, advancing a biologically driven model of gender difference. His discussion of men's and women's different communicative styles included terms like "hard-wired" and "cognitive processing." In a lecture segment that lasted about twenty minutes, the chaplain discussed the menstrual cycle, pregnancy hormones, and menopause in women and the sex drive in men as physiological "communication filters" that negatively impacted marital relationships. Twice, he recommended the *Men Are from Mars, Women Are from Venus* book series published by John Gray.[12] And although the chaplain explicitly argued against the assumption that women should be solely responsible for housework and raising children, he repeatedly referred to the biological and sociological differences that distinguished the two sexes.

A second area of Chaplain Buckman's presentation that was not directly taken from the PREP Leader Manual focused on the effects of language and cultural differences in a marriage. In his attempt to tailor lectures to an audience largely composed of American/Okinawan couples, the chaplain talked about the frustration of not being able to communicate with one's spouse about important issues or feelings due to a language barrier. This discussion developed after one of the male participants commented that "sharing emotions is harder because they [Okinawan fiancées] don't know the language that well." Later, the chaplain asked the group how they might resolve an argument that had arisen because the husband had not spoken clearly. In response, one military participant called out "Japanese classes!" Everyone laughed, and the chaplain dismissed the comment as a joke. "What's that? Japanese classes. Yeah, yeah. What else could be done?" The chaplain's discussion of cultural differences paralleled his discussion of gender differences. Within his lectures, American culture and Okinawan culture were presented as polarized, each a distinct and internally cohesive bundle of traits, in much the same way as male and female. "If you analyze some of your experiences in Okinawan culture, saving face and being polite is absolutely integral to their belief system. Now listen, 90 percent of you are entering into a cross-cultural marriage. If you don't think that is going to affect your intent-impact, you're crazy. If you as an American with your let-me-wear-it-on-my-face attitude go and get all over your wife—you may be wrong, and she may *know* that you're wrong, but her belief system will filter that through, and you'll get a silent polite response, even though you're creating a time bomb on the inside." A second example came from the chaplain's discussion about the different expectations that partners in an intercultural relationship brought to a marriage. Concerning spirituality, the chaplain asked, "Now you guys who are marrying Okinawans, how much research have you done into the spirituality of the Okinawan people? How's it going to work on a Sunday when you want to go to church as a family?" The chaplain went on to explain that major life events, like the birth of a child or the death of a parent, tended to make even the most unreligious persons reconsider their spiritual beliefs and commitments. "For the Okinawans—correct me, please, anybody, if I'm wrong—but the ancestral resting place with the bones, and all of the ceremony and ritual that goes with them, is a very sacred thing. And you would be wise to be prepared for the death of a parent, if you're not living in Okinawa, to make arrangements so that your spouse, either accompanied by you or not, is available to be part of that ritual. And I think there's—I took a class in this, but I'm a little bit rusty. Every so many years, you have to go back to the exact same tomb. I mean, it's just a whole different approach." The chaplain's point seemed to be well taken by the service members present, but there was no extended discussion and no contribution from the Okinawan women in attendance.

Taken together, the chaplain's lectures on gender and cultural difference supported an overall theory of marital conflict as a set of biologically and culturally determined misunderstandings between men and women and partners from different cultural and linguistic backgrounds. This approach to gender and cultural difference normalized power inequalities within relationships and represented them as just another component of the "natural" differences between American men and Okinawan women. For example, language-related miscommunication between partners was framed as a result of Okinawan women's imperfect control over English and their culturally determined inability to express emotions. The chaplain and seminar participants laughed at the possibility of military men learning Japanese. Needless to say, a long history of unequal power relations between Americans and Okinawans structures the use of language in Okinawa, making English the primary language of interaction. These power relations were made invisible within the chaplain's lectures.[13]

Modeling the Ideal Military Family

Military institutional models of gender, race, and nation contributed to the content and organization of Chaplain Buckman's presentation. Gendered formulations of cultural citizenship were especially evident in imagery of the ideal military family that circulated throughout the seminar. The first theme, discussed above, was that men and women were essentially dissimilar. The PREP Leader Manual took the following approach: "We and others are discovering that there are pivotal sex differences in how men and women in marriage handle conflict: men tend to withdraw and women tend to attempt to get men to communicate. We suggest that contrary to conventional wisdom, men are *not* deficient in intimacy skills, but *do* have increased problems handling conflict and negative feelings, compared to women" (Markman et al. 1999, 18). In the first lecture of the manual, the "classic pattern" of "female pursues discussing issues" and "male withdraws from discussing issues" was presented and explained as a result of physiology and socialization (47). The manual, however, instructed the workshop leader to emphasize that many patterns were possible: males could also pursue and females could withdraw, or neither could pursue or withdraw. In the seminar that I observed, the "classic pattern" was the only one discussed, and the physiological explanation for gender differences was underscored.

A second theme also resonated, that the husband-wife bond was the most fundamental kinship relation, and nuclear family households were therefore the norm within U.S. military communities. From the opening discussion of Relationship Trouble Spots to the discussion of culturally different spiritual practices, the chaplain referred to conflict, negotiation, and compromise solely between husbands and wives. Children were discussed as a possible source of disagreement, and parents and in-laws appeared as potential distractions pulling one away from one's primary familial obligations to spouse and children, as in the discussion of Okinawan women flying home to Okinawa to attend memorial services for a deceased parent. No mention was made of everyday interactions with members of extended families, financial aid to American or Okinawan relatives, travel back and forth in order to maintain family ties, communication difficulties with in-laws, or family opposition to marriage—all situations frequently encountered by military international couples. A clear separation was established between one's natal family (more important in the past) and one's spouse and children (more important in the future).

Finally, a third key assumption that structured premarital seminar discourse was that service members' intimate relationships were heterosexual by definition. Operating at the level of the taken-for-granted, the chaplain was completely silent on the matter. Under the "Don't Ask, Don't Tell" policy in effect at the time of my observation, military officials, including chaplains, were not permitted to ask about, open investigations into, or harass service members on the basis of sexual orientation. Service members, on the other hand, could be discharged for living openly as homosexual or bisexual.[14] One effect of this contradictory policy was that in settings like the premarital seminar, military families continued to be imagined as exclusively heterosexual, reinforcing the general supposition that there were only two genders and that each was "naturally" attracted to the other. Feminist scholars have argued that the notion of men and women being absolutely and essentially unlike—pervasive in military circles—serves as the basis for a key military ideology that men serve their country by participating in combat while women serve their country by supporting their military husbands.[15] The idea of an autonomous nuclear family binds civilian spouses to their service member husbands and to the military community, while reducing competing interests and obligations due to outside relationships. Moreover, the assumption of exclusive heterosexuality is fundamentally tied to institutional notions of combat bonding between men (Harrison and Laliberte 1997). The objective is to encourage military personnel and their spouses to build relationships that further the aim of combat readiness.[16] Combat-ready units like those in Okinawa once discouraged marriage altogether—hence, the oft-quoted saying, "If the Marine Corps wanted you to have a wife, they would have issued you one!" Later, they pushed the primacy of the nuclear family. In the early 2000s, amid increased deployments to Iraq and Afghanistan, a rising divorce rate, and recruiting shortfalls, the Marine Corps increased funding and support for marriage enrichment programs like the premarital seminar and couples counseling workshops that were available at Camp Foster and Kadena Air Base. One battalion commander explained, "This is absolutely a retention issue. We are trying to get spouses involved so they don't want their Marines to leave the service" (quoted in Rogers 2005). The strategy was apparently successful; divorce rates have fallen since 2011 (Bushatz 2016).

Limiting the participation of prospective Okinawan spouses in the marriage process fit neatly with the objective of combat readiness. Marriage procedures set up Okinawan women to be passive recipients of military decisions, while military personnel had some agency in the process. Civilian women were not authorized to perform most of the activities required to complete the marriage package. Japanese and Okinawan wives had no legal rights on U.S. bases, not simply because they were Japanese but because they were not active-duty U.S. military personnel. Under the SOFA, the category of military dependents—defined as "(a) Spouse, and children under 21, or (b) Parents, and children over 21, if dependent for over half their support upon a member of the United States Armed Forces or civilian component"—marked military spouses of all nationalities as legally dependent, lacking autonomy in the eyes of the U.S. military and the Japanese government. Thus Okinawan spouses were given the same limited rights as American civilian spouses on U.S. military bases in Japan. Neither could sign legal documents, including those as simple as a verification of receipt when a package was delivered to their on-base home or a consent form allowing their children to participate in after-school activities. All legal activity had to be channeled through the active-duty military member.[17] Because of the gender makeup of the U.S. military in Okinawa, the dependence of civilian spouses took the form of a gendered hierarchy, with active-duty men holding legal authority over legally powerless women and children. The overall significance of marriage orders and the SOFA for Japanese and Okinawan spouses was that they occupied the lowest category of persons in a racial and gender hierarchy co-constructed by the U.S. military and the Japanese government.

Responding to Institutional Authority

The premarital seminar supported a model of the ideal military family and institutional ideologies that defined entitlement and belonging along gender and racial lines. But subjective experiences and responses to such ideologies continued to be multifaceted. Resistance to the institutional surveillance associated with the marriage package was a common reaction among service members and their families. American servicemen and Okinawan military spouses worked hard at distancing themselves from military stereotypes of couples who were "not serious" or who had questionable motives. Military marriage procedures, along with parental disapproval, also commonly induced an "us against the world" mentality expressed through references to self-reliance, responsibility, or independence. "We got married to finalize our feelings for one another. Plus, I'm in the military. If I go back to the States, they're not going to pay her way or let her live on base, or give her an ID card, or let her have medical. I'm one of those guys that likes to have everything squared away. If I decide not to get married, that's fine. But I want it to be my choice and my option, not the government saying, 'Oh, you don't have enough time.'" At times, such self-possession took on stronger tones: "At the meetings, the commander is directing you to do things. And it's like, he doesn't know anything about my love for this girl. The more he tells you that you can't do something, the more you want to do it. So in the case of a young guy, stubborn, trying to prove his manhood, he starts thinking, 'Well, I'm going to show them!'" Looking back, one serviceman explained, "I learned how to raise hell and stomp my feet and get the appointments I needed to get it done." This attitude, too, ultimately serves the purposes of the military institution. Encouraging the development of personnel and families who are strongly committed *and* independent, who are prepared to get by without institutional support and without consuming military resources, intrusive and time-consuming marriage procedures benefited the military in multiple ways.

However, burdensome procedures and the headstrong mentality they sometimes engendered did not always benefit couples, particularly Okinawan wives. Amid deployment cycles associated with the wars in Iraq and Afghanistan, official programs for military personnel and spouses began to integrate frank discussions of marital infidelity and divorce, sometimes fueling even more flagrant displays of domination and control by military husbands. Citing rumors concerning a growing number of "Dear John" letters from unfaithful military spouses, the marine husband of one Okinawan woman I spoke with transferred the couple's jointly earned savings into accounts accessible only to him.

Okinawan family and community opposition to military marriage often contributed to a similar "us vs. them" mentality among Okinawa military spouses.

Yuki Eisner left Miyako Island against her father's wishes and migrated to Naha, the capital of Okinawa Prefecture, when she was eighteen. On weekends, she frequented dance clubs that catered to GI customers from nearby bases. In 2002, Yuki married Josh, an enlisted marine. Believing that her father wanted her to stay on Miyako Island to care for him and his wife as they grew older, Yuki adopted a combative tone and foisted this responsibility onto her older brother, calling it the *chōnan*'s (eldest son's) duty (see chapter 5). Strategically manipulating an important Okinawan kinship norm in order to justify her decision to leave Miyako, Yuki simultaneously justified her decision to marry an American serviceman. Ultimately, Yuki's oppositional stance dovetailed with the military institution's image of the ideal military family, a nuclear family independent from extended family obligations and ready to mobilize when called upon.

Brief Comparison with Procedures for Military Divorce

Divorce, although it also required cooperation between the U.S. military and Japanese governments, was a far simpler process. Indeed, the apparent lack of institutional concern with divorce, child custody, and child support has become a key focus of women's political activism in Okinawa. Comparing U.S. military and Japanese government approaches to marriage versus divorce further illuminates the assumptions that have shaped U.S. military and Japanese government approaches to international marriage, as well as how such procedures are used to police national borders. According to Okinawa Prefecture, 422 divorces involving Japanese women and American men were registered during the seven years from 2009 to 2014 (calculated from data compiled by the Japanese Ministry of Health, Labour and Welfare). The majority were "mutual consent divorces" (*kyōgi rikon*) accomplished by a simple registration procedure at the local municipal office. U.S. servicemen are not required to notify and obtain command approval for such divorces, and the Japanese government does not require any official documentation from the military (parallel to the Affidavit of Competency to Marry). In comparison to the marriage process, the procedures involved in divorce are simple, fast, and inexpensive. What's more, the United States has no treaty with Japan concerning the collection of child support payments from noncompliant military fathers, as it does with Germany, Britain, and Sweden (U.S. Department of Health and Human Services 2017). While this is at least partially a consequence of Japan's own lack of a mechanism for enforcing child support payments, the presence in Okinawa of an estimated four thousand children abandoned by their U.S. military fathers (Sims 2000b) has made this issue a rallying

Active-duty marine and spouse

point for women's groups and other political groups protesting the U.S. military presence in the prefecture.

Military international marriage (but not divorce) thus appears to be a key site of military, U.S. government, and Japanese government intervention, a border-crossing that is carefully monitored and policed. International couples blur national, cultural, and racial boundaries when they move from one country to another and bear children who have dual citizenship. Elaborate marriage, immigration, and citizenship procedures allow governments to redraw the lines of separation, firming up the edges of designated social categories. Curiously, by virtue of the SOFA, U.S. service members occupy an ambiguous status in relation to these border-policing systems. The SOFA dictates that while U.S. personnel are subject to the laws of Japan insofar as marriage is concerned (that is, their marriages must be performed by the government of Japan in order to be considered legal), they are at the same time exempt from Japanese laws and regulations concerning the registration and control of aliens. Service members and their families need not carry passports; their military IDs suffice. From the Japanese government perspective, such persons belong first to the U.S. military and only incidentally to the United States. Military international couples thus constitute a uniquely ambiguous legal category, subject to different degrees and types of surveillance from other international couples in Japan. Once again, Okinawa departs from the national pattern, and focusing on military international couples reveals the contradictions embedded within the U.S.-Japan political alliance.

U.S. Military Retirees: SOFA Status versus Japanese Residency

U.S. military retirees and other former-military personnel married to Okinawan women may no longer be covered by the status of forces agreement once they retire or separate from the military. In order to stay in Okinawa, they may reacquire SOFA status by working as a civilian on a U.S. military base, or they must apply for Japanese residency through the Immigration Bureau of Japan.[18] Civilian jobs on U.S. military bases are limited, with many employers giving preferential consideration to applicants who already have SOFA status (for example, spouses of active-duty personnel). Some positions do however offer SOFA status to new hires who do not have it. If a former-military husband manages to be hired for a civilian position offering SOFA status, then he does not need to apply for Japanese residency. This was a popular option among the American husbands I interviewed. Ralph Dickson (preface), Ray Horner (chapter 1), and Hank Megason (chapters 1 and 5) held civilian positions with SOFA status on U.S. military bases after retiring from the military and were able to remain in Okinawa for years without having to navigate Japanese immigration. Stew Brown (chapter 1), however, had difficulty finding and keeping such positions, contributing to community perceptions of him as economically and socially unstable. I met many former-military men, as well as several active-duty personnel who were considering separating from the military, for whom SOFA status was a coveted prize. This orientation reinforced their ties to the U.S. military and the U.S. government, despite their stated goal of establishing long-term residence and being accepted within the Okinawan community. These men were prepared to continue submitting to military institutional surveillance and discipline, to which they were already accustomed, in order to avoid having to learn a new system (Japanese immigration). This suggests an important point not covered in the above discussion of marriage protocols and procedures: for many U.S. military men, and perhaps some Okinawan spouses as well, subjection to U.S. military disciplinary power

generates a sense of safety, security, and constancy, along with financial opportunity, national cultural identity, and perhaps even pleasure.

Ralph Dickson and Hank Megason eventually applied for Japanese residency
after retiring from their on-base civilian positions. The Japanese Immigration
Bureau grants residency to spouses of Japanese nationals for three years, after which
it must be renewed. For Ralph and Hank, then in their sixties, this move was advantageous since it allowed them access to benefits (such as health care) available
to residents of Japan, alongside the benefits they received as U.S. military retirees. By 2009, Hank had decided to apply for Japanese permanent residency, which
would allow him to stay in Japan indefinitely, regardless of his marital status. Having lived in Okinawa for more than twenty-five years, he could not contemplate
returning to the United States and starting over again, which he would have to
do if his wife died before he did. While spouses of Japanese nationals may apply
for permanent residency after three years, the status is also dependent on the applicant having paid national and residential taxes, contributed to the national pension system, and stayed clear of all legal trouble, including minor traffic violations.
As of December 2017, only 4,737 individuals residing in Okinawa Prefecture held
permanent residency, out of 15,847 total foreign residents (Japanese Ministry of
Justice 2017).[19] When I returned to Okinawa in 2012, Hank proudly displayed
his permanent resident card. I discuss Hank's shifting sympathies and self-
identification from U.S. marine to Okinawan villager further in the next chapter.

"Properly trained, soldiers develop strong loyalties, pride, and self-confidence.
They also gain a sense of superiority over civilians," asserted Lt. Col. Andrew Cernicky of the Strategic Studies Institute, U.S. Army (Cernicky 2006, 46). In Okinawa
and throughout the global U.S. military, marriage and family regulations are
important techniques of governance aimed at producing military service members
and families that conform to institutional requirements regarding operational
readiness. The 2001–2002 marriage package and premarital seminar reinforced
institutional models of military marriage and family as relationships that were
necessarily subordinated to the mission of the service member's unit. Engendering
a sense of entitlement, as well as responsibility and self-reliance, these programs
also contributed to particular formulations of cultural citizenship among U.S.
military personnel.

Prior to the signing of the Plaza Accord (1985), socioeconomic disparities between American service members and Okinawans contributed to a sense of cultural superiority comingled with responsibility toward Okinawan civilians among
many U.S. military personnel.[20] This was evident in interviews with men who
married Okinawan women prior to reversion: "Her mother always chaperoned

our dates. Her dad had died in the war, and they were very poor, and I had this car. We went to the beach, and we went to the northern part of the island. Her mother was so happy because she had never gotten out before. I enjoyed seeing her get so excited. I felt like Santa Claus." Such feelings of entitlement and responsibility were reinforced by military commanders and chaplains during premarital counseling sessions and by U.S. consulate representatives during the visa application process. As recently as 1987, the U.S. consulate in Naha allegedly told one newlywed air force officer inquiring about a spouse visa, "You can't just take her back to the States. She's just going back there to get her citizenship. Eventually, she's going to leave you." This angered the officer, prompting him to search for a workaround. Ultimately, he returned to the States alone, and his wife entered separately on a tourist visa. Once in the United States, they were able to find a more sympathetic audience (and an easier paperwork route) at the local Immigration and Naturalization Service (INS) office. Institutional discourse prioritizing American culture and U.S. military lifestyles continued to circulate in the premarital seminar in 2001–2002. Marriage package procedures and the premarital seminar assumed the primacy of the serviceman's language, family, and career, creating a diversity of unequal subject positions and differentiating participants along lines of gender, nation, and race. In Okinawa, then and now, military institutional formulations of cultural citizenship are reinforced by historically constituted relations of power resulting from Japanese colonialism, American occupation, and the continuing presence of U.S. military bases in the prefecture—all of which are profoundly gendered. Consequently, most Okinawan wives do not expect their husbands to learn Japanese. Instead, they strive to learn English, a skill that they hope will help them access new career opportunities and legitimize their claims to global citizenship.

Similar formulations of cultural citizenship can be found throughout the global U.S. military empire. As in Okinawa, they are backed by location-specific marriage procedures and family regulations. Hegemonic ideas about belonging and not belonging in gendered and cultural terms conceal the political and social inequalities that enable the maintenance of U.S. troops, especially in economically or politically subordinate nations and provinces. While resistance to institutional surveillance and control is a common reaction among service members and their families, the ways in which such resistance engages power inequalities are not always predictable. Cumbersome marriage procedures often contribute to the development of self-reliant service members and families. Ultimately, this serves the purposes of the military, although it does not always benefit couples, especially foreign spouses. Even so, individuals adapt. Bill Brenner's wife, Junko, told me, "He controlled the money—while he was in the service and after he got out. I didn't know how much we had, and then I found out we didn't have any! . . . He has a strong personality, and he was really bossy. Well, I have a strong personality too, and I don't keep my mouth shut anymore."

By 2009, the status of Josh and Yuki Eisner had evolved. After a brief tour of duty in the United States, the Marine Corps had granted Yuki command sponsorship. The couple enjoyed institutional support in the form of family health care, moving assistance, on-base housing, and monetary compensation when they lived off base. Yet the Eisners recalled the cramped apartment in Kita-Nakagusuku with fondness. More than mere nostalgia, they agreed that it was the best accommodation they had lived in during their married life. Military housing and other institutional incentives and rewards were not as comfortable as they had once imagined. The responses of military service members and their spouses to military marriage procedures contribute to the ongoing negotiation of cultural citizenship and identity in Okinawa and throughout the global U.S. military, with important implications for the cultural reproduction of U.S. empire.

CREATING FAMILY AND COMMUNITY
ACROSS MILITARY FENCELINES

We were the first patrons to arrive at the trendy *izakaya* in Nago one evening in March 2017. As the hostess led us to our table, Mutsuko reassured Hank that this was indeed the place where they had eaten with their daughter several weeks before and that he had enjoyed the food. Hank had suggested that we meet early to complete the follow-up interview before ordering, but as soon as we slipped off our shoes and sat down, the couple picked up menus and began to scan the offerings. Hank quickly flipped through the pages and announced that Mutsuko would do the ordering since it was all written in Japanese. Using his limited language skills, he requested a beer for himself and then switched to English to order beverages for Mutsuko and me. Mutsuko clarified his order with the server and requested an assortment of dishes for us to share. While waiting for drinks, Hank pulled out his smartphone to show me recent images of him and Mutsuko dressed in formal kimono, celebrating their seventy-third birthdays at the Henoko *kominkan* (citizen's hall).[1] In one image, Hank stood tall and proud in a black *haori* jacket and pleated gray *hakama* trousers, with Mutsuko at his side dressed in a black and gold kimono bearing her family crest. In another, the smiling couple was seated at a table trimmed in gold cloth, the remains of an elaborate boxed meal before them. In a third, Hank danced the *kachāshī* with a young Okinawan girl, his granddaughter. As I admired the images, Mutsuko reached into her purse and pulled out a handful of worn and faded photographs and laid them on the table. The first was a close-up of Mutsuko taken by Hank in 1979. The couple's paths had first crossed during the late 1960s, when Hank stopped in Okinawa for several months on his way to Vietnam. Mutsuko was a waitress at the Hilltop Club at Camp Schwab. Ten years later, Hank returned to the island for a three-year tour. By then, Mutsuko had been promoted to office manager at the USO. She was in the process of divorcing her first husband, a U.S. marine whom she had met during the intervening years, and she was struggling to obtain Japanese permanent residency for her daughters, who held American citizenship. In 1982, Hank was promoted to sergeant major, the Marine Corps's highest enlisted rank, and reassigned to Cherry Point in North Carolina. They continued to date long-distance until he returned to Okinawa two years later. Once Mutsuko's divorce was finalized and she gained custody of her younger daughter Miya, they were married. The final photograph was a formal portrait taken on the occasion of Hank's retirement from the Marine Corps in 1990. He wore his green service uniform, and Mutsuko was dressed in a conservative linen suit. Fourteen-year-old Miya stood above the seated couple, smiling down at them. After retiring, Hank took a civilian position at Camp Schwab. They built a house in Henoko, on the hilltop next to the base, in the neighborhood that had once hosted the village's booming Vietnam-era entertainment district. Mutsuko's mother lived with them for five years before moving to a public nursing facility. Now Miya and her husband and children occupied the first two floors of the house, and Hank and Mutsuko lived in an apartment with separate entry on the third floor.

Lining the photographs up alongside the smartphone, Mutsuko laughed heartily, pointing out their progressively graying hair and extra pounds. I remarked that their easy smiles seemed not to have changed at all. What was apparent from the photos, however, was a shift in Hank's social identity, from uniformed marine entrenched in U.S. military social networks and most comfortable in on-base settings, to "uniformed" Okinawan elder, relaxed and at home in the kominkan among his fellow villagers. This contrast was further reinforced when the conversation turned to Henoko politics. When I first met Hank in 2001, he was heavily involved in activities that promoted Camp Schwab, hobnobbing with local military leaders and probase politicians from Nago, teaching English at the Nago City International House, and serving as English-language emcee for Henoko's annual hārī event.[2] He and Mutsuko had considered themselves a bridge between the military base and the local community, Mutsuko playing her part as president of the Women's Association for the greater Higashi area. Outspoken in their support of the proposed new U.S. Marine Corps facility in Henoko, Hank had explained that they would gladly accept the Japanese government's measures to mitigate increased noise, such as double-paned windows and reduced utility costs so that they could afford to run the air conditioner all of the time. "That's the price you have to pay for the security of knowing you are protected from an outside threat. Freedom doesn't come cheap."

Family portrait

In 2017, Hank still openly endorsed the proposed base, but I sensed a shift in his reasoning. For one thing, he seemed more aware of and sympathetic to the concerns of the opposition. The two main arguments against the base, he told me, were that many believed the presence of the U.S. military increased the likelihood that Okinawa could become a military target and, secondly, that the land occupied by U.S. bases would be more profitable if developed for tourism. But, he countered, too many tourist traps had been envisioned and built in northern Okinawa and failed. He listed a number of attractions in Nago City, including Furutsurando (Fruits Land) and Nago Pineapple Park, that have contributed to severe traffic congestion without generating significant jobs and economic growth for the community. He then voiced a long-standing complaint that Henoko citizens bear most of the inconveniences associated with hosting Camp Schwab, yet Japanese government subsidies are piped through Nago City, and villagers see little benefit. "That is why we are working with the national government to receive direct subsidies for the new base," Mutsuko added (see *Japan Times* 2015). Hank's points now centered around the needs and sacrifices of Henoko citizens rather than abstract understandings of military objectives and national security, as had been the case fifteen years earlier. As if to underscore his transition from U.S. marine to Henoko villager, Hank returned to the pictures of their seventy-third

Seventy-third birthday celebration

birthday celebration. Even the current Nago City mayor, whose politics were un-ambiguously antibase, had approached them to say hello and warmly congratulate them on their achievement. Expressing his commitment to the local community, Hank explained, "I don't go down to the McDonald's with all the other retireds and tell war stories. Those other guys are just passing through. I'm here for the long haul. My friends are in the village. They even let me vote for Henoko section mayor. They had a special council meeting and decided. It was unanimous."[3]

Hank's situation may be unique, but the processes of negotiation that he and Mutsuko engage in—balancing commitments to the military, extended family, and local community, conforming to American and Okinawan cultural expectations, and contending with challenges to their relationship from both sides of the fences—are experienced by most military international couples. This sort of maneuvering affects the long-term success of intimate relationships, as well as popular attitudes toward interracial marriage and children and broader formulations of Okinawan and U.S. military community. Against the backdrop of Okinawa's long-standing antibase movement, international couples like Hank and Mutsuko also influence military-host community relationships and community politics. This chapter examines the strategies Okinawan-U.S. military couples employ to navigate life across the fencelines and achieve acceptance for themselves and their children. Active-duty couples living in central Okinawa, especially young Okinawan women who make use of military support services, may successfully integrate into the U.S. military community. The International Spouses Program at Camp Foster is one avenue through which Okinawan spouses learn what services are available and how to take advantage of them. However, military resources tend to cluster on the bases in central Okinawa, where multiyear accompanied tours and family housing and support services are available. For unmarried couples, retired personnel, those who have left the military, and civilian employees, military resources may be more difficult to procure. Retired (and even active-duty) couples in northern Okinawa, without access to or living far from the mid-island bases, tend to rely more on Okinawan family and community organizations for support. Normative discourses on family and community are invoked by local officials, women's organizations, and family members to police the intimate choices and behaviors of individuals, and shape communities in ways that disadvantage international couples. But by strategically invoking these same discourses and taking advantage of the actual flexibility of Okinawan family and community models, couples may successfully manipulate important tenets of Okinawan culture and gain acceptance. Military international couples thus utilize their position at the legal and social margins of the U.S. military and Okinawan communities to tap resources across the fencelines. In doing so, they may "reposition their own identities to bend lines of power and create an altered space for self-configuration" (Knauft 1996, 168).

International Spouses in the U.S. Military Community

For active-duty married couples living in the vicinity of large U.S. military installations in central Okinawa, the military offers a variety of support services and opportunities for community-building to help mitigate the financial challenges and social-emotional demands of military employment. The International Spouses Program (ISP) at Marine Corps Camp Foster was organized in early 2001 by Karen Hanovitch, an American spouse who worked for Marine Corps Family Team Building (FTB), to help ease the transition of new Okinawan and other foreign-born spouses of U.S. military personnel into the U.S. military community.[4] After researching similar programs in Korea, Hawaii, and mainland Japan, Hanovitch designed a three-day workshop for Okinawan wives and their husbands that focused primarily on explaining American and U.S. military lifestyles, customs, and holidays, and included a trip to the commissary. Early on, the program drew criticism, primarily from husbands who objected to the idea of Americanizing their wives. A number of men also criticized the name Foreign-Born Spouses, which Hanovitch had borrowed from the Hawaii group. One high-ranking officer reprimanded her in an email, "*We* are the foreigners here!" Hanovitch changed the name to International Spouses and limited membership to military spouses, although their active-duty husbands continued to be invited to occasional dinners and parties.[5] Greater emphasis was placed on helping the women take an active role in managing a military household, including understanding their husbands' jobs and paychecks, handling checkbooks and credit, navigating the military health care system, and understanding the legal basis for powers of attorney and other documents frequently used in overseas U.S. military communities.

During 2001–2002, I regularly attended ISP workshops and classes. Workshops were held three mornings a month and lasted from 9:00 a.m. until noon. During this time, attendees listened to presentations concerning the military lifestyle and on-base family support services. Japanese translation was provided by an Okinawan military spouse who had graduated from the program the previous year and now worked in the FTB office. In addition, many of the women gathered for monthly classes to refresh their knowledge and enjoy less structured time together while visiting on-base recreation facilities, cooking and sharing meals, and celebrating American holidays with parties and gift exchanges. Classes were attended by five to fifteen spouses, depending on the month. Almost all of the attendees were young Okinawan women in their twenties and thirties, although a number of women in their forties also joined the group from time to time. I met approximately forty Okinawan women married to U.S. military men through ISP. The following narrative, while not necessarily representative of this diverse group, demonstrates some of the common themes that emerged in interviews with ISP participants, including the cultural "transparency" of U.S. bases for young Okinawans, who have no memory of the occupation and little interest in the contemporary antibase movement, the continuing opposition of many Okinawan parents to military marriages, and the agency exercised by some Okinawan spouses in learning about and utilizing military family services.

Akiko Jones, age twenty-eight when we first met in 2002, was a regular participant in ISP. She had learned of the group's existence from a flyer posted at the Personal Services Center at Camp Foster.[6] I also ran into her at the Family Support Center on Kadena Air Base, where she was enrolled in ESL classes, and again at the quarterly International Spouses workshop for air force spouses held at Kadena's Schilling Community Center. Compared to other participants, Akiko was outspoken and assertive, projecting an unusual degree of self-confidence whether speaking in Japanese or English. She seemed determined to take full advantage of on-base services available to Japanese spouses of active-duty service members.

Significantly, her husband, Aaron, an enlisted navy corpsman, also joined ISP classes from time to time, supporting her and learning for himself more about military family services. I met him on three occasions, at a Thanksgiving dinner cooking class, an information session on the Tri-Care health care system, and Akiko's graduation from ISP L.I.N.K.S.[7] Together, they were becoming well-informed and proactive members of the U.S. military community.

The two had met when Akiko posted a request for an American pen pal in the classifieds section of an online news site. Aaron had been among the dozens of young American servicemen who responded to her posting. "A lot of the people asked me if I was looking for a boyfriend or interested in having a relationship. My husband wrote to me about everyday stuff, 'This morning, I went running outside. The weather was nice,' things like that. Afterwards, we started to write back and forth." A month later, they decided to meet in person, and from that point on, whenever possible, Aaron rode the free military bus to Camp Foster, near Akiko's mid-island home. I asked Akiko about her initial impressions of the U.S. bases. "Oh, I always felt comfortable on the bases. My aunt married an air force guy when I was three years old. I've known him almost my whole life. Through him, I was able to touch American culture even as a small child." Several months later, Aaron informed her that his tour of duty in Okinawa would end the following year, and that he would likely be transferred back to the United States. They discussed their feelings for one another and decided to marry. At the time, Akiko lived at home with her parents in Chatan, where her father was a prominent member of the town's Base Affairs Committee. More than half of the land area of Chatan is occupied by U.S. military bases, and the relationship between the town and the military was at a postreversion low due to the internationally publicized rape trial of air force staff sergeant Timothy Woodland, who was later convicted of assaulting an Okinawan woman in the parking lot of a Chatan shopping mall (*New York Times* 2002a). Akiko's father was especially disappointed in her involvement with Aaron because of a family history of GI marriage and divorce.

> My father was upset. I have three aunts who married GIs—my father's sister, my mother's sister, and my grandmother's sister. My mom's sister is still married, but the other two are divorced. My dad's sister remarried another GI and then divorced again. My father told me, "You know that your aunt has gotten divorced from GIs *twice*. How can you even think of marrying an American?" I brought Aaron to the house, but my father was too upset to speak with him. Finally, he had a change of heart. He got out the dictionary and sat down with my husband to discuss his intentions and plans for the future. They talked for almost six hours, and afterwards my father supported us.

As time dragged on, and Aaron had still not found time to research the navy's overseas marriage procedures, Akiko went online and discovered a series of how-to sites written by Japanese women who were married to American military men. From that point forward, she directed their document-gathering efforts. Because Aaron served with a Marine Corps unit, they were subject to the marriage package described in chapter 4. After six months, the Marine Corps issued approval, and they were married. When I interviewed Akiko, she was in the process of applying for a Y-plate for her car.[8] Having a Y-plate would enable them to purchase gasoline on-base at less than half the town price. She was also researching the steps necessary to obtain a laboratory technician's license in the United States so that she could begin working soon after their transfer. In Okinawa, she held a well-paying job as a lab technician at the Adventist Medical Center, and they could not afford to lose her income.

For the past fifteen years, Akiko and Aaron have rotated in and out of Okinawa and various duty stations in the United States. In 2017, Aaron retired from the navy, and they settled permanently in Arizona. They now have two children, and Akiko travels with them to Okinawa every other summer to visit her family. In a recent email exchange, she wrote at length about the importance of effectively utilizing on-base and off-base resources—from family and professional connections to online resources and military benefits related to their SOFA status—and how this had contributed to the success of their marriage and continued relationship with her family. She proudly used the term "international spouse" to describe herself and the other women at ISP, who had integrated into the U.S. military community while maintaining close ties to family in Okinawa.

While the U.S. military tends to use "international" as an equivalent of "foreign" or "foreign-born," young women like Akiko embrace the term because it carries fewer negative connotations than the phrase "military wife" or historically, "war bride." Utilizing the more generalizable language of international marriage, which in Japan carries connotations of cosmopolitan experience, romantic love, and greater gender equality, these women attempt to change how their relationships are perceived by removing them from the more controversial local context of U.S. military occupation and reframing them as something to be admired. For example, many young women describe their American husbands as more affectionate and more helpful than Japanese men. Yuki Eisner, a regular ISP participant, provided an example:

> In Japan, dads are never home, moms are always home. Dads work late, moms watch kids even when dads *are* home so that they won't bother them. Japanese husbands go out with their friends whenever they like, even when they have young babies at home and their wives are tired.

American guys stay home and take care of the kids to give their wives a break. My husband loves to babysit. He changes diapers and feeds bottles. Japanese guys can't do those things. They never learned how.

Portraying their husbands as considerate, willing to share in the housework, and more inclined to view their wives as equals, these women participate in what Karen Kelsky (2001) has called the discourse of "Japanese women's internationalism," part of a self-building project that draws on popular images of Western men in order to challenge traditional Japanese gender roles. In Okinawa, however, such language serves not only as a method for resisting Japanese gender norms but also for avoiding negative stereotypes of Okinawan-U.S. military intimacy, as Akiko Jones's story illustrates. One of Akiko's main arguments to her father, which may have influenced his change of heart with regard to her relationship, was that not all military personnel are alike, and he should take the time to get to know her husband. Thus, Aaron was not a "typical" GI, and her relationship was not a "typical" military-Okinawan relationship. Her focus on legal and bureaucratic hurdles similarly reframed her marriage as a partnership of equals, in which both individuals had important roles to play as they negotiated their legal status and financial responsibilities across two different nation-states. This represents a departure from popular views of military intimacy as a legacy of war and continuing (gendered) subordination to the U.S. military and Japanese nation-state. The approach of young women like Akiko thus pushes military fencelines into the background, while state boundaries and associated legal structures continue to loom large as a set of hurdles to be negotiated. Within their narratives, intimacy across the fencelines increases a couple's negotiating power.

Challenges of Living across Military Fencelines

Reframing and distancing one's relationship from contentious local politics is often difficult for individuals who lack support, either inside or outside of the fences. Military resources may be difficult to access for couples who are unmarried, not command sponsored, or not active-duty military personnel (who have left the military or retired, or who are civilian employees). Lack of support from parents and other family and community members make these relationships difficult to sustain. The following narrative illustrates some of the challenges that couples face and how difficulties follow from or affect larger social and political contexts.

Bill and Junko Brenner met and married in 1971, as Okinawa was preparing to revert to Japanese sovereignty after more than two and a half decades of U.S. administration. The political situation was tense, and public protests against the conditions of U.S. occupation, nuclear weapons, and the war in Vietnam drew tens of thousands of participants.[9] Meanwhile, many American GIs tended to view Okinawa as little more than an R&R stopover on the way to and from Vietnam, and intimate Okinawan-U.S. military relationships were popularly associated with the sex trade. Junko and Bill met at the USO club on the Onna Point installation. Twenty-four years old, Junko had taken a part-time job dancing with marines at the USO. Bill was a nineteen-year-old lance corporal, a low-ranking enlisted marine, on his way to Vietnam when he was "blue-tagged" (that is, his orders were canceled). Washington's decision to pull troops out of Southeast Asia meant that his unit would not go to Vietnam. While awaiting orders for the next nine months, he was drawn into the island's live-today-die-tomorrow military leisure culture and developed a severe drinking problem.

On their first date, Bill purchased a Japanese-English dictionary for Junko and scrawled a message on the inside cover: "To my darling Yuko—October 1971." She had given him a false name, not sure if she should trust him. Her parents were strongly against her dating an American GI, so she asked Bill not to come to her neighborhood. They met elsewhere: at the USO, coffee shops, and a particular bar on B.C. Street in Koza. In January, she moved out of her parents' house and rented an apartment in Kin village with a friend. "Thirty years ago in Okinawa, it was a real no-no to move out before getting married," she explained. "Only bad women did that. But I wanted to see Bill more often, so I did it anyway." Bill eventually moved in with Junko and her friend. Her parents had no idea that they were living together. "The first time I met her mother, we had a party at the apartment in Kin, a bunch of guys and gals. The next morning, her mother came knocking on the door. There was a bunch of drunks still lying around on the floor, and the house hadn't been cleaned up yet. So we woke people up and got them out of there. Her mother was standing there in the room crying because this was her little girl."

Learning that he would return to the United States in June, Bill asked Junko to marry him. His parents in the United States were not pleased with his decision but said that they would support him and welcome his wife into the family. The couple spent their first month of marriage on leave with Bill's family in Seattle. He contemplated reenlisting with the Marine Corps in order to take advantage of the large bonuses associated with the military's new all-volunteer force (1973). Ultimately, his father persuaded him to reenlist, and the couple traveled by bus to Quantico, Virginia, his next duty station. Junko was disappointed when she saw her new home. "You had to pass through the town to get to the base. The whole town was only a couple of blocks. If you blinked, you would miss it. And everything was so old—the trees, the bushes, the houses. I was young, and I wanted to experience an American city and a new, modern life. But Quantico's image was completely different. I was so disappointed." Fortunately, she found a job working as a seamstress at a local tailor shop owned by a Japanese woman. Bill's salary was not sufficient to cover their living expenses and his drinking habit. At work, she developed the language skills and self-assurance to survive in the United States. She was able to find work sewing nearly everywhere they lived from that point forward.

Bill stopped drinking in 1974, but their money problems continued, ebbing and flowing according to his on-again, off-again relationship with the military. Twice over the course of their marriage, Bill left the Marine Corps to open his own business. Both times, these enterprises consumed what little savings they had but brought no returns. The first time, he reenlisted; the second time, he took a civilian position on base. Both times, he returned to government work at Junko's urging. Her own work was continually interrupted by their frequent moves and by the births of their two children. Severe morning sickness and distance from her family compounded her anxiety about finances.

> In Quantico, I was pregnant and his drinking was getting worse. From that point on, I started to believe that my husband was no good. He was an alcoholic. We had money problems. He was always having problems at work. I thought to myself, "My husband cannot do anything. Why did I marry him? What am I going to do?" I wanted to go back to Okinawa, but I didn't want my daughters to grow up half-Japanese, half-American with no father. I didn't want people to say, "I told you so."

Junko felt overworked, anxious about money, and resentful of Bill's chauvinistic attitudes toward marriage.

> He was just like a Japanese husband. "You do what I say." When I first married him, I didn't know any better because I grew up in Japan, where the man is always boss. I acted like a Japanese wife should, following him around even though I was pregnant and sick and tired. Sometimes, we would be sitting on the sofa watching TV, and he would say, "I need a drink." I would jump up and bring him a beer. If he said, "I don't have a cigarette," it was "Okay, here's a smoke." It didn't bother me at first. I don't remember when I woke up and started Americanizing.

The peak of their troubles came in 1984, while they were living in Oceanside, California. They had finally saved enough to put a down payment on a house. Junko had a good job managing the tailor shop at Camp Pendleton. Bill had been sent to Memphis for training. One morning, Junko arrived at work to discover that her supervisor had absconded with a large sum of money, and there were no funds to pay the workers. Her paycheck bounced, causing their first house payment to bounce. Working with military lawyers to ensure that the workers were paid, Junko had a breakdown and was hospitalized. The Red Cross contacted Bill, and he returned to California to pack up their belongings. He rented the house to friends, and Junko returned with him to Memphis. When they returned to California four months later, they discovered that their friends had disappeared along with their furniture and that all of the intervening house payments had been left unpaid. Junko called her parents in Okinawa to borrow money so that they would not lose the house.

In 1986, Bill left the military for the second time. Two years later, he took a civilian job at Camp Pendleton, and in 1996, he was offered a job working for the U.S. Army in Okinawa. With the exception of two short visits in the late 1970s, this was the first opportunity they had had to return to the island since 1972. Their children accompanied them initially, but within a year, both had left for college. For Junko, this period represented a turning point.

> I started to feel empty. The kids were gone, and I was starting to go through menopause. I was hospitalized several times, and there I started thinking about my life. I had always blamed everyone else for my misfortunes. I had a bad husband. America was a difficult place to live. I don't remember when I finally realized that I had to take responsibility for my life. I started talking to Bill, expressing my feelings. I told him, "You have to help me more with the house. I'm working eight hours a day too." The more we talked, the more we could understand one another.

Bill had a different view of how their marriage had evolved.

> We've been here [in Okinawa] for seven years now. Before we came back, she was completely Americanized. But our communication has gotten worse. She has reverted to communicating in the Japanese fashion, and she now runs on one speed, and that's slower than mine. Before we came back here, I said, "We're going back to Okinawa, but I don't want you to get involved in your family's business." They do the markets, they rent space and sell goods. I told her, "I work from eight to five. If you want to work, work from eight to five. Other than that, be a housewife." Well, she's gotten involved with her family's business anyway, and she's never home. She works twelve hours a day.

Bill's concerns with the family business went beyond Junko being away from home. He was worried that she would be accused of black-marketing and that her military ID card would be revoked. "Her sister has asked her to buy all sorts of things since we got back. I finally put my foot down. I said, 'Baby, you lose your ID card, we go back to the States. Period.' I won't put up with it." Bill and Junko both told me separately that they wanted to return to the United States when Bill left his job with the army. Bill did not want to live in Okinawa without access to the bases. Junko wanted to be closer to her children and grandchildren.

For Bill and Junko, like Akiko and Aaron Jones, maintaining access to military resources was an important strategy for preserving financial stability and marital wellbeing. At key junctures—such as when Junko was hospitalized for anxiety while Bill was away—they had depended on the military to help solve problems that were personal in nature, yet interfered with military priorities and thus were critical to the institution as well. Overall, however, due to interruptions in Bill's military employment and his current status as a civilian employee in Okinawa, their access to the base exchange and military support services had been inconsistent and promised to be unreliable in the future. The support of Junko's parents had also been important at times, such as when they sent money to help cover delinquent house payments. Yet the couple had had problems with trust and support from off-base sources as well. Both Junko's and Bill's parents were initially opposed to the marriage, friends in Oceanside stole from them, and in Bill's view at least, Junko's siblings in Okinawa pressured her to make unlawful purchases from the base exchange. Managing the interplay between military and family/community resources and support was difficult for the couple, and as a result, military fencelines had operated as a barrier. While they had successfully positioned themselves on one side or the other at various times, they had not maneuvered the two sides together into a cohesive set of strategies for living across the fencelines. Consequently, their narrative highlighted addiction, chronic financial troubles, and difficulty relating to one another. Looking back on their life together, Bill commented, "My wife and I have had communication problems for the last thirty years. Daily communication problems. I'm saying one thing, and she's hearing another. It's difficult enough when two people are both born and raised in Texas. Well, we went halfway around the world, where people have different languages and different cultures." Junko summed up similarly. "Life is not easy when you marry someone from another country. The most difficult thing for us has been that I have trouble expressing myself. Even now, when I try to talk to him, I don't feel comfortable. I feel like there's a wall between us, like there's something missing."

Social Isolation and Loneliness in Military International Marriages

Emotional distance and social isolation were key themes that emerged in the stories of women like Junko who had spent a decade or more married to U.S. military men and shuttling back and forth between the United States and Okinawa. Junko's success in developing marketable skills as a seamstress and finding work on and off base was notable, however, since spouse employment is often identified as both difficult to sustain due to frequent moves and an effective strategy for combating loneliness. Katsuko Horner, who also married during the early 1970s, discussed the extreme social isolation she experienced when her husband, Ray, an air force linguist, received orders to report as an instructor at Goodfellow Air Force Base in San Angelo, Texas. Intimidated by her lack of proficiency in English, Katsuko rarely left the house and had few friends. Eventually, they moved into base housing, and she was able to meet other Japanese spouses. But she continued to feel homesick, and her once-comfortable relationship with Ray deteriorated. When Ray was sent to Maryland for training, Katsuko and her son moved in with Ray's parents. Conflict developed with her mother-in-law over how to raise the child, and Katsuko left for Okinawa, telling Ray that they could work out the divorce agreement after he finished school. Their marriage survived. "At first, I thought, 'To hell with this!' But I really missed her. Then, she came to Korea [his next duty assignment] to visit me, and I went down to Okinawa to visit her. And we started dating again." During subsequent duty assignments in the United States, they worked hard to make sure the same thing would not happen again. Katsuko applied for a driver's license, took a job in a local slipper factory, and enrolled in macramé and pottery classes. Ray made an effort to spend more time with his wife and son. They joined a bowling league and bought season tickets for the local football team. These activities helped Katsuko integrate into the community and soothed her homesickness. In 1982, they moved back to Okinawa, where they continued to prioritize Katsuko's employment. She worked as a dependent hire on Kadena Air Base, first at the makeup counter at the base exchange, and then as a catering manager at the non-commissioned officers club. She also went back to school for certification to teach *ikebana* and kimono-wearing and then to complete her high school diploma. She later attended and graduated from a two-year college.

In 1986, Ray retired from the air force and began teaching at the Okinawa branch of an American community college. Katsuko was hired as an instructor of Japanese culture at the Air Force Family Support Center. Her training in Japanese culture enabled her to frame her difference as a foreign-born spouse as valuable cultural knowledge and skills that could be applied in the service of the military institution. Her classes focused on *ikebana*, kimono-wearing, papermaking, and other traditional crafts, supporting the institution's goals of teaching cultural awareness and appreciation to American service members and their families. Viewed critically, Katsuko's classes conflated Japanese and Okinawan culture, reducing both to a series of discreet and commodifiable aesthetic practices and artifacts. This approach exoticized Okinawan culture and depoliticized the relationship between the military and local people. Yet, for Katsuko, the benefits included bridging on- and off-base worlds and minimizing the effects of social isolation, not only for herself but potentially for American military personnel and their families as well.

Another set of factors contributing to the isolation and loneliness of Okinawan spouses relates to expectations regarding the behavior of military spouses and their participation in social functions and volunteer activities. Officers' wives, in particular, are expected to fulfill social obligations associated with their husbands' rank that differ dramatically from norms of husband-wife interaction in Okinawa. Hiroko Wolf, thirty-nine years old, had attended university in the United States and adapted quickly when they were transferred to an air base in Florida, but she had trouble adjusting to her responsibilities as an air force officer's wife. What kinds of situations and activities made her uncomfortable?

> Coffees. *Nan tte iu n ka naa?* [How can I explain this?] The other wives wouldn't talk to me. They would say, "Hi. How are you? What's your name?" But then I didn't know what to say because I didn't know them, they weren't my friends. And soon they would just ignore me. At first I thought it was because my English was not good enough. Then I met a lady from Switzerland, and she said, "Oh, Hiroko, don't worry about it. You'll get used to it." I felt relieved, but I also think she had an easier time because she looked the same as them. She was white.

Likewise, Mariko Burgess, who married a Marine Corps communications officer during the early 1990s, found that she had little in common with American officers' wives. She became active in the International Spouses group at Camp Pendleton, but her friends there were mostly married to enlisted men. Eventually, she stopped attending Marine Corps functions altogether. Her husband, who supported her decision, explained that she wasn't interested in whether a person was married to an officer or an enlisted man. She refused to recognize rank, whereas many of the American wives were "very into that." While Hiroko attributed her marginalization to American racial prejudice, Mariko blamed the rank/status divisions within U.S. military base communities. Both were quick to point out that expecting wives to socialize publically with their husbands' colleagues and colleagues' wives was not a common practice in Okinawa.

As an aside, Mariko's husband, John, believed that American racial attitudes had contributed to his wife's discomfort. He explained that she worked at an on-base Taco Bell, "not because she has to, but because she wants to." The hours were good, and she enjoyed the people she worked with. "Plus," he continued, "she doesn't go in for the usual volunteering because she believes that you should be paid for your time." But she was often treated badly by her American customers. "They seem to think that because she is an Okinawan standing behind the counter at a fast-food restaurant that she isn't smart, that she can't speak English, and that the only reason she has work at all is because the military bases are here." He then described a situation in which a lieutenant colonel's wife entered the restaurant wearing her husband's rank on her lapel and began talking down to Mariko. "The woman didn't realize that she was talking to a major's wife." John did not believe that these racial and class prejudices were widespread. "Maybe 10 percent of officers and other ranking persons plus their dependents think that way. But that 10 percent sure seems to like tacos."

American military wives living on U.S. military bases overseas experience many of the same challenges as international spouses, including separations, frequent moves and interrupted employment, along with pressures to conform to expected "appropriate" behavior. However, Okinawan and other foreign-born spouses also confront additional complications related to language and culture difference, along with the prejudice of their American counterparts. Especially when husbands are assigned to installations in the United States, geographic and social distance from Okinawan friends and family often results in feelings of alienation. Maintaining employment and reaching across military ranks to make friends and find support are strategies that some women have adopted to mitigate their loneliness. In comparison to the young Okinawan wives who participated in ISP, men and women who met and married during the turmoil of reversion (1972) and the decades immediately following seem to have experienced these challenges to a greater degree. A closer look at changes taking place within the U.S. military institution during this period is critical to understanding these couples' experiences.

Military Fencelines and the Transition to an All-Volunteer Force

The individuals discussed in this section—Bill and Junko Brenner, Ray and Katsuko Horner, Hiroko Wolf, and John and Mariko Burgess—married during a period of considerable transformation of the U.S. military. Coinciding with the withdrawal of troops from Vietnam, the United States moved from conscription to an all-volunteer force in 1973. The draft was terminated, and spending was increased to support recruitment and advertise military service as an attractive career choice. Congress voted to boost military pay and benefits—by more than 60 percent for enlistees in 1973, with additional double-digit increases across the board in 1981 and 1982—and technologize equipment and training facilities (Yuengert 2015). A variety of programs, including family support services, were expanded or newly created to increase retention rates and morale among service members and their dependents.[10] The Marine Corps lagged in these efforts, and at the time of my initial research in Okinawa (2001–2002) still had the reputation of being relatively unsupportive of families, despite ISP and other programs operating through Marine Corps Community Services.[11]

Sociologist Charles Moskos (1977a, 1977b) famously analyzed these changes as a shift in the overall model of military organization from institutional to occupational. "Instead of a military system anchored in the normative values of an institution, captured in words like 'duty,' 'honor,' 'country,' the Gates Commission [which studied and recommended the all-volunteer system to Congress] explicitly argued that primary reliance in recruiting an armed force should be on monetary inducements guided by marketplace standards" (Moskos 1977a, 45). For enlisted personnel, military service was reformulated as a set of responsibilities to meet contractual obligations in exchange for a competitive salary and benefits rather than a vocational calling. Over time, this attracted a different type of service member. Trends included an overall reduction of force strength, longer periods of enlistment (a result of efforts to retain older and more highly educated recruits), greater numbers of married enlisted personnel, more female recruits and assignment of women to a greater range of occupations, and the expansion of civilian positions within U.S. military communities. Not surprisingly, these trends have had a significant impact on military families. In an important 1986 article in *Armed Forces & Society*, Mady Wechsler Segal argued that the shift to an all-volunteer force had led the institutions of the military and the family—both "greedy institutions" which "seek exclusive and undivided loyalty and attempt to reduce the claims of competing roles and status positions on those they wish to encompass within their boundaries" (1986, 11)—to compete with one another for members' attention in new and often confounding ways. Generally speaking, "The family was expected to adapt to the 'greediness' of the military institution and support the service member in meeting military obligations" (13). Yet societal trends and military family patterns during the 1970s and 1980s challenged this norm, including changes in American women's roles in society (especially labor force participation rates), increases in the number of married junior enlisted personnel, single parents, active-duty mothers, and dual-service couples. Segal recommended that the military adopt the following measures in response: provision of on-post housing for young enlisted families, offering opportunities for junior enlisted families to develop informal social support networks, incorporating enlisted wives into the military institution in the same way as officers' wives, and accommodating the employment needs of military spouses. As of 2001, many of these recommendations had been phased in, as is evident in the stories of young participants in ISP. Yet couples who married during the 1970s, 1980s, and early 1990s continued to struggle as the military adapted too slowly to meet their needs during the early years of their marriages.

Segal's analysis, while instructive, fails to account for many of the special needs and experiences of international military families in Okinawa. Grounded in American conceptions of the family (and rather narrow military ideals at that) and without an adequate modeling of the competing loyalties and shifting relations of power that characterize communities surrounding U.S. military bases overseas, Segal's analysis misses the many fencelines, both physical and symbolic, that structure such communities and which international families must negotiate. The gendered and racialized power differentials associated with U.S. colonialism and empire explored in previous chapters are of particular relevance. Nonetheless, military sociologists like Moskos and Segal are antecedents for this study in their focus on the social impacts of the all-volunteer force, and the kinds of questions they ask may be extended to examine the nature of military fencelines, including their variable importance, permeability, and strategic utilization by individuals in specific locations.

The requirements of the all-volunteer force have led to a shift in the relationship between military bases and surrounding communities. Downsizing and privatization have led to the growth of some bases due to the realignment of functions and the closure of others, with significant economic consequences for local communities. An increasing number of married enlisted personnel live off base, which draws their lives away from military installations. And within communities themselves, social impacts are far-reaching. In the United States, for example, researchers have documented less racial segregation in housing and less racial inequality in employment in U.S. communities with a major military presence, whereas gender discrimination in employment is higher in such communities (Segal 2007). Meanwhile, in Okinawa, perceptions of race, class, and gender have become increasingly tied to the U.S. military presence, as discussed in chapters 2 and 3. The social contours of surrounding communities in both the United States and Okinawa have become militarized, creating or transforming fencelines beyond the physical barriers that enclose military installations.

International couples often have access to resources on both sides of the fences in overseas military base communities. They are also subject to multiple and conflicting norms and expectations. In Okinawa, with a military ID card and SOFA status, local spouses can use the commissary, base exchange, and other services.

If they are command sponsored, the couple may qualify for base housing. At the same time, couples may circumvent military restrictions like those placed on the number of vehicles a service member owns by registering a car with the Japanese Land Transport Bureau under the local spouse's name. They can live off base near Okinawan family members while having their air conditioning bill subsidized by the Japanese government (as long as the spouse is command sponsored) like other U.S. military members. With Okinawan friends and neighbors, they may take advantage of courtesies accorded to foreigners while reaping the benefits of membership in Okinawan extended families. Okinawan-military couples are simultaneously Okinawan, Japanese, and American, white, black, or Hispanic, and Asian. These different facets of identity may be manipulated, along with the rights and obligations that are associated with them.

The following discussion examines an area that military international couples negotiate in complex and creative ways—family. As demonstrated in the analysis of the premarital seminar, the Marine Corps, like other major branches of the U.S. armed forces, puts great effort into socializing service members and their spouses to adopt a standard notion of the ideal military family, one that is considered optimal for maintaining readiness and supporting service members' missions. While this model may be embraced at times by military-Okinawan families, it exists alongside other models of family from across the fencelines, including well-codified notions of the Okinawan family. International couples may draw on these alternate formulations of family, modifying them as needed, to resolve conflicts in their lives and advance their own interests. Utilizing strategies that involve family, many couples on the fringes of the U.S. military community, including Hank and Mutsuko Megason and others in northern Okinawa, live effectively beyond military fencelines.

Creating Families and Community across Military Fencelines

Individuals in military international marriages continually emphasized the importance of Okinawan family, not only when recalling initial support or opposition to their marriages but also for developing meaningful interpersonal relationships and community ties. A surprising number of American military husbands described camping trips with their wives' families, beach barbeques with aunts, uncles, and cousins, and funeral-related gatherings with their in-laws' neighbors and distant relatives. They spoke of a sense of belonging to family networks that spanned the main island of Okinawa and often extended to the outer islands as well. Even couples who spoke candidly about strained relations with parents and in-laws described trips to their wives' hometowns, visits with relatives, and, in several instances, distant relatives offering to help buy property and build houses when parents were not immediately supportive. Terrance Carter told me the following story:

> One of my wife's distant cousins, *ushinseki* as they say here, works at the company with us. He came up to me one day and said, "I heard that you are marrying my cousin." I said, "Yes." And he said, "I also heard that her father doesn't like the idea. Tell you what, I'll give you the land and the money to build a house. Because you are a good boy, and [her father] is being an idiot." I was really touched by that. To me, the gesture meant more than actually taking it. I said, "Thank you very much," and my wife and I got a government loan and built the house ourselves.

Receiving assistance from Okinawan family members while establishing residency, buying land, and building houses was mentioned by several interviewees. Ralph Dickson, Hiroko Wolf, and Hank and Mutsuko Megason were all given land or the money to buy land by Okinawan relatives, enabling them to settle permanently in Okinawa. Indeed, the support of Okinawan family, both practical/financial and social/emotional, was the greatest single factor impacting the opportunities and choices available to couples who decided to remain in Okinawa long term. For those anticipating future tours of duty or settling in the United States, the support of American parents and siblings was also important, but arranging for return trips to Okinawa remained a priority. Many couples told me that relationships with Okinawan family were their top concern due to the overall importance of family within Okinawan culture.

Public discourses on the Okinawan family are central to the construction of personhood and social identity in Okinawa, including claims to uniqueness vis-à-vis Japan and the United States. An example appeared in a 1999 issue of *Okinawa Living*, a magazine produced by Marine Corps Community Services to introduce U.S. military personnel and their families to local military bases and Okinawan culture. The column's author, Makiko Shimanaka, uses *shima-naichā* (mainland Japanese persons who have settled in Okinawa) as an entrée to her usual topic, Okinawa's distinctive island culture.[12]

> One of the mysteries for *shima-naicha* is the close tie that binds Okinawan parents and children. You might have already found that many Okinawans who are old enough to set out on their own still live in their parents' houses. In the mainland, however, it would become embarrassing and uncomfortable to stay with the parents. *Shima-naicha* find the deep understanding and tolerance in these parent-child relationships unusual. Moreover, *shima-naicha* notice that the family clans and the

regional communities function as support groups to help people who are divorced or are unemployed. In time, *shima-naicha* can become part of an extended Okinawan family group and enjoy the benefits of family support (Shimanaka 1999, 7).[13]

For most American readers, Okinawans *are* for all intents and purposes Japanese. The specifics of Shimanaka's contrast are therefore less important than the contrast itself. The lesson is that close family and community ties are an integral part of local culture that set Okinawans apart, even from other Japanese. Differences between Okinawan families and American families must truly be monumental.[14]

Such discourses may be used to dissuade or condemn local women who date and marry U.S. military personnel. Marriages to military men are popularly associated with the breakup of families due to the frequency of divorce. They may also symbolize a disregard for the wishes of parents, a deliberate decision to leave Okinawa, and the embrace of an American lifestyle that appears to be the very antithesis of traditional Okinawan values. These same discourses, however, are often appropriated and creatively redeployed by international couples themselves, either to demonstrate their own proximity to the norm or to legitimize alternative choices and behaviors. Discourses on the Okinawan family thus function as technologies of power deployed by local officials, women's organizations, and families to construct and regulate subjectivity and social reproduction, and by couples themselves to exercise agency and independence.

The Chōnan's Duty

Ideas concerning appropriate marriage partners, an eldest son's privileges and responsibilities, and traditional gender roles were frequently discussed. For example, Okinawan military wives often referred to normative ideas about birth order and gender roles when discussing their marriage choices. In Okinawa, I was told, the *chōnan* (eldest son) typically assumes responsibility for the care of elderly parents and the family ancestors. More specifically, the *chōnan*'s wife is expected to perform eldercare as needed, along with much of the ritual activity surrounding the family mortuary tablets (*tōtōmē* or *ihai*).[15] Other individuals may take over if circumstances prevent a family from following the norm, but the negotiation of these duties may cause conflict among family members. Anthropologist Matthews Hamabata (1990) has written about a scandal involving the *tōtōmē* that erupted in a family that he was working with in Tokyo. One morning, one of his research participants received an agitated phone call from her mother, who reported that an aunt whom no one liked had entered her grandfather's empty house, gathered up the family *ihai*, and taken them to her own house where she had prepared a *butsudan*. She then called the participant's mother and apologized for having been remiss and not taking the initiative earlier. As wife of the eldest son of the household, she would assume the responsibility for the *ihai* as was appropriate. This aunt's husband was the grandfather's son by his first wife, while the participant's husband and siblings were born to the grandfather's second wife, and there was constant friction between the two sides of the family. The other wives could do nothing, for the aunt was merely behaving according to the rules of filial piety. As angry as everyone was that the aunt had "stolen" the *ihai*, the consensus was that it had been a shrewd move on her part, and they were all were forced to telephone and thank her for her generosity of time and spirit (Hamabata 1990, 113–114).[16]

In quite the opposite kind of move, Yuki Eisner invoked the image of the *chōnan* in order to absolve herself of family responsibilities. Yuki, who had left her home on Miyako Island and come to Naha to attend college when she was eighteen, was adamant about not "getting stuck" taking care of her parents. "That is my brother's job. He is *chōnan*. My father is *chōnan*. My grandfather is *chōnan*. My grandfather's father is *chōnan*. As the youngest daughter in that kind of family, I won't get any land or money when my parents die. My mother told me when I was a little girl that they wouldn't be able to will me anything, but that they would pay for my education, so I made sure that I went to university. If they ask for my help, I will help them, but I won't let them control my life." Yuki left Miyako against her father's wishes. Interpreting his desire to keep her at home as an attempt to ensure that she would take care of him and his wife as they grew older, she foisted that responsibility onto her older brother, calling it the *chōnan*'s duty. Yuki strategically invoked the image of the *chōnan* in order to legitimize her decision to leave Miyako and marry an American military man.

Okinawan military wives also frequently drew attention to the flexibility of Okinawan family models. While the static language of normative statements may create the impression that Okinawan families are bounded organizations with a stable membership, in practice real Okinawan families are extremely flexible social units with varied memberships and roles that change over time in response to everyday contingencies. The Nakasone family, with whom my husband and I spent New Year's Day 2002, was a case in point. Yasuhiro, the eldest and only son, and his British wife, Carolyn, had invited us to join them at his father's house so that we would not be alone on such an important holiday. Soon after we arrived, Yasuhiro's father invited us to kneel on a floor pillow opposite him in front of the family altar. He said a brief prayer asking for continued success and good relationships during the upcoming year. Afterwards, Carolyn and her three-year-old daughter appeared from the kitchen with large trays of specially prepared

foods recalling the distinctive cuisine of the Ryūkyū court. They placed these on
the family altar and bowed low while inviting Grandmother (recently deceased)
to come and join the New Year's feast. They then moved the trays to the family
dining table, and we began to eat. Yasuhiro and Carolyn brought out individual
bowls of *nakami-jiru* (pig stomach soup) and pink rice made with azuki beans. I
asked where Carolyn had learned to make the dishes, and she laughed telling me
that she had ordered everything but the rice and soup from the local San-e su-
permarket. Yasuhiro's mother had died shortly after the couple had married, and
there was no one available to teach her how to prepare the festival foods. Actually, Yasuhiro confessed, his mother had also ordered the dishes from the super-
market. Yasuhiro himself had prepared the rice and soup. They giggled about the
soup—they had found two family recipes, each of which called for a different
amount of *nakami* (pig stomach). They combined the recipes but were certain
that there was far too much *nakami* in the final product.

Okinawan military wives also took advantage of the flexibility of Okinawan
norms of succession. Haruko Benjamin, for example, lived in the United States
eight months of the year with her American husband, a retired army special forces
officer whom she had met and married in Okinawa before reversion. She spent
the remaining months living in her deceased parents' house in Yabu village, just
west of Nago. Haruko had five living brothers and a sister, all of who resided in
Nago, but her eldest brother had passed away while he was still young and unmarried. Since she was the eldest daughter (*chōjo*) and was the sibling most interested in upholding family traditions, she elected to take over care of the *tōtōmē*.
Her back-and-forth living arrangement helped Haruko maintain close ties with
her siblings despite her marriage to an American man and move to the United
States. Moreover, during her months in Okinawa each year, she had the opportunity to study and perform Ryukyuan folk dance, which she taught in California.

American military husbands may also carry out responsibilities that are typically associated with the *chōnan*'s family. When I first interviewed Hank Megason,
he was involved in planning the *shīmī* festival at Mutsuko's family tomb, located
in Kadena township.[17] Hank explained his role:

> We'll take Mutsuko's mother down to the *haka* [tomb] a week from this
> Sunday, and we're going to do *shīmī*. I'm gonna clean the tomb on Sat-
> urday. I already went by and did a recon of it, and it's got some serious
> grass to cut. And then the following Sunday, we'll take her mother down
> there. It's a very large *haka* for the whole family. But Mutsuko's uncle
> told me that they're planning to put a road through that area, so we may
> have to move it. In fact, we've already talked to the people at the He-
> noko village office about moving it up here.

This is an extraordinary arrangement—a retired American military husband involved in planning important family rituals like *shīmī*. Hank's involvement in his wife's family affairs, however, is not entirely incompatible with Okinawan notions of family. Mutsuko's older brother (the *chōnan*) had died young, while his own son was still a child. Mutsuko and Hank had stepped in as guardians to care for the family ancestors until their nephew was capable of performing the duties himself. Coupled with observable demonstrations of sincerity—which Hank performed by giving up a weekend every spring to cut weeds around the family tomb and transport his ailing mother-in-law to the *shīmī* gathering—normative discourses on the Okinawan family are an important means by which military-Okinawan couples may legitimize their position within Okinawan extended families.

Finally, military-Okinawan couples often have options when it comes to residency, eldercare, and ancestor care that are not available to Okinawan-Okinawan couples. Katsuko Horner returned to Okinawa from the United States in 1982 to care for her aged mother. While performing the necessary care, she developed strong feelings of resentment and vowed never to place her son in a similar position.

> I'd like to stay here in Okinawa as long as I am healthy. But if I get sick, then I don't want the responsibility of caring for me to fall on my husband and my son. When my mother was sick, my sister and I stayed overnight in the hospital to care for her—changing her diapers, washing her clothes, giving her baths, feeding her. In Japan, these things are the family's responsibility, not the nurse's. And burial too—in Okinawa, there is a very heavy responsibility on the eldest son. He has to visit the tomb four times a year and hold memorial services. And if he is not doing these things properly, he will have trouble fitting into the community. People will say that he does not respect his parents and that he is not trustworthy. I don't want to put this pressure on my son. That's why I want to die in America.

Whereas Yuki Eisner invoked the *chōnan*'s duty to absolve herself, as youngest daughter, of family responsibilities, Katsuko Horner assumed that her son would be saddled with such duties even though his father was not Japanese. She and Ray had therefore decided to retire in the United States. Haruko Benjamin and Mutsuko and Hank Megason, on the other hand, had undertaken the *chōnan*'s duties themselves, and this had helped to cement their position as vital members of larger extended families. In each case, normative discourses on the Okinawan family were summoned and adjusted as necessary to resolve conflicts and advance a couple's self-interest as they negotiated a place for themselves in Okinawan society.[18]

Prescriptions Regarding Marital Commitment and Divorce

International couples also engaged normative discourses concerning marital commitment and community participation. Since reversion, Okinawa Prefecture has vied with Hokkaido for the highest divorce rate in Japan.[19] Scholarly explanations for Okinawa's high divorce rate have focused on the retention of pre-Japanese attitudes toward marriage and the historically high status of women, related to their religious authority during the Ryūkyū Kingdom period (see, for example, Sered 1999; compare Kawahashi 2000).[20] At the time of my research, however, divorce carried a stigma. As in mainland Japan, it was often viewed as "an embarrassing public revelation of private disorder" (White 2002, 2). A friend and colleague, Toshiko, related the following conversation from a recent high school reunion. She had just finished writing a book based on a year of research in the United States, and her classmates congratulated her on her accomplishment. One of her classmates gushed over how lucky she was to have a husband who would allow her to spend a year away in the States, and Toshiko answered matter-of-factly that she and her husband had recently divorced. This statement was followed by an awkward silence. Another classmate attempted to relieve the tension by telling a joke, but Toshiko was irritated and moved away to join a different group.

Feminist scholars and antibase activists have argued that Okinawa's high divorce rate is related to the presence of U.S. military bases within the prefecture.[21] Divorce, they claim, is common in the United States because Americans place emphasis on romantic love. "Falling *out* of love" is thus seen as a legitimate reason for dissolving a marriage. Hirata Masayo, a counselor at the Okinawa Gender Equality Center (Tiruru), reported that her Okinawan clients often complained about their American husbands' weak commitment to marriage. "I cook for him, I keep his house clean, I love and nurture his children. There is no reason for him to want a divorce." Romantic love is nice if you have it, Hirata-san told me, but in Okinawa it is not thought to be necessary for a successful marriage. Okinawa's high divorce rate is thus explained as a direct consequence of marriage to U.S. military men, or indirectly, as a result of the Americanization of Okinawan ideas about marriage.[22] Many Okinawans can indeed point to relatives who have married and subsequently divorced American GIs, as Akiko Jones's father did when trying to persuade her not to marry Aaron. In this way, military relationships continue to be ideologically linked to the moral rupture of the close-knit, mutually supportive, multigenerational Okinawan family.

Nonetheless, most women—even those who had openly defied their parents—emphasized the importance of marrying a man their parents could be proud of.

Noriko Sacca, from Ogimi Village in northern Okinawa, referred to norms of marital commitment and community participation when discussing her relationship with Tony, an enlisted marine stationed at Camp Schwab. Noriko had met Tony while she was still in high school, and they spent the first year of their courtship meeting clandestinely at night. After Noriko graduated and moved to Naha to attend college, the couple began to appear together in public, but she continued to hide her relationship from her parents. Finally, after completing her degree, she approached her parents to explain about her relationship with Tony. "I went to my father's work by myself one day and told him that there was someone that I wanted him to meet. I told him that the guy was a really good person, but that he had green eyes. My father warned me about how hard it would be to live with someone from a different background, and then told me that if I decided to marry Tony, I shouldn't bother him with my plans. 'You do whatever you want, but don't try to change me.'"

Some weeks later, when Noriko and Tony drove to Ogimi to meet her parents, her father refused to turn and face Tony. Her mother sobbed hysterically and beat Tony with her fists. "My father told me not to come back to the house, so we didn't. When there was a big family event, I would go, but my father never talked to me in public. And then, after that, we moved to the States." After the couple had lived in the United States for a year, Noriko's sister called from Okinawa to report that their father was sick. He had been diagnosed with cancer with only three months to live. Her mother was also ill and in the hospital. Tony researched flights and bought Noriko an airplane ticket. She flew back to "put in her time" alongside her older sisters and brother. She stayed in Okinawa for six months, until her father died and her mother was released from the hospital. "I was there when they needed help, and I think that changed the opinions of a lot of people. My mother's friends all told her, 'Look how good Tony is to send Noriko home to Okinawa when her family needs her. Not all men would do that. She got a really good husband.' My mom finally told me that she agreed with her friends, and after that, she stopped trying to hide that I was married to an American." Tony was reassigned to Camp Schwab in 1995 and over time developed a warm relationship with Noriko's mother. "Now, when they have some kind of event or festival up in Ogimi, we go, and Tony always participates. Do you know the *sabani hārī* [dragon boat races]? Well, he has done that several times. And now everybody in the community knows him, and probably, a lot of people have changed their minds about Americans."

Okinawan wives like Noriko insist that their marriages are not as far outside the norm as people assume. They too have chosen husbands their parents can be proud of, who value close family relationships and contribute to the local community. In northern Okinawa, it is not uncommon to see American husbands working and socializing alongside Okinawan relatives at family events, community festivals, or at the grocery store, post office, or bank. Like Hank Megason and Tony Sacca, they contribute to their wives' families and the local community by fulfilling regular obligations such as traffic guard duty at school crossings, participating in neighborhood cleanups, or joining the local retirees' gateball team. Okinawan-military couples often gauge the success or failure of their family-making efforts based on how well they are able to approximate or renegotiate the norms of Okinawan family and community. With paternal grandparents and aunts and uncles living far away in the United States, they do not have the extensive paternal kin networks that characterize traditional Okinawan families. Their family-oriented activities involve maternal relatives. Even so, many invoke and embrace normative ideas, turning them to their own ends. They hope, as Noriko did, that by identifying themselves with Okinawan family and community norms, they will be able to renegotiate the boundaries of what is considered normal. Through their efforts, the fencelines that structure Okinawan communities may be moved or dismissed altogether.

Military international couples that I interviewed put great effort into creating functional and fulfilling lives across the various fencelines that divide Okinawan communities. Their interactions with friends and neighbors and decisions concerning residence, employment, education, and childrearing involved navigating boundaries of nationality, SOFA status, location, generation, race, and class. Younger couples were able to access a variety of military support services, and this provided them with additional options for creating balanced and secure lives. Akiko Jones's adoption of military language (such as the term "international spouse"), along with her focus on legal and bureaucratic hurdles, enabled her to frame her marriage as a partnership of equals, while removing it from contentious base-related politics. In another example, Yuki Eisner, who had not yet told her parents that she was married to a U.S. marine, announced: "When my parents discover that I am married, we will be able to show them that we are doing the right thing. We have this much in savings. We have a plan for the future." This was a lesson that she had taken from ISP, where it appeared in a module on family readiness. For both women, military experiences and resources provided potential solutions for countering negative community stereotypes associated with Okinawan-U.S. military intimacy.[23] My recent communications with Yuki Eisner and Akiko Jones suggest that their efforts to integrate into the U.S. military community via participation in ISP have paid off. After serving as the translator for ISP in Okinawa, Yuki was able to find employment at Family Team Building offices on Marine Corps bases in the United States. Akiko has settled permanently in Arizona with her husband and two children. Both women are still married and view their marriages as successes.

U.S. military-Okinawan couples who married earlier, during the 1970s, 1980s, and early 1990s following the establishment of the all-volunteer force, did not have access to Family Team Building and other family services early in their marriages. They spoke of continuous financial/practical and social/emotional difficulties while trying to navigate the military system, along with difficulties related to unreliable employment, language and cultural differences, and racism. Their stories were filled with references to illness, money troubles, addiction, domestic violence, communication problems, and divorce.[24] However, I encountered many couples who married during this period who had successfully integrated into local Okinawan communities. Some maintained ties to military networks, but most spoke only of sporadic outings to the commissary and base exchange. For these couples, the support of Okinawan families and participation in local communities were the basis for their most meaningful social relationships. Such couples often invoked and adapted Okinawan family norms to normalize their familial arrangements. A significant number had become important members of Okinawan extended families by shouldering responsibility for the upkeep of the family tomb, like Hank Megason, or caring for the *tōtōmē*, like Haruko Benjamin. Similarly, women like Noriko Sacca self-consciously associated their relationships with the values of traditional Okinawan families, asserting that they too had chosen men who valued close family relationships and contributed to the local community. Okinawan family values remained strategically important to these men and women, even as they struggled to renegotiate for themselves, their families, and their communities a more accepting approach to military international marriage.

For all of the couples mentioned here, support *within* their marriages was critically important for maintaining functional relationships. The social isolation that Katsuko Horner experienced in Texas illustrates some of the potential difficulties. Katsuko's alienation was due to a lack of interaction with other Japanese speakers, to separations when her husband was temporarily assigned elsewhere, and to Ray's attitude of indifference. To save the marriage, they made decisions that would help mitigate her loneliness, including joining a bowling league together and prioritizing Katsuko's employment. Among younger couples, Aaron Jones's attendance at Akiko's ISP functions demonstrated his support as she learned to utilize military family services. Among couples in northern Okinawa, Mutsuko Megason's near-constant support of Hank in social interactions requiring

Japanese—ordering for him at the *izakaya* restaurant we visited together, for example—was critical to their ability to retire successfully in Okinawa.

Finally, living across and beyond military fencelines depends on a couple's ability to provide a safe and loving family and community environment for their children, one in which they are treated fairly and able to thrive socially. Although the situation of Amerasian children has not been explored in detail in this book, it is of critical importance to military international couples, as well as to Okinawan and international advocacy groups. I offer the following stories and comments to conclude this discussion of resources, negotiation, and family.

Midori Pineda, wife of a Filipino American Marine Corps officer, was troubled by the way Okinawans stared openly at her and her children when they climbed into the family's Y-plate vehicle. Because of her husband's Asian features, their children looked like any other Okinawan children. She explained, "Those people are probably thinking, 'How did those little Okinawan children come to belong to that Y-plate car? They must be her *tsureko* [a pejorative term denoting children from a prior marriage].'" For Midori, it was inexcusable that derogatory stereotypes associated with military international intimacy were used in ways that hurt defenseless children. Similarly, Terrance Carter reported that his son, who had African American features, was called "American" by the children at his Japanese elementary school. In such a context, this label is also pejorative. How do U.S. military-Okinawan parents, who are engaged in demonstrating the normalcy of their own relationships vis-à-vis Okinawan family practices, respond when a son or daughter is being teased or taunted by others for being different? For Terrance Carter, the challenge was to teach his son to "be his own man," to be an individual, which he understood as a distinctly American concept that went against the grain of Japanese cultural norms. Other parents acknowledged that they had deliberately placed their children in Department of Defense or international schools to avoid these kinds of situations. Once again, these solutions involve utilizing resources on both sides of the fence. Unfortunately, children educated outside of the Japanese education system often have difficulty attaining full literacy in Japanese language.

Children were thus considered vulnerable and in need of protection, but they were also held aloft as an embodiment of hope. Younger couples who did not yet have children spoke idealistically about raising sons and daughters who would speak both languages and feel equally at ease in Japan and the United States. Marshall and Hiroko Wolf declared with pride that their children were able to operate in military and Okinawan social settings with equal facility. A number of interviewees employed the term *daburu* (double), meaning two cultural heritages, as opposed to the negatively nuanced term *hafu* (half, meaning half-Japanese). Children were thus invested with their parents' hopes and dreams, not only concerning individual achievement but also concerning society as a whole. Children, it was hoped, would someday reap the benefits of their parents' efforts to navigate U.S. military and Okinawan communities and live effectively across the fencelines. In the meantime, they taught their children that sameness and difference do not, in themselves, qualify human beings as worthy of love and respect. "Love yourself. Respect yourself," Mutsuko Megason urged her daughter Miya. "You are the future."

Conclusion

ON STORIES AND SILENCES

Okinawa patterns differently from mainland Japan with regard to international marriage due to a history of Japanese colonialism, devastating war, U.S. military occupation, and continuing disproportionate U.S. military presence. Today, U.S. military bases with their barbed wire fences are the foremost symbol of Okinawa's continuing subordination to Tokyo and marginalization within the Japanese nation-state. International marriages involving U.S. military personnel call attention to the intensive militarization of Okinawan society, penetrating the most intimate spaces and relationships. U.S. military-Okinawan marriage thus involves more than differences of nationality, language, and culture, but also engages social, political, and economic inequalities at all levels. Military international marriage evokes internal forms of inequality, such as those that structure differences between individuals from different regions of Okinawa and members of the former gentry versus commoners, because of its symbolic prominence within overarching notions of "marrying out." Okinawans use a common set of discursive frames, tropes, and assessments when discussing various types of exogamous relationships, including tropes of romantic love and fated first meetings. The social and economic conditions of Okinawa's base towns have meant that "outsider" Okinawans (such as those from working-class backgrounds, from the northern region, or from outer islands) are symbolically associated with U.S. military customers and military international sex and marriage. Tracing these connections sheds light on the various symbolic fencelines—some associated with the U.S. military presence and others based in prewar and wartime experiences of Japanese colonialism and the Ryūkyū Kingdom—that shape changing distinctions among insiders and outsiders in Okinawan society. Through these linkages, military transnational intimacy directs attention to the ways in which military and political domination have affected all aspects of Okinawan society and structured all manner of relationships, including notions of Okinawan-ness itself.

This book traces the historical emergence and transformation of popular imagery and stereotypes of U.S. military men, Okinawan women, and military international sex and marriage from the early years of the U.S. occupation through the postreversion era. Today, racialized and sexualized stereotypes of U.S. military men surface especially in connection with family opposition to military marriages. Negative attitudes are explained and justified with reference to the collective past, particularly the U.S. occupation period, when Okinawans attempted to reconstruct and reinvent their lives while living alongside a foreign military force and coping with the traumas of war and survival. Drawing on official histories, popular imagery, and personal experience, memory narratives tend to portray African American soldiers in particular as disorderly, dangerous, and prone to sexual violence. Okinawan women who date and marry American military men are racialized as well, according to the skin color of their sexual partners and husbands. Class-based stereotypes and assumptions of sexual promiscuity also adhere to women who date and marry U.S. servicemen. Women who married before reversion in 1972 are commonly presumed to have met their husbands while working as bargirls or prostitutes, whereas younger women may be labeled with the derogatory term *amejo*. The strategies that women employ to distance themselves from these socially damaging stereotypes—from conducting their relationships in secret to transferring negative imagery onto Other women (for example, mainland Japanese women and Filipinas)—more often than not reproduce the very beliefs and conceptual categories that marginalize military international couples and their children. The precise articulation of race and class within such discourses demonstrates the localized character of the symbolic fencelines that fragment Okinawan society.

In collaboration with the Japanese and U.S. governments, the U.S. military institution plays an important role in structuring opportunities and interpretations of international sex, marriage, and family. Aspects of international intimacy are monitored and regulated through a variety of official directives and procedural routines. In Okinawa, these have included the regulation of military prostitution; authorizing marriage, on-base residence, and other privileges through the marriage package and command sponsorship; managing the legal rights of foreign spouses and children; and facilitating immigration and residency in the United States or Japan. Through these mechanisms, the military exercises surveillance and control over personnel and their families, while encouraging particular gendered and racialized notions of cultural citizenship. The Marine Corps premarital seminar propagates a model of the ideal military family that centers on the husband-wife bond rather than parent-child relationships and prescribes specific gendered roles to spouses in support of institutional priorities associated with operational readiness. The underlying message is that men can best serve their country by participating in combat while women support their military husbands. The family ideologies embedded in military orders and procedures, together with the legal statuses established by the SOFA, tend to reinforce a sense of cultural superiority and entitlement among U.S. service members. For men who marry Okinawan women, the cumbersome procedures may also engender feelings of self-reliance and responsibility as they struggle to complete marriage paperwork or find ways to circumvent institutional hurdles. For Okinawan spouses, the marriage process highlights their position at the bottom of institutional race and gender hierarchies. The responses of U.S. service members and their spouses to marriage procedures, whether compliant or resistant, contribute to the ongoing negotiation of cultural citizenship and identity in the U.S. military and Okinawa, while revealing the limits of the military's disciplinary power. The agency of U.S. military personnel and their families, including their complicity or rejection of institutional mandates, factor importantly in the processes through which military fencelines are erected, challenged, and reproduced.

Military international couples' experiences forging emotional intimacy with their partners, social relationships with immediate and extended family members, and a sense of belonging in the Okinawan and U.S. military communities—in other words, their ability to craft lives across military fencelines—vary according to individual circumstance. However, generational and geographical patterns are discernible. Notably, couples' ability to creatively tap resources and support on both sides of the fences has shifted alongside changing political-economic trends associated with Okinawa's reversion to Japanese sovereignty in 1972 and the U.S. government's transition to an all-volunteer force in 1973. Okinawan women who married U.S. military men during the 1960s, 1970s, and early 1980s often experienced severe social isolation and loneliness due to the frequent separations, moves, and distance from family that characterize military lifestyles. Military support for families was relatively weak, and foreign wives were often marginalized within military base communities. Those who failed to garner support from their husbands and extended families relate stories of chronic financial trouble, mental and physical illness, and controlling or abusive husbands. Since the late 1990s, active-duty couples have drawn valuable support from new and expanded military family services. In Okinawa, support programs like the International Spouses Program at Camp Foster provide young wives with additional tools for building community, cultural knowledge, and logistical competence. In addition to enjoying the benefits of subsidized groceries and gasoline, on-base housing, and government employment opportunities, some wives have strategically adopted U.S. military language and cultural frames as a means for combating negative stereotypes in the Okinawan community. Correspondingly, some husbands have secured a place in Okinawan families and communities by investing in relationships with their wives' relatives and embracing and manipulating Okinawan family norms. Strategic manipulation of U.S. military and Okinawan resources, legal statuses, and cultural and linguistic norms has thus enabled some couples to develop highly successful approaches to living across the fencelines. These strategies pattern generationally and geographically, as well, with many retired and other former military couples integrating successfully into Okinawan families and local communities in the northern region. Ultimately, the flexibility of military-Okinawan married couples who cross fencelines leads to a blurring of the boundaries that circumscribe the spaces and people of U.S. military empire.

Several stories in this book suggest that military international couples and their children directly impact Okinawan society, not only as symbols of U.S. military incursion but also as political agents. Hank Megason's recognition as a member of the Henoko community, permitted to vote in local elections on critical issues like the new Marine Corps facility under construction, demonstrates the extent of military international couples' involvement in local politics. Another area in which military international families have been particularly influential involves the rights and acceptance of Amerasian children. It was a group of single mothers of children with U.S. military fathers who formed the study group that culminated in the opening of the AmerAsian School in Okinawa (AASO) in 1998. Unable to afford the tuition rates of DoD schools and existing private international schools, and with their children the targets of bullying in Japanese schools, the mothers worked to formulate a bilingual (or "double") educational model that would provide children with an opportunity to learn English alongside other required subjects, positively affirming their dual-heritage identities. The school, which at first involved one American teacher and thirteen students meeting in a house, opened as a nonaccredited free school in 1998. In 2000, it received formal accreditation from the Okinawa Prefectural Assembly and moved to a facility owned by Ginowan City. In addition to AASO, there are a number of other organizations and groups in Okinawa that have provided support to Amerasian children and their families, including the Pearl Buck Foundation, International Social Services Okinawa, Okinawa Gender Equality Center (Tiruru), Big Bear Club (a playgroup for Amerasian children), and various legal offices and church-sponsored organizations. Together, these organizations have supported countless Okinawan women and children while slowly changing perceptions of Amerasian children. Often, however, the groups have been divided among themselves due to personal and political differences. Some, for example, take a hard-line approach against the U.S. military presence, while others gladly accept donations and military volunteers.

Since reversion, military international intimacy has also affected local U.S. military policy, from the initial orientation and instructions given to newly arriving personnel to the development of a Marine Corps all-island premarital seminar and International Spouses Program, to periodic curfews and restrictions on off-base alcohol consumption. Ultimately, supplementary agreements to the SOFA have been signed in response to rapes and sexual assaults committed by U.S. personnel. Following the 1995 rape of a schoolgirl from Kin village, for example, the United States officially agreed to "favorably consider" handing over U.S. military suspects in serious cases like rape and murder to Japanese authorities before they had been formally indicted, per Japanese criminal justice protocols. While the SOFA does not prohibit U.S. military suspects from being tried in Japanese courts, it does specify that U.S. service members be retained in U.S. custody until they are charged. The policy change reflects a compromise designed to quell popular protest and resentment against the privileged legal status of U.S. military personnel and the use of U.S. military fences to shelter criminals. In January 2017, following the 2016 rape and murder of an Okinawan woman by a civilian contract worker and former U.S. marine, the United States and Japan further clarified the protections afforded to civilian employees of the U.S. military under the SOFA. Under the new agreement, only contractors who are considered "essential to the mission of the United States armed forces and have a high degree of skill or knowledge for the accomplishment of mission requirements" will be covered under the civilian component of the SOFA (Mie 2017). While such modifications are welcomed by Okinawans, women who have married or conceived children with U.S. servicemen have long complained that the fences of U.S. bases have been used to shelter abusive husbands and those who seek to avoid acknowledging paternity or paying child support. Examples are well documented by Okinawan women's organizations. Given the high stakes, monitoring and regulating military international sex, marriage, and family remain a critical concern for those formulating local U.S. military policy. This suggests that military international couples and their families possess considerable latent political power, far beyond their relationships at the village level and activism on behalf of Amerasian children.

This book, with its many stories, is marked by a number of silences. The first concerns occupation-era sexual violence. Although it is widely acknowledged that rapes committed by U.S. military personnel were common in the early months and years of the postwar occupation, personal experiences are rarely discussed by female victims or their families due to lasting trauma and shame. The taboos surrounding such stories are illustrated by the resistance of local villagers and U.S. military officials to investigating the Katsuyama cave incident. This silence has been filled to a certain extent by Okinawan writers of the postwar generation. In recent decades, instances of rape have been co-opted by politicians and activists to mobilize local people against the U.S. bases. While arguments concerning the links between sexual violence, U.S. military training, and the ongoing U.S. military presence may be legitimate, the power of military rape as a political symbol has also contributed to the dehumanization of female victims (Angst 2003). The second silence concerns Okinawan women's experiences in the occupation-era sex trade. According to popular stereotypes, most women who met and married American husbands prior to reversion worked as bar workers or prostitutes. While some women told me that they had met their husbands at dances and several mentioned that they had worked as bartenders, none were comfortable framing their relationships as transactional or in any way related to prostitution. Association with the occupation-era sex industry was simply too damaging for women who had already paid significant social costs for marrying U.S. military men. Instead, they emphasized romantic love, the benefits of having husbands who helped with housework and childcare, and their own personal fulfillment within international relationships.

A final resounding silence that lingers beyond the edges of the stories in this book concerns domestic violence and other abusive intimate relationships. Several interviewees indicated that they had been involved in abusive relationships before meeting their current spouses. Katsuko Horner told me that during the mid-1960s, she had fallen in love with a U.S. soldier, her son's father, only to learn that he became violent after consuming alcohol. She fled their shared apartment one night after he "nearly killed" her. Leaving her infant son with relatives, she returned to her bartending job in Koza but kept her distance from U.S. military customers. When Ray Horner met her two years later, describing her as "unlike the other buy-me-drinkie" girls he had met in Okinawa, he was likely referring to her careful self-presentation, born of fear and self-preservation. According to Okinawan social workers and legal professionals, spouse and child abuse are commonly cited by Okinawan women as reasons for separating from their American husbands. While lobbying for children's educational rights, Midori Thayer (principal of the AmerAsian School) and other women have publically shared their experiences as victims of domestic violence. In a letter to President Bill Clinton, Thayer demanded that the U.S. government accept responsibility and provide assistance to women like herself, who have little recourse once their husbands seek refuge inside U.S. military bases. Thayer has told me that in her work as an activist and school principal, she is "surrounded by failed relationships" similar to her own. Stories like these, common in Okinawa although rarely shared publicly, are the basis for claims by local politicians, feminists, and advocacy organizations that the U.S. military presence has been especially dangerous and oppressive for

Okinawan women. Focusing exclusively on stories involving American men, however, may have the unintended effect of concealing domestic violence and other abuse committed by Okinawan husbands and fathers.

Finally, this book develops the concept of fencelines in ways that may be generalizable to U.S. military base communities in other parts of the world. Military fencelines in Okinawa denote miles of barbed wire and chain links, the material fences that surround U.S. military installations. The term also refers to the symbolic boundaries that divide military from civilian, American from Okinawan, and white from black and Filipino service members. They also divide Okinawans themselves according to place of origin, hereditary status, kinship ties, and wealth or education. All of these distinctions index relations of inequality in Okinawan society, and all have been thoroughly affected by the sustained U.S. military presence. The concept of fencelines thus captures the processes and products of militarization, including deepening distinctions between "us" and "them," and shifting views and subjective experiences of sex, marriage, and family. Such fencelines are not static; they run throughout Okinawan society, shifting with changing political-economic circumstances. Moreover, at times they are porous and permeable, enabling the emergence of new alliances across social boundaries. At others, they are solid and impenetrable, a basis for exclusion and discrimination. As such, fencelines are conduits for militarization, while also serving as a basis for antibase political mobilization. An example involves the Nago City Fisheries Cooperative Association, which has switched allegiance in the struggle over the new Marine Corps facility in Henoko several times. Initially opposed to the new base because it would restrict access to fishing grounds and risk polluting the water, association members cooperated with activists manning the protest tent in Henoko by sharing parking and hiring out boats to protestors. The association later changed its stance when new economic opportunities arose in connection with the Japanese Defense Ministry's maritime survey. In January 2017, the association bequeathed its rights to the Henoko/Oura Bay area altogether, literally redrawing military spatial boundaries and making way for construction of the new base.

Military fencelines are thus conditioned by economic factors relating to the growth and development of local communities, as well as larger state and state-institutional forces. However, individuals' responses are critical to understanding how fencelines are negotiated, and how they affect daily life. Fencelines are for this reason an important site of individual and group maneuvering. Discursive maneuvering—involving among other things the reframing of emotion and experience, the use of common tropes or allegory, the assertion of causality, and the adoption of supportive or oppositional stances—is an important aspect of this process. Discursive maneuvering accompanies the strategic utilization and manipulation of material resources and support on all sides of the fences. Ethnography is an effective method for investigating the nature of military fencelines in specific locations, including their variable importance, permeability, and strategic utilization by local people.

How generalizable are the findings detailed here regarding military international intimacy? Much of the scholarship on U.S. empire highlights global patterns related to the uniform nature of U.S. military training, overarching command structure, standardization of military base design and construction, and military leisure culture. Comparative studies of the U.S. military's impact on specific communities are less common (compare Höhn and Moon 2010). Ethnographic accounts of military international sex, romance, and marriage in a single place (such as Korea) suggest important similarities to the Okinawan case, although the military personnel that I interviewed pointed out significant differences in how off-base entertainment was organized and monitored in the two countries, and differences in how they experienced interactions with local people. Media accounts of military international romance and marriage in locations outside of Asia suggest striking similarities as well. In early 2004, the news program *60 Minutes II* aired a segment on military international marriage in Iraq (CBS 2004). The storyline, about an enlisted army sergeant who married an Iraqi doctor he had met at Baghdad Hospital, resonated with the stories I had documented in Okinawa. Deliberately disobeying his commanding officer, the young sergeant converted to Islam in order to meet the requirements of Iraqi marriage law and then married the woman in the presence of her parents and members of his unit. When his battalion commander discovered that the wedding had taken place, he shipped the soldier home ahead of his unit, saying that he could not trust the man's judgment. Six months later, after leaving the army with an honorable discharge, the man reunited with his wife, whom he had not seen since their wedding day. At the time of the CBS broadcast, the couple was living in Jordan, waiting for her visa to enter the United States.

The similarity of the couple's narrative to stories told by men and women in Okinawa led me to pause. *60 Minutes* filmed the Iraqi woman as she searched for the right words: "I saw a tall, shy, handsome—he had the most beautiful eyes I ever saw. He's so honest, he's so kind, and when he came, my heart started beating like I was a teenager . . . . Sometimes, you just fall in love and you don't know why. I think it's our fate. I think we're meant to be together." Compare the words of Katsuko Horner in Okinawa: "The first night we met, I noticed that his eyes were the most beautiful eyes I had ever seen. To this day, my husband and I believe that it was love at first sight. I cannot explain what it was that I was feeling, but I was thinking, 'Wow, maybe this is it.'" Likewise, Katsuko's husband Ray told me, "Meeting Katsuko was one of those things of fate. It was Valentine's Day, as a matter of fact." The young sergeant in Iraq explained, "We were brought to-gether by some higher force than ourselves. It was meant to be, and I wasn't gonna let anybody stop that." Ray and Katsuko Horner met and married in Okinawa during the late 1960s. The couple on *60 Minutes* met and married in Iraq in 2002. Despite the two different times, locations, and cultures, shared processes of cul-tural production were clearly at work.

The Iraqi case suggests the following comparative questions: Which aspects of military international intimacy (in Iraq, Okinawa, Guam, Taegu, or Fayette-ville) are due to the specificities of local society and culture, and which follow di-rectly from official U.S. military policies concerning fraternization between military personnel and local citizens? How do experiences with local people at previous duty stations, both stateside and overseas, affect the way U.S. service members approach relationships with local people when they are transferred to new locations? To what extent do current U.S. military policies, as well as the at-titudes of individual commanding officers, recall previous U.S., European, or Japanese colonial arrangements, and how do they articulate with postcolonial dis-courses in military base communities around the world today? Finally, what dis-tinctive strategies do couples adopt in different locations to gain the acceptance of their families and home communities, as well as others within the military com-munity? The answers to these and other questions require careful ethnographic and historical analysis. Comparisons across communities hosting U.S. military bases are critical for understanding the processes of militarization that follow global U.S. military expansion during wartime deployments, when new bases are constructed, and as a result of joint training exercises with the militaries of other nations. Feminist scholars have paved the way for this sort of analysis by identi-fying patterns in the ways militaries and militarization have affected women's lives as wives, mothers, soldiers, and sex workers. A specifically anthropological con-tribution to the study of global U.S. military power involves reading the effects of power not at the macro-level of governmental politics and policies, but at the micro-level of the production of cultural meaning and everyday relationships be-tween U.S. service members and local persons.

I end with stories from Ralph Dickson, the recently widowed retired Marine Corps officer introduced in the preface, who took a chance on me and shared his experiences while mourning the death of his wife. Ralph visited Okinawa for the first time in 1955 on a Navy LST (a tank landing ship) that anchored off Nami-noue Beach in Naha. On his first trip to shore, he set out in search of the famous Teahouse of the August Moon.[1]

> I wandered about the streets. Naha was 90 percent trees, one paved street in town, and the rest of it was white coral roads. There weren't many

buildings. An old Okinawan lady pointed me to the place. The Teahouse of the August Moon was a single story building with a sliding front door and an open-air courtyard. It was a very humble establishment, a typical Okinawan place. They had electrical power from five in the evening until about ten, but the beer was warm. An older woman came out to talk with us. She was wearing battle fatigue trousers and had a rope holding her trousers up. They were much too big for her. She had a little bag of sugar candy. She had black sugar candy and white sugar candy, and she wanted to know, "Which one do you want?" I think I took the white one.

From the time of this first experience in Naha, Ralph began to develop empathy for local people and a new sense of self situated in Okinawan settings. From 1956 to 1958, he came and went from Okinawa, working mostly for the laboratory implementing the VD contact tracer. During the 1960s, he rotated through California and Hawaii, and then returned "home" to Okinawa.

Ralph met his future wife, Chiemi, at a village festival in 1967. Over the next two years, they developed a friendship, meeting at the club where she worked and visiting Okinawan sacred sites together while Chiemi prepared to become a *yuta* (shamaness).[2] "My wife talked to God and to dead people. Well, I do that myself, but they talked *back* to her. In the West, they might label someone like that 'psychiatric,' but here, it's a part of life. When there's an unexpected problem, it means that a dead relative is unhappy or is trying to ask a living relative to do him a favor. And you have to go to a specialist to find out what that dead relative wants. My wife was one of those specialists." It was during these drives with Chiemi that Ralph developed a lifelong interest in Okinawa's distinctive history and culture, and it was to these same sites that he brought my husband and me during our first year in Okinawa. I can only think that these tours were part of his healing process.

Ralph and Chiemi argued from time to time, but divorce, he told me, was never an option. "We took out the dictionary and turned to the D's. We cut out the word 'divorce' and then framed the page, hole and all, and hung it on the wall next to the telephone." One day, as Ralph and I were driving through the mountains in his beat-up pickup truck, I asked him, "What do you most want to tell young military guys who are getting married in Okinawa today?" He answered, "You ask them: Do you love her? Do you *love* that girl? You have to love her like your own hand. If your hand hurts, you don't cut it off. You treat it, you heal it. You can't do without it." In 2000, Chiemi became ill and died. When I met Ralph, he was living in their apartment above the pineapple cannery with Chiemi's daughter and her two children. His military retirement and pension from the postretirement civilian position were the primary sources of income for the household. Gradually, over the course of the next year, Ralph resumed social activities, joining a cycling club and volunteering at local schools. Shortly before I returned to the States, he showed up on my doorstep with a friend, Tatsuko Lee, an Okinawan woman who was herself recently widowed. Months later, he wrote to tell me that the two were getting married. He had given the cannery to Chiemi's daughter and moved south to Tatsuko's home in Yomitan.

Four years passed before I returned to Okinawa. Upon arrival, I learned that Ralph had died in a cycling accident the previous year. As I reflect back on the time I spent with him, I am struck by the many life lessons embedded in his stories, lessons that he wished to share with me and with others. He talked of love and commitment, conflict, forgiveness, companionship, loneliness, and letting go. I recall him asking once if I was going to become a counselor. "No," I replied, "but I've talked to lots of counselors. I am interested in people's stories." "Are you going to write a book, then?" he asked. "I think that all this stuff you're asking about would make a good book." Ralph, I have finally written that book.

METHODOLOGICAL NOTES

This book draws on ethnographic research conducted in Okinawa beginning in 2001–2002, with additional research trips in 2006, 2009, 2012, 2014, 2016, and 2017. I have conducted participant observation in a variety of sites, from formal seminars and workshops offered by the U.S. military to less structured observations at beaches, restaurants, shopping areas, museums and war memorials, bars and clubs, and community festivals. I was even honored to receive an invitation to attend an Okinawan-U.S. military wedding. In order to meet and build rapport with U.S. military-Okinawan couples and families, I volunteered with the Nago City International Friendship Committee and the Yanbaru Language Volunteers.[1] In central Okinawa, I volunteered with a playgroup for Amerasian children. Organized by the children's mothers, the group created opportunities for boys and girls who had no contact with their American fathers to interact with American volunteers, most of whom were active-duty U.S. military personnel, in on-base settings. In November 2001, I was invited by a representative of the Camp Foster Family Team Building office (FTB) to participate in the Marine Corps International Spouses Program (ISP), described in chapter 5.[2] I met approximately forty Okinawan military spouses through ISP. Participants invited me into their homes, introduced me to their spouses, and included me in family activities. My involvement with ISP led to further contacts within the U.S. military community, including introductions to the coordinators of the Marine Corps premarital seminar and the Air Force Family Life Education and Assistance Programs.[3]

A key methodological concern arose from the ways in which networking proceeded. Especially during the early months of research, I was continually steered toward married couples with relatively stable and successful relationships. This occurred despite my declared interest in a range of intimate military international relationships (including marriages but also sexual encounters, dating, and divorce). My research sample therefore contained few participants who had been involved in Okinawan-U.S. military marriages that ended in divorce.[4] Although there are no comprehensive statistics on divorce among Okinawan-U.S. military couples, it is popularly assumed that the divorce rate is quite high.[5] One navy chaplain estimated that as many as 80 percent of couples eventually divorced. Although this figure may be exaggerated, my sample still appears strongly skewed toward couples who stayed married. One curious effect of this bias is that interviewees tended to deemphasize conflict within their marriages while emphasizing conflict between themselves and their natal families and the surrounding community. Interviewees (women, especially) often spoke of being ostracized from their natal families because they had married military men, but few expressed regret that they had moved ahead with the marriage. Individuals who did speak frankly about marital difficulties tended to frame such difficulties as obstacles that had been overcome within larger narratives of marital success.

Recognizing the limitations as well as the importance of data I collected in interviews, I have drawn extensively on other sources as well, including interviews with social workers and marriage counselors, written accounts of Amerasian children who grew up without knowing their U.S. military fathers, and available statistical evidence. I consulted government studies of military international marriage, divorce, and children, including the helpful "Handbook of Japanese-American Marriage, Divorce, and Children—Investigation of Women's Problems Deriving from the Presence of the American Military Bases," published by Okinawa Prefecture (*Okinawa Josei Zaidan* 1999). I also gathered materials from the U.S. military pertaining to overseas marriage and divorce, including official military orders governing overseas marriage and two chaplains' handbooks for the Marine Corps premarital seminar. In analyzing these materials, I noted the ways in which Okinawan and U.S. military sources characterized intimate international relationships, what legal and social obstacles seemed to be emphasized, and what kinds of advice were offered.

The true heart of my data collection centers on a series of thirty-eight semi-structured personal interviews with twenty-four Okinawan women and fourteen American men who were at the time or had previously been involved in military international marriages. Within this sample, all of the women were born and raised in Okinawa, while the men had initially come to the island as active-duty U.S. servicemen. Interviewees ranged in age from twenty-one to sixty-nine. About one-third of the respondents had married prior to reversion (1972). Of the total number of marriages, 57 percent involved white servicemen and 14 percent involved African American servicemen, with the remainder involving Japanese American servicemen, Filipino servicemen, and one husband who identified himself as racially mixed. In over half of the respondent groups, the husband was active-duty; the remaining husbands had either "separated" from the military short of retirement or were collecting a retirement pension. Over half of the total number of marriages involved men affiliated with the Marine Corps, followed by an equal number affiliated with the navy and the air force; a small number involved army men. Two-thirds of the marriages involved enlisted men; the remaining one-third involved officers.[6]

Nearly half of the interviews took place in the interviewees' homes. Other locations included out-of-the-way tables at restaurants, coffee shops, public sitting areas in indoor shopping malls, the FTB office at Camp Foster, the International House in Nago, and my office at Meio University. I interviewed each individual one or more times; many I met repeatedly. Interviews were conducted in English and Japanese, according to the habit of the interviewee. Questions concerned the interviewees' personal and family history, as well as their experiences in international relationships. With married individuals, I asked about first meetings, first impressions, courtship, family reactions, the decision to get married, marriage procedures, and married life. I elicited information about communication, everyday life on and off base, children, work, friends, community, and future plans. I have maintained contact with many of these individuals and interviewed them numerous times over the years, building long-term relationships and following their lives. Their updates are integrated as relevant throughout the text.

INTERVIEWEE PSEUDONYMS WITH RELATIONSHIP TO THE U.S. MILITARY

ID	PSEUDONYM	GENDER	INTERVIEWEE IN MILITARY?	INTERV./SPOUSE'S MILITARY STATUS	BRANCH	RANK
1		F	No	Separated	Army	E1-E4
2		M	Yes	Separated	Army	E1-E4
3		F	No	Separated	USAF	Enlisted
4	Thomas Cooper	M	Yes	Separated	USN	O4-O10
5	Haruko Benjamin	F	No	Not Specified	Army	Unknown
6	Asato Katsuko (Horner)	F	No	Retired	USAF	E7-E9
7	Ray Horner	M	Yes	Retired	USAF	E7-E9
8	Miyagi Satoko (Wilson)	F	No	Retired	USMC	E7-E9
9	Junko Brenner	F	No	Separated	USMC	E5-E6
10	Bill Brenner	M	Yes	Separated	USMC	E5-E6
11	Tatsuko Lee	F	No	Retired	USN	O4-O10
12	Ralph Dickson	M	Yes	Retired	USN	O4-O10
13		F	No	Separated	USMC	E5-E6
14	Mutsuko Megason	F	No	Retired	USMC	E7-E9
15	Hank Megason	M	Yes	Retired	USMC	E7-E9
16	Hiroko Wolf	F	No	Active Duty	USAF	O4-O10
17	Marshall Wolf	M	Yes	Active Duty	USAF	O4-O10
18	Midori Pineda	F	No	Active Duty	USMC	O1-O3
19		M	Yes	Active Duty	USMC	O1-O3
20		M	Yes	Reserves	USMC	E5-E6
21	Noriko Sacca	F	No	Active Duty	USMC	E7-E9

(continued)

ID	PSEUDONYM	GENDER	INTERVIEWEE IN MILITARY?	INTERV./SPOUSE'S MILITARY STATUS	BRANCH	RANK
22	Harumi Olsen	F	No	Active Duty	USMC	E1-E4
23		F	No	Active Duty	USMC	E7-E9
24	Tony Sacca	M	Yes	Active Duty	USMC	E7-E9
25	Terrance Carter	M	Yes	Separated	USAF	E1-E4
26	Kaneshiro Kaoru	F	No	Civilian	USN	GS-13
27	Mariko Burgess	F	No	Active Duty	USMC	O4-O10
28	John Burgess	M	Yes	Active Duty	USMC	O4-O10
29		F	No	Active Duty	USN	Unknown
30	Chieko Pierce	F	No	Active Duty	USAF	E7-E9
31		F	No	Active Duty	USMC	E7-E9
32	Yuki Eisner	F	No	Active Duty	USMC	E1-E4
33	Josh Eisner	M	Yes	Active Duty	USMC	E1-E4
34	Akiko Jones	F	No	Active Duty	USN	E1-E4
35	Nakamura Miki	F	No	Active Duty	USMC	E5-E6
36	Iha Mayumi	F	No	Active Duty	USMC	E1-E4
37		F	No	Active Duty	USMC	O1-O3
38		M	Yes	Active Duty	USMC	O1-O3

Notes

INTRODUCTION

1. Officially, the U.S. Department of Defense owns or leases 4,855 sites worldwide, including 576 in foreign countries and 110 in U.S. territories outside of the fifty states (U.S. Department of Defense 2015). These numbers do not include "forward operating sites" in Iraq, Afghanistan, and elsewhere, nor do they include "cooperative security locations" maintained throughout the world by host nations or contractors for occasional use by the U.S. military.

2. The U.S. Department of Defense controls thirty-four sites in Okinawa, including installations for the army, navy, air force, and Marine Corps (U.S. Department of Defense 2015). As of January 2016, this accounted for 73.9 percent of U.S. military installations in Japan (Okinawa Prefectural Government 2016). In December 2016, Tokyo and Washington announced the return of approximately four thousand hectares of the Northern Training Area, the largest land parcel to be returned since Okinawa reverted to Japanese sovereignty in 1972. According to the Japanese Defense Ministry, the hand-back reduced Okinawa's share of U.S. military-exclusive facilities to 70.6 percent. U.S. facilities now occupy 14.6 percent of the main island of Okinawa (Mie 2016). The 2016 return, however, was contingent upon the construction (paid for by Japan) of six new landing pads for U.S. Osprey helicopters in the remaining area of the installation, and thus met with fierce opposition from local residents and environmental groups.

3. Defense planners propose collaboration in the areas of noise, facility maintenance, health care, family services, utilities, recreation and education facilities, and environmental conservation (Powledge 2008; Harmon et al. 2014; Association of Defense Communities 2016). A recent report explains, "Changing missions, evolving weapons systems and capabilities, budgetary challenges, expanding availability and improving quality of goods and services provided by local economies, aging infrastructure, and generational changes in culture and social attitudes all bring into question the current support structure of military bases that developed during the Cold War" (Association of Defense Communities 2016, 1). Planners claim that increased collaboration will lead to more efficient and ultimately more secure bases of the future. Reducing military expenditures on noncombat functions by contracting them out to local communities is clearly a motive.

4. Admiral Richard C. Macke, commander of U.S. Pacific Command, responded to a journalist's question about the 1995 rape of a twelve-year-old Okinawan girl by three U.S. servicemen with the comment, "I think it was absolutely stupid . . . For the price they paid to rent the car, they could have had a girl" (quoted in Enloe 2000, 117). Okinawans were outraged by the comment and joined international activists in pressuring the Department of Defense to offer Macke early retirement with a demotion. Feminist scholars argue that military prostitution has been institutionalized in Okinawa and throughout the Asia-Pacific region as a means for constructing a standard type of militarized masculinity central to the culture of military combat (Enloe 1989, 2000; Sturdevant and Stoltzfus 1993; Lee and Lee 1995; Takagi and Park 1995; Moon 1997).

5. In 2015, the rate of international marriage in Okinawa was 4.2 percent (365 of 8,695 total marriages); 3.2 percent (281) of marriages involved Japanese women and foreign men,

and 86.8 percent (244) of foreign grooms were American (Japanese Ministry of Health, Labour and Welfare 2016).

6. Originally signed on September 8, 1951, alongside the San Francisco Peace Treaty, the U.S.-Japan Mutual Cooperation and Security Treaty was a ten-year renewable agreement that outlined a security arrangement for Japan in light of the new peace constitution. Surviving in revised form today, it grants the United States the right to military bases in the Japanese archipelago in exchange for a U.S. pledge to defend Japan in the event of an attack. The U.S.-Japan Status of Forces Agreement (SOFA) further outlines the rights and privileges of U.S. personnel, including entry into and exit from Japan, tax liabilities, employment of Japanese nationals on U.S. bases, and civil and criminal jurisdiction over U.S. bases and personnel.

7. In 2011, 47,300 U.S. military personnel, civilian employees, and family members were stationed in Okinawa Prefecture (Okinawa Prefectural Government 2013).

8. A similar criticism has been leveled at ethnographic accounts of antibase movements in places like Okinawa, the Philippines, and Puerto Rico (see, for example, McKaffrey 2002; see also Ben-Ari 2004).

9. Following reversion in 1972, the number of Okinawans employed by the U.S. military declined from a peak of thirty thousand. Okinawan employees, whose salaries are now paid by the Japanese government, have numbered around eight thousand persons in recent decades (Arasaki 2000, 125; LMO/IAA 2013, 14). The LMO/IAA is a civilian contractor of the Japanese Ministry of Defense charged with managing USFJ employees in Japan.

10. These figures may appear to suggest a measure of economic dependence on the U.S. bases. However, recent studies show that land occupied by U.S. bases generates income well below the per-square-kilometer average in Okinawa (Yoshida 2015). At the time of reversion, U.S. forces–related revenue constituted 15.5 percent of gross prefectural income, but by 2008 this ratio had decreased to 5.3 percent (Okinawa Prefecture n.d.).

11. In Okinawa and elsewhere, the self-conscious discursive construction of U.S. bases as insular and self-sustaining "local" spaces—what Erin Fitz-Henry (2011) refers to as "scaling down"—has been purposefully utilized by U.S. military spokesmen to discredit the "globalizing" politics of antibase movements. The particulate structuring of the U.S. military may thus be understood as part of a "strategic vision for controlling a large swath of Asia and, with it, the global economy, dating to at least World War II" (Vine 2009, 188). In his account of the U.S. Navy in Diego Garcia, David Vine traces the evolution of the military's "Strategic Island Concept" and today's "Lily Pad" basing strategy, in which the United States builds installations that are "isolated from population centers, have limited troop deployments, and instead rely largely on prepositioned weaponry for future (un-) anticipated conflicts" (186). Vine argues that the forced removal of local people to make way for new bases is a deliberate empire-building strategy, designed to protect military interests from potentially antagonistic local populations.

12. The guest pass allowed me to enter Camp Schwab and use the library, restaurants, and recreation facilities, and talk to the Okinawans and military personnel I met there.

13. In addition to my own dissertation (2004), two English-language dissertations have explored intimate relationships between U.S. military men and Okinawan women. Ayako Mizumura (2009) examined the changing "gaze" of Japanese war brides and Okinawan military wives and their decisions to enter into relationships with American men. Chris Ames (2007) discussed the marginalization and agency of Okinawan women involved with U.S. military personnel as part of a larger argument about Okinawans' ambivalence vis-à-vis the U.S. military presence. In addition, Kaori Miyanishi (2012) published a Japanese-language study of Okinawan military wives based on her observations while interning at Marine Corps headquarters at Camp Butler. These studies focused mainly on active-duty couples living in the central region. Due to my geographical base in northern Okinawa

and my lack of direct association with the U.S. military, my participant sample was broader, including active-duty and retired couples, former military personnel and other local hires, and DoD civilians. The analysis is also broader in scope, exploring intimate encounters with U.S. military personnel as sites of symbolic negotiation in which gender, race, and class meanings are constructed and challenged.

1. INTERNATIONAL MARRIAGE IN JAPAN'S PERIPHERY

1. Hank and Mutsuko Megason's stories are explored in more detail in chapter 5.

2. Recent declines are attributed to changes to the Immigration Control Act in 2005. Revisions tightened requirements for entertainer and other visa types, resulting in decreased opportunities for Japanese men and women to encounter foreigners at home in Japan.

3. Significant numbers of Filipina women were also recruited to work as hostesses/entertainers and, more recently, as nurses/care workers throughout Japan, contributing to the high rate of international marriages between Japanese men and Filipina women (Suzuki 2003, 2007, 2009; Faier 2009).

4. An abundance of Japanese-language websites help potential suitors find foreign spouses, and many popular books and television programs focus on the lives of international couples. In 2014–2015, for example, Japan's public broadcasting company, NHK, ran a morning television drama entitled *Massan* that tells the story of a Japanese-Scottish couple's efforts to establish a whisky distillery. The story was based on the lives of Nikka Whisky founder Taketsuru Masataka and his Scottish wife, Jessie Roberta "Rita" Cowan (Nippon.com 2015).

5. Of note, Japanese government international marriage statistics include marriages between Japanese persons and resident Koreans, Chinese, and others whose parents or grandparents were brought to Japan as imperial subjects during the early twentieth century. Many chose to remain in Japan after the war, even though under the terms of the San Francisco Treaty (1952), they lost the Japanese nationality they had possessed as subjects of the Japanese empire. Their descendants have thenceforth been classified as foreigners, despite having been born and raised exclusively in Japan and speaking Japanese as a first language.

6. *Kokusaika* (internationalization) is a popular term that refers to interactions between Japan and the rest of the world in situations as varied as the diffusion of Western culture during the eighteenth century, foreign citizens living within Japan and the emigration of Japanese persons to other countries, legal processes associated with citizenship and naturalization, the liberalization of trade policy, and attaining foreign language competence (Befu 1983). As a common gloss for westernization (*seiyōka*), modernization (*kindaika*), and liberalization (*jiyūka*), *kokusaika* is strapped with the ideological nuances of each of these terms. Consequently, *kokusaika* has been implicated in the ideology of Japanese nationalism. Befu and others have argued that linguistic and cultural misunderstandings between Japanese and non-Japanese reinforce the belief that Japan is a homogenous society whose members are united by a common race, language, and culture (Miller 1982; Befu 1983; Yoshino 1998). Marilyn Ivy writes that the rhetoric of *kokusaika*, above all, serves a conservative political agenda: "While internationalization elsewhere implies a cosmopolitan expansiveness (even while retaining the national frame), the Japanese state-sponsored version tends toward the domestication of the foreign. Schemes to internationalize the communications industry, education, and the citizenry index the pressures on the state to give the appearance, at least, of openness, while carefully circumscribing the problem of identity and difference" (1995, 3). In short, Ivy argues that the political project of *kokusaika* is fundamentally linked to the erasure of difference through its repression, absorption, or outright exclusion.

7. Two other prefectures with similarly high percentages of American grooms, although not as high as Okinawa, were Aomori Prefecture, at 70.5 percent and Nagasaki Prefecture

at 64 percent (Japanese Ministry of Health, Labour and Welfare 2016). Aomori is home to the large combined joint service (U.S. military/Japanese Self-Defense Forces) installation of Misawa Air Base. Nagasaki hosts the U.S. Fleet Activities naval base at Sasebo.

8. *Uchi/soto*, along with the conceptual pairs *omote/ura* (front/back) and *tatemae/honne* (surface/hidden), figure prominently in studies of Japanese self, society, and language (Doi 1985; Rosenberger 1992; Bachnik and Quinn 1994). Bachnik's (1989) approach to *uchi/ soto* as a referentially empty set of categories that take on meaning only within specific contexts has become standard. *Uchi/soto* and other related dualisms perform the twin functions of indexing close/far and defining an axis of similarity/difference, allowing Japanese individuals to situate self within an ever-changing social context.

9. Ethnographic studies of intimate relationships between Japanese men and Filipina women have added much-needed perspective to the literature on international marriage in mainland Japan (for example, Faier 2009; Suzuki 2009).

10. In contrast to whiteness, which "signifie(s) upward mobility and assimilation in 'world culture'" (Kelsky 2001, 145), blackness is conspicuous (*medatsu*) and racially marked. The Japanese term *gaijin* (foreigner, literally "outside person") tends to be reserved for light-skinned foreigners, while the term *gaikokujin* (literally "outside nation's person") is generally used if the individual is dark-skinned, including African American and non-Japanese Asian. Befu has illustrated this asymmetry by evoking the improbable image of Japanese schoolchildren pointing at Koreans and shouting "*Gaijin, gaijin!*" (1983, 242–243). The cognitive dissonance associated with this image makes it recognizable as a joke. As in the United States, the Japanese words *kokujin* (black person) and *hakujin* (white person) stand in polar opposition to one another. These terms, however, never achieve total oppositional equivalency, not only because whiteness is seen as somehow transcending race (Kelsky 2001), but also because Japanese themselves seldom view their difference from white foreigners in terms of skin color (Russell 1998, 2017; see also Molasky 1999, 72–75). Rather, white foreigners tend to be marked as *culturally* different from Japanese.

11. During the Sanzan period (1314–1429), the main island of Okinawa was divided into three major principalities: Hokuzan (Northern Mountain) based in Nakijin, Chūzan (Middle Mountain) based in Urasoe and later Shuri, and Nanzan (Southern Mountain) based near Itoman. Of these, the king of Chūzan, the most economically prosperous of the three kingdoms, was the first to establish a tributary relationship with Ming China in 1372. The Chūzan king also received tribute from the southern island groups of Miyako and Yaeyama. King Shō Hashi of Chūzan conquered Hokuzan in 1416 and Nanzan in 1429, unifying the main island of Okinawa and surrounding island groups into the Ryūkyū Ōkoku (Ryūkyū Kingdom). Ryūkyū monarchs later extended the kingdom to the Amami Islands, located in present-day Kagoshima Prefecture, and the Sakishima Islands near Taiwan.

12. Universal education in standard Japanese language was instituted in Okinawa in 1890. Pupils were punished for speaking Ryukyuan languages and made to wear *hōgen fuda* (dialect tags). Students who spoke Ryukyuan were forced to wear the tags around their necks until they could identify others who spoke the language, at which point they could pass the tags on to the new transgressors. Students who wore tags at the end of the school day were punished by the teacher.

13. The adoption of Western notions of unilineal social evolution, which inspired Fuyū, Yanagita, and others to approach Okinawa in this way, is discussed in chapter 2.

14. After reversion, officials changed the city's name from Koza to Okinawa City (written in *kanji*) and attempted to establish a new postoccupation identity for the city. Today, promotional materials celebrate the area's hybrid culture and attempt to reinvent the city's bars and brothels, which now cater mainly to Japanese tourists, as hip night spots (Angst 2001).

15. Here, I refer to village studies conducted by occupation-era American ethnographers, along with works published by Japanese folklorists, anthropologists, and sociologists, including Japanese native ethnologists and folklorists of the prewar period (see Beillevaire 1999). While some of these were salvage attempts (that is, concerned with reconstructing kinship patterns that no longer existed at the time of research), others aimed to document patterns the researchers observed in the countryside or outer islands of Okinawa. Under Japanese colonialism, in the aftermath of war, or in the midst of foreign military occupation, these patterns could hardly be viewed as normal, and I do my best to situate them historically. Within such studies, Okinawan families were treated as surface manifestations of underlying systems of ideal kinship relations. Consequently, these accounts tend to erase the impact of historical change and colonial configurations of power on Okinawan culture and society.

16. The *munchū* is a large patrilineal descent group that traces its roots back to a common founding ancestor (Lee 1995). The practice of recognizing membership in a *munchū* began in the seventeenth century among the gentry class in Shuri, which kept elaborate genealogical records for purposes of determining rank. Gradually, the practice spread to commoners, although the existence of *munchū* is not evenly distributed throughout the islands.

17. Occupation-era ethnographers noted that this system was recognized more in the breach than in practice due to the destruction of family registries and other genealogical records and the loss of family members during the war.

18. During 1899 to 1903, the new prefectural government privatized all communally held land, with ownership passing to the national, prefectural, and local governments (McCune 1975). Individuals were able to buy land as well, encouraging the spread of the Japanese system of patrilineal succession and inheritance. After the U.S. military assumed control of Okinawa in 1945, little attempt was made to change this system of land tenure and inheritance. The 1946 Japanese Land Reform Law and the 1947 revision of the Japanese Civil Code, implemented in mainland Japan by SCAP to eradicate "feudalistic" family relationships, were never introduced in Okinawa. Even so, other factors besides sex and birth order figured importantly in determining a successor, and households headed by younger sons or women existed in all villages. Under the new Civil Code, which finally came to Okinawa upon reversion in 1972, inheritance of all property—money, house, land, goods, and so on—was equalized among siblings, regardless of sex or birth order. A useful overview of the history and revision of the Civil Code can be found in Steiner (1987).

19. Lee (1995) discusses the survival of this "loosely structured" family system into the 1970s in villages in northern Okinawa, with reference to the kinds of tombs (*haka*) and burial practices found in village cemeteries. Based on this evidence and personal interviews, he argues that the Okinawan household (*yā*) represented a functional unit including whichever relationships were considered most important in a given historical moment, rather than a lineal structure whose membership stayed constant through time.

20. This accords with a story I was told about the difficulties a participant's aunt endured when she moved from her parents' village in Motobu to her husband's community in Nakijin during the early postwar period. Although the two villages were located immediately next to one another, perhaps a twenty-minute walk apart, she had trouble communicating with her husband's family due to dialect differences. The participant remembered his cousins and other family members making fun of her speech and ignoring her during family gatherings. He supposed that she must have felt extremely lonely and suffered greatly due to the alienation.

21. Prohibitions concerning the residence and movement of commoners were also lifted at this time, and many people from the outer islands of Okinawa came to the main island to work. The new prefectural government set up special development funds to encourage

emigration and cultivation of lands in northern Okinawa, Miyako Island, and the Yaeyama island group (Kerr 1958; Yoshikawa 1996), and by the turn of the century, organized emigration to Japanese colonies in the Pacific and outside of the Japanese empire to Hawaii, Peru, and elsewhere had begun (Kerr 1958; Nakasone 2002). In the midst of these massive dislocations, the trope of the *yādui* (rural villages settled by the deposed Ryukyuan gentry) emerged as the object of nostalgic longing among those who traced their lineages back to Shuri (Nelson 2008).

22. That the two classes did in fact mix frequently, even during the Ryūkyū Kingdom when laws prohibited such unions, is evident from the fact that during the 1960s a number of commoner *munchū* claimed upper-class status based on descent from liaisons between unmarried upper-class men and commoner women (Lebra 1966, 159).

23. While prejudice and discrimination against Okinawans was rife among Japanese colonial administrators, more research is needed on Japanese-Okinawan sexual relations during the colonial period. Japanese businessmen sent to Naha during the early decades of the twentieth century, like Satsuma merchants and Chinese investiture officials before them, were known to frequent Tsuji, Naha's brothel district (Christy 1993, 621–622; Barske 2013). Moreover, a number of lower level Japanese administrators assigned to rural districts married Okinawan women and started families. Scholars have reported that Japanese assimilation policies in other colonies (for example, Korea) encouraged intermarriage between Japanese colonialists and conquered peoples (Oguma 1995; Suzuki 1992, 78–87, discussed in Morris-Suzuki 1998, 96).

24. The Okinawan term *naichā*, referring to persons from mainland Japan, often carries the negative undertones of an ethnic slur.

25. The concept of interdiscursivity refers to "semiosis across encounters" (Gal 2007) or how connections operate across multiple discursive encounters where cultural understandings and social identities are being formulated and contested. Interdiscursive linkages involve lifting a given element of discourse (for example, a particular phrase or metaphor, a set of value judgments, or other framing device) from one setting—that is, decontextualizing it—and inserting it into another setting where it is recontextualized (Bauman and Briggs 1990). When a piece of discourse is moved from one context to another, it carries along aspects of the earlier context, but it is also transformed in the new context.

26. Davinder Bhowmik has written that themes of love and adventure, typical of more affluent regions, have not gained much traction in Okinawan prose fiction (2008, 180). Rather, she argues, Okinawan literature has dwelt on questions of identity and power. The examples that I examine here demonstrate that the two sets of themes need not be mutually exclusive. Within the folk stories and literary examples I have compiled, it is precisely in stories of unsanctioned relationships characterized by social inequality that themes of romantic love tend to occur.

27. Historically, Tametomo's shipwreck would have occurred during the 1150s. According to Japanese chronicles, Tametomo was exiled to Izu Oshima by the Taira clan following the Hōgen Rebellion (1156). There, he committed *seppuku*, probably the first known case in Japan (Turnbull 1977, 37). The tale recorded in the *Seikan* picks up from this time as Tametomo attempted to flee to Okinawa. Written after Satsuma's invasion of Ryūkyū in 1609, the *Seikan* narrative was likely constructed by court regents to connect and legitimize the relation of Japan's imperial family with the Ryūkyū Islands (Kerr 1958). The Minamoto family was founded in the tenth century by a grandson of the Emperor Seiwa. The legend of Tametomo in Okinawa was later resurrected to legitimize the annexation of the Ryūkyū Kingdom by Japan in 1879 (Loo 2014).

2. RACE, MEMORY, AND MILITARY MEN'S SEXUALITY

1. The psychological and social consequences of military training are a matter of public concern in U.S. military base towns worldwide. Professional counselors and feminist scholars discuss a systematic relationship between militarized masculinity and violence against women (Kim and Sawdey 1981; Enloe 2000), and Okinawan feminists have drawn on this work in their analyses of crimes committed by U.S. servicemen in Okinawa. The military itself has sponsored studies of violent acts committed by off-duty personnel, exploring for example the allegation that spouse abuse occurs with greater frequency in the military population than among civilians (U.S. Department of Defense 2003).

2. Popular images are also daily reinforced by the behavior of some U.S. service members who seem unconcerned with how they are perceived by Okinawans. At the Nago City Fisheries Cooperative Association *hārī* races in 2002, for example, two members of the U.S. Marine Corps team from Camp Schwab showed up bared to the waist, faces and torsos painted in greens and browns. During the event, these two cheered aggressively for the Camp Schwab team, screaming until they were hoarse and beating their chests, drowning out the other spectators. They were frightening. The military leadership educates troops about appropriate off-base behavior, but the current mandatory orientations are seemingly inadequate.

3. *Kurombō* is a strongly pejorative term used to refer to persons of African descent. The term is commonly translated as "negro" due to its reference to black skin, but the Japanese term carries much stronger negative connotations (see Russell 2009).

4. According to the Okinawa Prefectural Government, 5,919 crimes were committed by U.S. military and civilian personnel from 1972 until 2016. Of these, 576 were heinous offenses, including 129 cases of rape (Okinawa Prefectural Government 2018). Feminists argue that these numbers represent only the tip of the iceberg since such crimes often go unreported. No comparable statistics are available for the period before reversion to Japanese sovereignty (1972). During the occupation, Okinawan police were not permitted to arrest U.S. personnel or conduct investigations. All cases were handled by U.S. military police and U.S. courts martial. Following reversion, U.S. jurisdiction in criminal cases came under the purview of the 1960 status of forces agreement. Article xvii (3) (c) states that U.S. authorities may retain custody of accused U.S. service members and civilian employees within the confines of U.S. military bases until they have been formally indicted by Japanese authorities. Okinawan critics argue that this stipulation results in delayed investigations and sometimes avoidance of criminal prosecution altogether when accused service members receive orders to return to the United States.

5. Sexual violence against children and women outside of entertainment areas was a rallying point. The rape and murder of a six-year-old girl in September 1955 (the so-called Yumiko-chan incident) sparked public outcry and alongside the resistance of local landowners to land appropriations galvanized the popular movement for reversion to Japanese sovereignty (Tanji 2006). The U.S. soldier who committed the crime was sentenced to death by a U.S. court martial but was later transferred back to the United States without notifying Okinawan authorities and given a reduced sentence (Tanji 2006, 71).

6. Molasky has written about the appropriation of the female body by male Okinawan writers in order to establish male victimhood, allegorically linking the rape of individual women to the rape of Okinawa. "Colonial or military transgression of geographical territory is conjoined with sexual transgression of the individual body. These and related tropes rely on a logic that conflates individual body with national body and designates the transgressed body as female, emphasizing her subjugation and helplessness before the dominant male intruders" (1999, 28).

7. The shame is partly associated with the circumstances surrounding so-called group suicides. Koji Taira (1999) has written on the problematic usage of the Japanese phrase

shudan jiketsu in Japanese history textbooks to describe wartime suicides in Okinawa. The word *jiketsu*, he writes, connotes a heroic, awe-inspiring, splendid act. The phrase is used to honor and glorify a person who has had the extraordinary courage to kill his self. This interpretation of Okinawan deaths is offensive to many Okinawan war survivors, who insist that these "suicides" should instead be characterized as murders committed by the Japanese imperial army. In order to prevent Okinawans from divulging secrets about Japanese defense arrangements, the army undertook an extensive propaganda campaign to convince Okinawans that they would suffer less if they killed themselves than if they surrendered or were captured. Some were given hand grenades, and stories of groups of old men, women, and children huddling together around a single grenade to enhance its killing efficiency are common. Linda Angst (2001) has elaborated on other factors that inhibited women especially from sharing their wartime memories, including their socialization as Japanese colonial subjects during the prewar period, their experiences of powerlessness during the occupation, and their continuing marginalization within local political circles, which tend to be dominated by men.

8. Within interaction, identities emerge as macro-level demographic categories (for example, Okinawan, African American, soldier), as temporary and interactionally specific stances and participant roles (for example, narrator, listener, conversant), or as local ethnographically emergent cultural positions (for example, victim, survivor, occupier, outsider). Such identities are indexed linguistically through labels, implicatures, stances, styles, or linguistic structures and systems (Bucholtz and Hall 2005). Moreover, within interaction, identities are relationally constructed, depending upon the relative positions and relationships between speakers and listeners. Ultimately, a focus on social interaction reveals the co-constructed, contextually embedded, and fragile or fluid nature of identity constructs.

9. The term *script* is drawn from Ann Laura Stoler's (2002) essays on memory work in Java. Stoler uses the term in three distinct but overlapping ways. First, she discusses the kind of rehearsed memory stories that roll off the tongue, either because they have become well-honed through repeated telling or because they follow official history. Participants answered her questions with ease when these ready-made scripts could be brought to bear, but when no scripts existed for the time period and content she was interested in, informants tended to stumble through their answers—hesitating, evading, or falling back on disjointed, impressionistic images and avoiding use of the narrative form altogether. Second, the term *scripts* is used in a more active sense—for example, when participants who had worked as servants in the homes of Dutch colonials "reinscribed" colonial categories in their memory narratives, turning familiar Dutch tropes to different, often critical, ends. Finally, Stoler uses *scripts* in the prescriptive sense, discussing how colonial rhetoric positioned European women "as the guardians of morality in a range of imperial contexts. These were gendered assignments that scripted what women were compelled to do as mothers, daughters, sisters, and wives, what marriage choices they made, how they arranged their homes and schooled their young" (Stoler 2002, 211).

10. The first recorded encounter between Japanese and Europeans occurred in 1543 when a Chinese ship carrying several "strange looking" (*kikai*) Portuguese traders landed on Tanegashima, an island off the coast of Kyushu. According to a 1606 account, Chinese crew members from the vessel explained that the foreigners were "barbarian merchants from the southwest (*seinan banshu no kako*)" who "roughly distinguished between ruler and subject" as the Chinese and Japanese did, but who were illiterate and lacked table manners (quoted in Racel 2011, 42).

11. References to long hair, bushy eyebrows, beards, and body hair were also common in Japanese illustrations of Ainu and Ryukyuans, indicating their intermediate status between Japanese and barbarian outsiders (Gottlieb 2006, 80).

12. In Okinawa, the corresponding term *urandā* also referred to Dutch persons and white Europeans in general. Historian Sakihara Mitsugu's dictionary of *uchinaguchi* (Ryukyuan language), published posthumously in 2006, lists "Westerner," "European," and "American" as possible definitions (196).

13. Although overwhelmed militarily and economically dependent upon Satsuma for the metals needed for its tribute trade with China, many Ryukyuan intellectuals and government ministers looked to China for cultural expertise and practical models of governance. Ryūkyū's kings gained legitimacy through formal investiture by the Chinese emperor, regular tribute missions traveled from Naha to Fuzhou and Beijing, and the two countries conducted formal and informal educational exchanges. Shimazu lords supported these activities because they enabled Satsuma to trade indirectly with China despite failed negotiations between China and Japan.

14. *World Geography* was adopted as a school textbook during the early Meiji period and over one million copies were sold (Takezawa 2015). Fukuzawa first encountered the stage theory of social progress in nineteenth century American geography textbooks. He then pursued the origins of the idea in the writings of Adam Smith, Adam Ferguson, John Hill Burton, Francois Guizot, Henry Thomas Buckle, and other political economists (Craig 2009). Other Western thinkers popular among Meiji intellectuals included Charles Darwin—several translations of *The Descent of Man* were published during the Meiji period—and Herbert Spencer. Approximately thirty translations of Spencer's works appeared in Japan between 1877 and 1900 (Russell 2007, 32).

15. The group included Jahana Noboru, Takamine Chōkyō, Nakijin Chōhan, Kishimoto Gashō, and Ōta Chōfu, all of whom played important leadership roles upon returning to Okinawa.

16. See Oguma Eiji (1995) and Morris-Suzuki (1998) for extended discussions of Japanese debates surrounding the racial origins of the Japanese, beginning in the Meiji period.

17. Isa Junko's story was initially published in Japanese in a volume of war testimonials of female survivors of the Battle of Okinawa (Keyso 2000, original volume not specified). The first postwar collection of three volumes of survivor testimonials was published under the title *Okinawa Sen* (Battle of Okinawa) by the Okinawa Prefectural Board of Education in 1971 and 1974. A fourth volume, based on historical documents and survivors' accounts was published in 2017 (Kimura 2017).

18. Kimberley Phillips (2012) argues that experiences of segregation and racial violence in the U.S. military played a role in motivating African Americans to mobilize and support the civil rights and black power movements in the United States. In turn, African American soldiers brought civil rights and black power discourses to Japan, Okinawa, and elsewhere, where they were embraced by local intellectuals and writers. John Russell notes that Japanese leftist writers of the 1960s and 1970s "were familiar with the works of James Baldwin, Richard Wright, and Frantz Fanon and supported the U.S. civil rights movements . . . . Blackness helped to add definition to their own ambivalent attitudes toward white America, their identity as Japanese, and their struggles against racism directed at Japan's internal minorities at a time when Japanese popular images of blacks were decidedly negative and public sympathies were with beleaguered whites" (1998, 120; see also Onishi 2013).

19. In both places, civilians saw themselves as having been liberated from social and political domination of the Japanese military. Okinawans, however, tended to see themselves as a historically separate subject population victimized by Japanese soldiers in a much more corporeal way, through propaganda-induced "suicides" and outright murder.

20. Simultaneous U.S. occupations of Okinawa and the Philippines enabled the circulation of U.S. military personnel and Filipino labor troops, as well as American racial ideologies, between the two imperial outposts throughout the postwar period (Zulueta 2017).

21. Hundreds of Okinawan women did marry Filipino scouts during the early postwar period. Colonel William S. Triplet (2001), commander of the 44th Philippine Scouts Infantry Regiment, discussed the earliest of these marriages in his personal memoirs. Translator Nakama Tetsu described to me his research on the experiences of such women: according to Nakama, the U.S. military arranged for the transport of hundreds of Okinawan women to the Philippines when their Filipino husbands were released from occupation duty and sent home in 1953–1954. The women were invited onto Kadena Air Base, asked if they were willing to accompany their husbands to the Philippines, and directed to sign a tall stack of papers. Many of the women did not read English and did not understand exactly what it was they were signing. As it turned out, they were signing away their Japanese citizenship and applying for Philippine passports. Nakama helped twenty or more women recover Japanese citizenship before leaving Okinawa, but he surmised that many more women, perhaps hundreds, had moved to the Philippines without understanding what had happened to them.

22. When personnel shortages and racial tensions became acute in the early 1950s, army officers in the Korean theater turned to desegregation as a solution (Mershon and Schlossman 1998). Desegregation evolved out of the process of troop replacement, beginning with informal agreements between officers of the Eighth Army and officers of particular divisions and regiments who were willing to accept African American soldiers as replacements. In July 1951, desegregation was formally authorized by the Department of the Army for the entire Far East Command. The process was completed by May 1952, and large-scale desegregation soon spread to other army commands in the United States and around the world.

23. The segregated 24th Infantry Unit was reassigned to Camp Majestic in Gifu Prefecture in February 1947, where they were integrated into the all-white 25th Infantry Division. Despite institution-mandated integration, African American troops continued to experience informal social segregation with limited contact and interaction with white troops. Okada (2011) examines evolving racial and gendered notions of justice, power, and identity among African American soldiers in Gifu within the parameters of the privileged position they enjoyed as members of the U.S. occupation forces, as well as the racial discrimination they encountered in the U.S. Army and in their interactions with Japanese citizens.

24. The narrative explanations of Iha Mayumi and Terrance Carter and the Katsuyama Cave incident story are examples of "racializing discourses," defined by Bonnie Urciuoli as language that "indexes notions about fixed social hierarchies and proper social location, notions that natural types of persons exist, notions about the natural properties of person that make up those types, notions about where those types are from in the world, and where they should or shouldn't be and why" (2011, E114). Such discourses work primarily through processes of social marking, "through which any diacritic of social personhood—including class, ethnicity, generation, kinship/affinity, and positions within fields of power—comes to be essentialized, naturalized, and/or biologized . . . into fixed species of otherness" (Silverstein 2005, 364). The examples in this chapter mark African American soldiers in relation to unmarked white soldiers, U.S. military personnel in relation to Okinawans, and Okinawans in relation to mainland Japanese. Narratives are a powerful means of communicating such models of identity, and recurring narratives are one mechanism through which relatively stable models of identity can emerge and become robustly associated with particular groups (Wortham et al. 2011).

25. Segregated recreation districts developed outside of U.S. military bases throughout Asia and the Pacific. "The Ville" was the name applied to areas that catered primarily to white soldiers whether in Okinawa, Tokyo, or Korea (Moon 1997; Millard 1999; Bird 2001). In Okinawa, the area for black soldiers was called "the Bush." In the Philippines, it was

called "the Jungle." Similar nomenclature across base towns suggests the overall uniformity of U.S. military leisure culture throughout Asia and the Pacific. A 1960 report filed by U.S. congressman Charles Diggs, who visited Okinawa to investigate complaints of racial discrimination against U.S. servicemen, concluded that the segregated pattern in Koza was due to a minority of white airmen who had, through systematic extortion, compelled other servicemen as well as civilian merchants to confine black airmen to the Teruya area (Mershon and Schlossman 1998, 278). In response to the Diggs report, the Government of the Ryukyu Islands passed laws making this sort of segregation illegal, but the laws proved difficult to enforce (McCune 1975).

26. From late 1945, the U.S. military venereal disease control system applied to all individuals whose occupations involved a possible threat of venereal disease transmission to American GIs, including dancers, waitresses, maids, and female employees of the U.S. occupation forces (Takeuchi 2010). The VD tracer involved finding women who were suspected to be sources of venereal disease and imposing examinations and medication. Infected soldiers were required to report to medical officers and were then turned over to the provost marshal to identify women with whom they had had contact.

27. Takushi Etsuko (2000) has explored the ways in which racial associations followed Okinawan women after they immigrated to the United States. According to Takushi, women who married white military men were viewed as white themselves, while women who married black soldiers were viewed as black. Once in the United States, these two groups of women rarely socialized with one another, constrained as they were by the segregationist practices of the white and black communities they married into.

28. Official histories note the important role played by Japanese American and Okinawan American members of the U.S. Military Intelligence Service, who acted as interpreters during the final days of the Battle of Okinawa. Speaking in Japanese and Okinawan over loudspeakers, these men attempted to persuade Okinawan civilians and Japanese soldiers to come out of the caves and tombs where they were hiding and surrender (Martin 1984; McNaughton 1994). Japanese American linguists were also instrumental in interrogating captured Japanese soldiers and facilitating cooperation between Okinawans and Americans in civilian resettlement camps.

29. The large number of marriages registered during this thirty-day period resulted from the passage of Public Law 126, also known as the Soldier Brides Act. Signed into law by President Truman on June 28, 1947, the law established a temporary reprieve of U.S. immigration quotas, allowing racially ineligible brides to enter the United States and join their husbands, as long as the marriage was performed between July 23 and August 21, 1947.

30. Hispanic/Latino service members are largely absent from personal statements and popular images of military international intimacy. None of the marriages in my interview sample involved Latino military personnel, although I did meet a Mexican American marine engaged to an Okinawan woman at the Marine Corps premarital seminar.

3. LIVING RESPECTABLY AND NEGOTIATING CLASS

1. Hokuzan was the northernmost of the three kingdoms that controlled Okinawa during the fourteenth century. Based in Nakijin, the kingdom flourished from 1314 until 1416, when it was conquered by King Shō Hashi of Chūzan.

2. Similarly, images of camp town prostitution adhere to Korean military brides (Yuh 2002). It is my impression that most Asian military spouses struggle with such imagery due to the sexual nature of U.S. military leisure culture throughout the Asia-Pacific region.

3. A similar system existed for bringing dance partners onto U.S. bases in wartime and postwar Britain. There, the buses were referred to as "passion wagons." Hiring women as

dance partners was one way that the military directly managed intimate encounters between U.S. troops and local women.

4. The latter type of relationship, common among American GIs and Japanese women in postwar Japan, is referred to in the scholarly literature as concubinage or cohabitation, and was known euphemistically as being a GI's *onrii* (or "only" girlfriend) in Japanese. Ayako Mizumura (2009) has collected the personal stories of Japanese war brides living in Kansas during the early 2000s. Several of Mizumura's interviewees described in detail their lives as *onrii* to consecutive U.S. military men before they met their husbands.

5. Japanese and Okinawan concepts of purity and contamination are not identical. With respect to religion and spirituality, occupation-era ethnographer William Lebra wrote, "In contrast to the Japanese, for whom spiritual purity in large measure implies physical purity, Okinawans tend to conceive ritual purity more as freedom from malevolent spirits . . . . Thus concepts of a need for physical cleanliness for ritual are relatively weak or nonexistent. Conspicuously absent from Okinawan shrine areas are basins for rinsing the mouth and hands, so commonly found within the precincts of Japanese shrines" (1966, 57). In contrast to Lebra's ritual-centered understanding of purity and contamination, I argue that concepts of moral purity—as in cultivating a pure heart and pursuing harmonious relationships, derived from Confucian doctrine—do exist in Okinawa, extending to notions concerning proper sexual relations. Sex workers and others engaging in sex with American military men have been considered by many to be tainted. Amerasian children have been similarly perceived and discriminated against.

6. Michiko Takeuchi (2010) has argued that recruitment practices for the RAA replicated the Japanese imperial military's "comfort women" system, illustrating the continuation of Japanese colonial policies toward lower-class women following surrender.

7. Okichi was the name of the young woman assigned as a consort for Townsend Harris, the first American consul in Japan after Matthew Perry and his "black ships" forced the country to abandon its policy of seclusion in the mid-nineteenth century. Okichi has been incorporated into modern Japanese mythology as a patriotic martyr who sacrificed her own virtue in order to protect the chastity of "good" Japanese women.

8. The speaker's preoccupation with black American GIs is a further example of the racialized memories discussed in chapter 2. Shima's narrative demonstrates the degree to which images of commercial sex and rape are intertwined with notions of racial difference and class respectability in narratives of occupation-era Okinawa.

9. Some Okinawan women's groups rejected the idea of special zones and spoke instead of protecting women's rights. Other citizens' groups discussed how the establishment of zones would enhance the ability of Okinawans to procure American dollars (Takushi 2000, 128).

10. U.S. military management of sexual encounters in Okinawa has included formal licensing systems for sex workers and regular medical checks for bar girls, inspections and certification of restaurants and nightclubs (the infamous A-sign system), and establishing regular procedures for contacting men known to be living off-base with local women despite orders prohibiting cohabitation.

11. Contributing to this shift, a planned depreciation of the U.S. dollar took place in 1985 as a result of the Plaza Accord, signed by the G5 nations: France, West Germany, Japan, the United States, and Great Britain. Intended to spur economic growth on a global level, the value of the yen increased from 242 yen to the dollar in September 1985 to 153 yen to the dollar in 1986. As a result, the purchasing power of U.S. dollar-holding American service members declined dramatically.

12. Yamada Eimi's 1985 novel *Bedtime Eyes* has been credited with sparking a full-scale "black boom" in Japan (Cornyetz 1994, 1996; Russell 1998; see also Molasky 1999; Kelsky 2001). Critics argue that Yamada's book and other works in the same genre dehumanize

black men, treating them as mere props in Japanese women's emerging body awareness. In Okinawa, the derogatory term *kokujo* (short for *kokujin jōgū*, "women who consume black men") refers to women who primarily date black men. During my initial field research in 2001–2002, the terms *amejo* and *kokujo* were used primarily by younger Okinawans.

13. This strategy was not used by the older women I interviewed, who had married U.S. military men prior to reversion. They might have feared that showing any knowledge of or interest in what goes on in Okinawa's entertainment districts could be enough to tie them to the occupation-era sex industry.

14. Several U.S. servicemen I interviewed who were married to Filipina women spoke of their wives' experiences of widespread prejudice and discrimination in Okinawa due to the association of Filipinas with the sex industry.

15. I have retained Nakama's real name and not altered identifying characteristics because his story is already well documented. I was put in touch with Nakama after an article appeared in the newspaper *Ryukyu Shimpo* describing his translation business and his work with international couples (January 16, 2002). He has also appeared in a number of local NHK documentaries concerning international marriage in Okinawa. Finally, the novel *Koibumi Sanjūnen* (*Thirty Years of Love Letters*), written by Saki Ryūzō (1986), is set in and around Nakama's translation shop.

16. Former women's counselor at the Naha City Women's Center and four-time Naha City assemblywoman Takazato Suzuyo has cochaired Okinawan Women Act Against Military Violence since its inception in 1995. Takazato's many public speeches and published works have been instrumental in bringing international attention to the pattern of sexual violence against women committed by U.S. military personnel in Okinawa. A quote from Takazato opens chapter 2.

4. THE MARINE CORPS MARRIAGE PACKAGE

1. Neither Japanese government nor U.S. military statistics are reliable indicators of how many U.S. military couples marry "out in town." Municipal offices process approximately two hundred marriages a year between American men and Okinawan women. Prefectural numbers do not include couples who fly to Guam, Hawaii, or the continental United States to get married. U.S. military records are even less comprehensive, as they only include couples who marry "by the book," while excluding those who marry without official military permission.

2. By 2017, marines assigned to III MEF were no longer required to submit an Application for Authorization to Marry to their command. Navy personnel were still required to comply with the updated COMNAVFORJAPANINST 1752.1R, with procedures virtually identical to those described here. The U.S. Marine Corps, Navy, Air Force, and Army all have regulations governing the marriage process, and there is considerable variation depending upon branch of service, region, time period, and among individual commanding officers.

3. As mentioned previously, status of forces agreements (SOFAs) are agreements between a host country and a foreign nation stationing military forces in that country. SOFAs establish the rights and privileges of foreign personnel within the host country, including issues such as entry into and exit from the country, tax liabilities, postal services, employment for host-country nationals, and civil and criminal jurisdiction over bases and personnel. General Orders of conduct establish proscribed or prohibited behaviors of personnel within a particular area of responsibility. For example, General Order No. 1, issued by the Department of the Army in 2009 for U.S. troops in Iraq and Afghanistan, prohibited sexual contact of any kind with local nationals or third-party nationals who were not members of coalition forces (*New York Times* n.d.).

4. During the same period, Congress was preparing to pass the War Brides Act of 1945, which granted entry to tens of thousands of European women who had married U.S.

servicemen and to several hundred Chinese GI brides, the latter group as a political reward offered to China for its loyalty during the Pacific conflict.

5. These marriages took place despite the continuing antifraternization policy. Antifraternization laws were in place in Japan for the first four years of the occupation. Koshiro points out that a similar law in occupied Germany lasted for less than five months and suggests that racism motivated such policies (Koshiro 1999).

6. On June 28, 1947, President Harry S. Truman signed Public Law No. 126, otherwise known as the Soldier Brides Act, which allowed racially ineligible brides to enter the United States and join their husbands as long as the marriage was performed between July 23 and August 21, 1947. The day after this thirty-day reprieve of existing immigration quotas, the Associated Press reported that a total of 823 marriages had taken place in occupied Japan between American men and Japanese women (Koshiro 1999, 157). In Okinawa, sixty-three couples filed marriage paperwork. Fifty-three of these marriages involved Japanese American military personnel (Takushi 2000, 117).

7. The description here applied to Marine Corps and navy personnel in Okinawa in 2001–2002. For air force personnel, marriage counseling, medical examinations, financial statements, and the Application for Authorization to Marry were all optional. Written authorization by a senior commander was required, but which documents were necessary and what form this authorization took were left to the discretion of the area commander. For nonmilitary personnel (that is, U.S. civilians employed by the U.S. Department of Defense), the Affidavit for Competency to Marry was issued by the U.S. consulate's office in Naha.

8. To apply for a U.S. spouse immigrant visa, Okinawan spouses had to repeat the medical examination and blood tests for an additional $250 fee. They were also required to obtain a Japanese police investigation certificate. Before the late 1990s, Japanese police certificates were required as part of the marriage package as well. At that time, the Japanese government performed police checks for the U.S. military as a courtesy, without requiring payment. By 2001–2002, the Japanese government had stopped this practice because it had become too expensive. Rather than pay for the checks, the Marine Corps had decided to discontinue the requirement altogether (interview with premarital coordinator Randy Tulabut, July 29, 2002). An overview of the U.S. spouse immigrant visa process, including required petitions, affidavits, fees, application forms, documentation including police certificates, interview, and medical examination and vaccinations appears on the U.S. Department of State website: https://travel.state.gov/content/travel/en/us-visas/immigrate/family-immigration/immigrant-visa-for-spouse.html.

9. The U.S. immigrant visa application requires police investigations to be conducted in the country of nationality and the country of residence, as well as all countries where the applicant has lived for longer than one year. One Filipina spouse told me she had met and married her husband in Korea, where she had lived and worked for several years, and then accompanied him to Okinawa when he was reassigned to Camp Hansen. When her husband received orders to return to the United States, they applied for an immigrant visa and had to order police certificates from the Philippines, Korea, and Japan. It took several months for the Korean police certificate to arrive, and they feared that she would be stranded in Okinawa.

10. Orientalist stereotypes of Asian and especially Japanese women are discussed at length in Johnson 1988; Ma 1996; Kelsky 2001; and Liu 2003.

11. Inclusion of a presentation on U.S. citizenship procedures in the premarital seminar suggests that service members and their prospective spouses regularly inquired about options for naturalization. Active-duty service members and veterans of the U.S. military may qualify for naturalization after just one year of military service. Japanese and other foreign spouses may also qualify for expedited or overseas naturalization. However, many of the Okinawan spouses I knew were not interested in becoming U.S. citizens because

this would mean giving up their Japanese citizenship. Japanese law does not permit dual citizenship except under limited circumstances. Under Japan's revised Nationality Law, passed in 1985, Japanese nationals are required to renounce their Japanese citizenship upon naturalization in a foreign country. Children with dual citizenship must make a "declaration of choice" between the ages of twenty and twenty-two, in which they choose to renounce either their Japanese nationality or their foreign citizenship. This was a matter of significant concern to the Okinawan spouses who participated in my research and likely was a key reason for including the U.S. citizenship brief in the premarital seminar. Of note, most couples with adult children whom I interviewed admitted that their children continued to carry multiple passports past the age of twenty-two despite the prohibition. Not a single American husband declared an interest in naturalizing and becoming a citizen of Japan.

12. Gray's published works (for example, Gray 1992) have been critiqued by feminist scholars for promoting essentialist thinking, reinforcing unequal power relations between the sexes, and privileging heterosexual intercourse over other sexual activities and sexualities (Potts 1998; Peterson 2000; Dozier, Raine, & and Schwartz 2001).

13. Attempts to promote PREP outside the United States have been mixed. In the introduction of the Leader Manual, the authors highlighted the results of two studies concerning the efficacy of PREP in Germany and Australia. In Germany, couples who took PREP communicated better than control couples who either had no special training or took the traditional premarital training offered by the German Catholic Church. In Australia, couples at low risk for divorce showed no significant advantage over low-risk couples who opted to participate in another intervention. High-risk couples, however, showed significant advantages over those taking the alternate intervention. The manual then ran quickly through a series of studies conducted in the Netherlands and the United States that found no differences between those taking the program and control couples. The authors critiqued the statistical validity of these studies and then moved on to a different study of premarital couples in the United States that was "greatly encouraging of prevention efforts" (Markman, Stanley, and Blumberg 1999, 12–14). No studies of international couples were cited.

14. "Don't Ask, Don't Tell, Don't Pursue" (Defense Directive 1304.26) was instituted by the Clinton administration on February 28, 1994, and remained in effect until September 20, 2011. Today, the policy is widely seen as a transition law situated between earlier all-out bans on military service by gay and lesbian individuals and later provisions which enabled individuals to serve regardless of openly expressed sexual orientation. In 2013, after the Supreme Court ruled the Defense of Marriage Act unconstitutional, the U.S. Department of Defense implemented policies to extend family benefits to same-sex spouses of U.S. military members. Osburn and Benecke (1997) outline the contentious political debates that surrounded the "Don't Ask, Don't Tell" policy at the time of my observation.

15. Harrison and Laliberté (1997) argue that the military uses a socially constructed polarity between masculine and feminine as the cementing principle that unites men into combat-ready units and justifies the extraordinary expectations placed on wives, who must assume all of a couple's domestic work and childcare while their husbands are deployed, relinquish their own paid employment every time their husbands are posted to a new place, and devote a significant amount of time to unpaid volunteer work within the military community. Although most combat billets are now open to women—the navy announced in March 2016 that the first female enlisted SEALS could be assigned to units in fall 2017 (Seck 2016)—Harrison and Laliberté argue that at an ideological level, the belief that combat is essentially a male activity has not been seriously challenged.

16. Put simply, "readiness" means that military personnel and their family members must be ready at all times to do whatever is necessary for the service member's unit to

successfully complete its mission. The *User's Guide to Marine Corps Values* contains the following statement about family involvement: "Clearly, unit readiness requirements are constant. But why are personal and family readiness such key components of making the Marine Corps 'the nation's force in readiness'? Because when personal affairs are in order, Marines and their commanders can fully focus on the mission. And while no amount of planning can provide for every eventuality, careful preparation in these areas will significantly reduce distractions, allowing the Marine's full attention to the military matters at hand. Distracted Marines can be a burden on their command and a danger to themselves and fellow Marines" (U.S. Department of the Navy 1998, 12, p. 1).

17. The inability of civilian spouses to sign legal documents becomes particularly problematic when the service member is deployed elsewhere for training exercises or combat. The military has developed a complex system of powers of attorney to compensate and keep military households functioning while service members are away or otherwise unavailable to take care of legal matters.

18. SOFA status is held by U.S. military and civilian personnel whose jobs are covered by the terms of the U.S.-Japan status of forces agreement. Dependents (such as spouses, children) of such individuals may also have SOFA status, which enables them to live in Okinawa without acquiring Japanese residency for the length of the service member's assignment.

19. Nearly 28 percent of all permanent residents in Japan who are U.S. citizens reside in Okinawa Prefecture (Japanese Ministry of Justice 2017). These numbers do not include military or civilian personnel and dependents with SOFA status.

20. As a result of the planned depreciation of the dollar agreed upon by the G5 nations in the Plaza Accord, the value of the Japanese yen increased from 242 yen to the dollar in September 1985 to 153 yen to the dollar in 1986. As a result, the purchasing power of American service members in Okinawa declined dramatically.

5. CREATING FAMILY AND COMMUNITY ACROSS MILITARY FENCE LINES

1. This event, known as *seinen iwai* (birth year party), celebrates important birthdays of elderly villagers who share the same Chinese zodiac sign. For example, in 2017, those turning sixty-one, seventy-three, and eighty-five years of age, all born in the year of the chicken/rooster, were honored together at community celebrations throughout Okinawa. Persons turning ninety-seven years of age were honored separately at a celebration called the *kajimaya*.

2. *Hārī*, or dragon boat races, are held in fishing communities throughout Okinawa during the late spring and summer. The races were traditionally held to give thanks to the sea god and pray for the safety and prosperity of fishermen (Nakachi 1996). Today, they continue to be sponsored by local fishermen's associations. Racing the length of the harbor in colorfully painted wooden boats (*sabani*), rowing teams sponsored by local businesses and organizations compete against one another while local citizens cheer noisily for friends and neighbors. U.S. military bases often sponsor teams at *hārī* events. Henoko's festival features a unique form of "street *hārī*," in which wheels are affixed to the boats, and teams "row" their way down the main street of the village.

3. Hank's decision to pursue Japanese permanent residency is discussed in chapter 4.

4. Marine Corps Family Team Building (FTB) is a multifaceted family training and readiness program that aims to provide military spouses with a better understanding of Marine Corps culture, as well as skills and resources for becoming resilient, self-sufficient, and self-reliant members of the military community. The Marine Corps program was adapted from Army Family Team Building, established during the early 1990s in response to problems encountered during the Gulf War. Diana Brancaforte's (2000) dissertation contains a detailed ethnographic description of the Army FTB program at Fort Huachuca, Texas. Brancaforte primarily discusses the disciplinary components of FTB, which resemble those discussed in

chapter 4 with regard to overseas marriage requirements in Okinawa. The discussion here focuses on the ways in which Okinawan military spouses utilize FTB programs like ISP as tools for self-empowerment and as a method for resisting negative perceptions of foreign-born spouses within the U.S. military and Okinawan communities.

5. Although the program in Okinawa was open to all international spouses of U.S. military personnel, the regular attendees were all women, and ISP information materials regularly referred to participants as "wives."

6. According to Karen Hanovitch, the biggest challenge facing ISP was how to reach Okinawan spouses. Most of the regular participants had learned about the program through word-of-mouth. Many of the spouses were not officially known to the Marine Corps. They and their husbands had not completed the marriage package and received official command approval to marry. Instead, like the Eisners in chapter 4, they had gotten married "out in town," and as a result were not command-sponsored. Attempting to include this population, Hanovitch designed the program so that spouses who completed the three-day workshop would earn the right to seek federal employment, a benefit normally reserved for command-sponsored spouses.

7. L.I.N.K.S. is an acronym that stands for Lifestyle, Insights, Networking, Knowledge, and Skills. The L.I.N.K.S. programs in Okinawa are mentoring programs for marine family members taught by marine spouses. Classes provide insight into the military lifestyle, giving family members a place to network with other military families. Participants learn about Marine Corps history and rank, local installation resources, services, and benefits, military pay, separation and deployment, communication styles, investing in the community, and Marine Corps traditions. In Okinawa, FTB has created L.I.N.K.S. sessions for children, teens, and American and Japanese/Okinawan spouses.

8. In Japan, vehicles owned by U.S. military personnel and their dependents under the status of forces agreement have special white license plates with a "Y" where the Japanese *hiragana* character is normally displayed. Personnel on "accompanied" tours are generally permitted two passenger vehicles and two motorcycles per licensed driver, whereas "unaccompanied" personnel are limited to one passenger vehicle and one motorcycle. Personnel deployed to Okinawan bases temporarily (without a permanent duty assignment) are not eligible to own vehicles.

9. Support for reversion had initially coalesced during the 1950s, in response to the U.S. military's expropriation of land for military bases. By 1966, annual reversion rallies were attracting tens of thousands of participants, and protests were growing against the use of Okinawa-based B-52s in Vietnam (Aldous 2003). In December 1970, public outrage over a string of acquittals by U.S. military courts of servicemen charged with crimes against Okinawans culminated in the Koza riot. In November 1969, President Nixon and Japanese Prime Minister Sato announced that the two governments would begin negotiations for the reversion of Okinawa in 1972.

10. The military began providing a variety of family support services in the 1960s, and these services were expanded during the 1970s and 1980s. Today, organizations such as Army Community Services, Navy Personal Services Centers, and Air Force Family Support Centers offer assistance directly to families, including legal advice, family counseling, financial help, English classes for non-native speakers, and relocation assistance.

11. Throughout the 1970s, the army and the Marine Corps failed to meet recruiting goals. In comparison with other branches of military service, both branches—associated with blue-collar work in combat situations—attracted disproportionate numbers of nonwhite recruits from lower socioeconomic backgrounds. With an institutional culture that encourages and rewards traditional warrior masculinity, the Marine Corps has identified in its own self-critique a chronic undervaluing of the supporting establishment, female recruits, and families.

12. The Okinawan term *naicha* or *naichā* may carry the negative undertones of an ethnic slur. Shimanaka does not mention such connotations, explaining that the term is used "in a very warm way" in order to "congratulate Japanese people who live on Okinawa and become part Okinawan" (1999, 7).

13. Shimanaka's description of Okinawan family and community relationships sounds remarkably similar to descriptions of families in mainland Japan, despite her assertion to the contrary. The primacy of parent-child bonds, especially mother-child bonds, over husband-wife relationships has been cited as a distinguishing feature of the Japanese family since the Meiji period (Vogel 1971; Hendry 1981; Uno 1999; Allison 2000; Rosenberger 2001; White 2002). Moreover, it is common for young people in mainland Japan to live with their parents until marriage, given the expense of establishing and maintaining a separate household (Ogasawara 1998; Rosenberger 2001). Indeed, Shimanaka's comments index, however unintentionally, the continuity between Okinawan and Japanese family norms, making Okinawan difference a matter of degree rather than type.

14. A detailed discussion of changing Okinawan family norms appears in chapter 1. While such norms are frequently cited, they do not often reflect Okinawan social reality. During the immediate postwar period, ethnographers claimed that residential households in Okinawa typically consisted of a man and a woman, their children, and sometimes one or more grandparents. Yet, as Maretzki and Maretzki (1966) noted, war-related dislocation and death substantially affected the composition of households. In the northeast village of Taira, only eighteen of sixty total households actually consisted of patrilineal extended families (Maretzki and Maretzki 1966, 50). The analysis here explores the conditions under which such discourses continue to be invoked and to what ends. Considering the gap between popular discourses on the family and the practices of real individuals and families, the actual flexibility of Okinawan families is explored.

15. The *tōtōmē* is a cabinet on the *butsudan* (family altar) which houses the *ihai* (mortuary tablets), small rectangular lacquered memorial tablets with the deceased's posthumous name engraved on the front and the pre-death name on the back. Traditionally, only the ancestors of the patrilineage were enshrined in the *tōtōmē*. The *tōtōmē* was ideally kept in the house of the oldest living generation, with the *chōnan*'s wife performing most of the daily ritual activities. Daily care for the *ihai* included incense burning, offering food and drink, placing fresh flowers, and prayer (Matayoshi and Tafton 2000). In addition to the *butsudan*, many households also contain a prayer spot next to the stove in the kitchen, referred to as a *hinukan* (literally, hearth deity), consisting of an arrangement of tea, rice, ash, a cup for *awamori* (Okinawan rice liquor), a vessel for burning incense, and traditionally, three stones from the beach. Okinawan women may pray to the *hinukan* deity for fortune and protection of the inhabitants of the home, informing the deity of important changes such as births, marriages, or deaths. The *hinukan* is believed to have been introduced from China to Okinawa during the Ryūkyū Kingdom era, whereas Japanese-style *butsudan* were adopted later, after Satsuma's invasion of Okinawa (1609).

16. My use of the example from Hamabata's (1990) ethnography of Tokyo business families is not meant to suggest that Okinawan and mainland Japanese altars and rituals are identical. Distinctive Okinawan beliefs and practices are discussed at length in Lebra (1966) and Matayoshi and Tafton (2000).

17. *Shīmī* (*seimeisai* in Japanese) takes place in April and is a time set aside to honor a family's deceased relatives. During this period, family members and extended kin gather at their ancestral tombs to clear away the underbrush and make ritual offerings, and then share a family feast and spend time together.

18. The discussion here has focused on social norms regarding succession and family-based rituals. Japanese law of succession, based on the 1947 revision of the Japanese Civil Code (applicable to Okinawa after reversion in 1972), however, recognizes relationships

and rules for succession that differ markedly from such norms. Under the revised Civil Code, all property—money, house, land, goods, and so on—was distributed equally among siblings, regardless of sex or birth order, diminishing the importance of the *chōnan*. Current Japanese statutory law provides for equal division of an estate between the spouse of the deceased (who inherits half) and the deceased's children (among whom the remaining half is divided). However, succession law also includes provisions for children to renounce their inheritance, an option which is commonly taken in order to avoid splitting up an estate. In such cases, the prerogative of the *chōnan* is often invoked as an explanation for why the decision was made.

19. In 2013, Okinawa's rate was 2.59 divorces per thousand people, while the national rate was just 1.84 (Japanese Ministry of Health, Labour and Welfare 2014a).

20. Under the Ryūkyū Kingdom, a hierarchy of female priestesses (*nuru, noro* in Japanese) parallel to the hierarchy of male political appointees held ultimate authority over ritual matters (Lebra 1966; Takara 1994; Wacker 2000). The head priestess (*kikoe-ogimi*) in Shuri was assisted by regional priestesses, who in turn coordinated with village-level priestesses. Today, *nuru* priestesses continue to perform prayer duties in communities throughout northern Okinawa, although they are no longer associated with any central authority.

21. According to Okinawa Prefecture, 422 divorces involving Japanese women and American men were registered during the seven years from 2009 to 2014 (calculated from data compiled by the Japanese Ministry of Health, Labour and Welfare).

22. The connection between divorce and U.S. military personnel has also become intertwined with the politically charged issue of Amerasian children abandoned by their U.S. military fathers (Negishi 2000; Sims 2000b; Curtin 2002b). However, the claim that Okinawa's high divorce rate is due to military international couples seems exaggerated since a smaller percentage of the overall number of divorces are registered by international couples in Okinawa than in mainland Japan (*Okinawa Josei Zaidan* 1999).

23. It is not clear how well military support services serve international spouses on military bases in the United States. At the time of Diana Brancaforte's research on Army Family Team Building at Fort Huachuca in the late 1990s, programs or accommodations for international spouses had not yet been developed. Brancaforte reported that foreign-born spouses thus experienced severe isolation and marginalization among U.S. army wives.

24. Anecdotal evidence suggests that even today these are common themes in the lives of military couples who do not have access to institutional or family and community support, including unmarried couples, noncommand sponsored wives and dependents, and separated or retired personnel living in remote locales like northern Okinawa.

CONCLUSION

1. The restaurant Teahouse of the August Moon, known in Japanese as *Matsu no Shita* (Beneath the Pine Trees), was opened in the Tsuji entertainment district in Naha by Uehara Eiko in 1952 (Junkerman 2014). Uehara had been raised in the high-class entertainment district, where she rose to prominence. By the 1940s, she had become a teahouse mother, looking after a group of young *juri* (Okinawan geisha). In 1944, restaurants in the district were converted into "sexual comfort facilities" for the Japanese military, and Uehara was assigned to attend to high-ranking officers. Tsuji was destroyed, along with much of Naha, in an American bombardment on October 10, 1944. With the American invasion, Uehara fled south with the Japanese military and hid for weeks in a limestone cave at the southern tip of the island. On June 23, 1945, she surrendered to U.S. forces and was raped by American GIs. After living for some time in the Ishikawa detention camp and working as a maid for American officers, she was recruited to train dancers and

entertain detainees in the camps. Around this time, she gained the attention of army intelligence officer Vern Sneider, who wrote the novel *Teahouse of the August Moon*, modeling the character of Lotus Flower after her. In 1952, taking advantage of her connections in USCAR, which governed Okinawa from 1950 until 1972, Uehara obtained approval to open a restaurant in the old Tsuji district, and named it the Teahouse of the August Moon, after the title of Sneider's book. Sneider's novel, which satirizes the U.S. occupation, was adapted as a play and debuted on Broadway in October 1953. A film followed in 1956, featuring Marlon Brando in yellow face as Sakini, an Okinawan interpreter for the U.S. military. The restaurant became a favorite among American GIs and later Japanese tourists. The restaurant remained in operation until 2007, when Uehara's daughter, Ivy Hosaka, decided to close its doors as its Japanese clientele began migrating to newer restaurants and music venues on Kokusai-dori (Fackler 2012).

2. The *yuta* role is performed by women who have the ability to communicate directly with the spirit world. Okinawans may consult a *yuta* when misfortune strikes or when unusual events transpire to determine the best course of action. *Yuta* identify themselves with a particular spirit, called their *chiji*, upon whom their access to the spirit world is based. Chiemi's visits to sacred sites were likely associated with a search for her *chiji*.

APPENDIX A

1. The Nago City International Friendship and Exchange Committee, a municipal government-sponsored group, coordinated a variety of exchange activities and events that brought Nago citizens together with U.S. Marine Corps personnel from Camp Schwab. The Yanbaru Language Volunteers consisted of Okinawans and foreigners living in the northern region who were fluent in English. The organization was originally established by the Nago City International House to help with preparations for the 2000 G8 summit. As an on-call volunteer, I was asked to provide interpretation and translation assistance at local community events. This afforded me a convenient vantage point for surveying the participants and spectators at the events, and also provided opportunities for informal conversations with my fellow volunteers, a number of whom were involved in international relationships.

2. While ISP no longer appears on the roster of programs offered by Marine Corps Family Team Building, a similar program called the Japanese Spouse Orientation remains on the list of advertised offerings (MCCS Okinawa n.d.).

3. I attended the Marine Corps premarital seminar in March 2002. Later that spring, I attended classes and workshops on Kadena Air Base, including the quarterly international spouses seminar, ESL classes, and couples communication seminars.

4. Of the thirty-eight individuals I interviewed, nine (three women and six men) indicated that they had been married before, with three of those prior marriages counting as Okinawan-U.S. military international marriages. Two women listed their marital status as divorced at the time of our initial interview. One woman was engaged to be married, and another identified herself as a widow.

5. Okinawa Prefecture reports that local, town, and village offices process approximately fifty to sixty divorces per year between Okinawan women and American men, but these figures do not include divorces that have been legalized outside of Okinawa. Neither does this statistic distinguish American men who are SOFA status from those who are not (calculated from data compiled by the Japanese Ministry of Health, Labour and Welfare).

6. These numbers include only Okinawan and U.S. military individuals who agreed to sit for formal tape-recorded interviews. Not included are the dozens of military international couples and individuals with whom I met and spoke to informally during the course of participant observation. Neither have I included the dozen or so non-military-affiliated international couples whom I interviewed for comparative purposes.

References

Akibayashi, K., and S. Takazato. 2009. Okinawa: Women's Struggle for Demilitarization. In *The Bases of Empire: The Global Struggle against U.S. Military Posts*, edited by Catherine Lutz, 243–269. New York: New York University Press.

Aldous, Christopher. 2003. "Achieving Reversion: Protest and Authority in Okinawa, 1952–70." *Modern Asian Studies* 37(2):485–508.

Alexander, Ronni. 2016. "Living with the Fence: Militarization and Military Space on Guahan/Guam." *Gender, Place & Culture* 23(6):869–882.

Allison, Anne. 2000. *Permitted and Prohibited Desires: Mothers, Comics, and Censorship in Japan*. Berkeley: University of California Press.

AmerAsian School in Okinawa. 2012. "Mission Statement." http://amerasianschool okinawa.org/.

Ames, Christopher A. 2007. *Mired in History: Victimhood, Memory, and Ambivalence in Okinawa Prefecture, Japan*. PhD diss., University of Michigan.

Angst, Linda Isako. 1997. "Gendered Nationalism: The Himeyuri Story and Okinawan Identity in Postwar Japan." *POLAR* 20(1):100–113.

——. 2001. *In a Dark Time: Community, Memory, and the Making of Ethnic Selves in Okinawan Women's Narratives*. PhD diss., Yale University.

——. 2003. "The Rape of a Schoolgirl: Discourses of Power and Women's Lives in Okinawa." In *Islands of Discontent: Okinawan Responses to Japanese and American Power*, edited by Laura Hein and Mark Selden, 135–157. Lanham, MD: Rowman & Littlefield.

Antze, Paul, and Michael Lambek. 1996. *Tense Past: Cultural Essays in Trauma and Memory*. New York: Routledge.

Arasaki, Moriteru. 1986. *Okinawa hansen jinushi*. Tokyo: Kōbunken.

——, ed. 2000. *Okinawa no sugao*. Tokyo: Techno Marketing Center.

Asad, Talal, ed. 1973. *Anthropology and the Colonial Encounter*. New York: Humanities Press.

——. 1991. "Afterword: From the History of Colonial Anthropology to the Anthropology of Western Hegemony." In *Colonial Situations: Essays on the Contextualization of Ethnographic Knowledge*, edited by George Stocking. Madison: University of Wisconsin Press.

Asakura, Takuya. 2002. "Foreign Brides Fill the Gap in Rural Japan." *Japan Times*, January 8. https://www.japantimes.co.jp/news/2002/01/08/national/foreign -brides-fill-the-gap-in-rural-japan/.

Association of Defense Communities. 2016. "The Base of the Future: A Call for Action by States and Communities." https://defensecommunities.org/wp-content /uploads/2015/01/The-Base-of-the-Future_v5.pdf.

Bachnik, Jane M. 1989. "Omote/Ura: Indexes and the Organization of Self and Society in Japan." *Comparative Social Research* 11:239–262.

Bachnik, Jane M., and Charles J. Quinn Jr., eds. 1994. *Situated Meaning: Inside and Outside in Japanese Self, Society and Language*. Princeton, NJ: Princeton University Press.

Barske, Valerie H. 2013. "Visualizing Priestesses or Performing Prostitutes? Ifa Fuyū's Depiction of Okinawan Women, 1913–1943." *Studies on Asia Series IV* 3(1):65–116.

Bauman, Richard, and Charles L. Briggs. 1990. "Poetics and Performance as Critical Perspectives on Language and Social Life." *Annual Review of Anthropology* 19:59–88.

Befu, Harumi. 1983. "Internationalization of Japan and Nihon Bunkaron." In *The Challenge of Japan's Internationalization: Organization and Culture*, edited by Hiroshi Mannari and Harumi Befu, 232–266. Tokyo: Kwansei Gakuin University and Kadansha International.

Beillevaire, Patrick. 1999. "Assimilation from Within, Appropriation from Without: The Folklore-Studies and Ethnology of Ryukyu/Okinawa." In *Anthropology and Colonialism in Asia and Oceania*, edited by Jan van Breman and Akitoshi Shimizu, 172–196. Hong Kong: Curzon.

Ben-Ari, Eyal. 2004. "Review Essay: The Military and Militarization in the United States." *American Ethnologist* 31(3):340–348.

Bender, Daniel E., and Jana K. Lipman. 2015. "Introduction: Through the Looking Glass: U.S. Empire through the Lens of Labor History." In *Making the Empire Work: Labor and United States Imperialism*, edited by Daniel E. Bender and Jana K. Lipman, 1–34. New York: New York University Press.

Bhowmik, Davinder L. 2008. *Writing Okinawa: Narrative Acts of Identity and Resistance.* New York: Routledge.

Bird, Sarah. 2001. *The Yokota Officer's Club: A Novel.* New York: Knopf.

Brancaforte, Daniela B. M. 2000. *Camouflaged Identities and Army Wives: Narratives of Self and Place on the Margins of the U.S. Military Family.* PhD diss., Princeton University.

Bucholtz, Mary, and Kira Hall. 2005. "Identity and Interaction: A Sociocultural Linguistic Approach." *Discourse Studies* 7(4–5):585–614.

Bushatz, Amy. 2016. "Military Divorce Rate Continues Slow but Steady Decline." April 22. http://www.military.com/daily-news/2016/04/22/military-divorce-rate -continues-slow-but-steady-decline.html.

Cabinet Office (Government of Japan). 2014. "Policies on Okinawa." Retrieved August 14, 2017. http://www8.cao.go.jp/okinawa.

CBS. 2004. "Love and War: U.S. Soldier and Iraqi Doctor Find Love and Romance in War Zone." *60 Minutes II*, May 3. https://www.cbsnews.com/news/love-and-war -03-03-2004/.

Cernicky, A. J. 2006. "Moral Power and a Hearts-and-Minds Strategy in Post-Conflict Operations." In *Strategic Challenges for Counterinsurgency and the Global War on Terrorism*, edited by Williamson Murray, 43–75. Carlisle, PA: U.S. Army War College, Strategic Studies Institute.

Cheng, Sealing. 2010. *On the Move for Love: Migrant Entertainers and the U.S. Military in South Korea.* Philadelphia: University of Pennsylvania Press.

Christy, Alan S. 1993. "The Making of Imperial Subjects in Okinawa." *Positions* 1(3):607–639.

Collier, Jane, and Sylvia Yanagisako, eds. 1987. *Gender and Kinship: Essays Toward a Unified Analysis.* Stanford, CA: Stanford University Press.

Constable, Nicole, ed. 2005. *Cross-Border Marriages: Gender and Mobility in Transnational Asia.* Philadelphia: University of Pennsylvania Press.

Cornyetz, Nina. 1994. "Fetishized Blackness: Hip Hop and Racialized Desire in Contemporary Japan." *Social Text* 41(Winter):113–139.

——. 1996. "Power and Gender in the Narratives of Yamada Eimi." In *The Woman's Hand: Gender and Theory in Japanese Women's Writing*, edited by Paul Gordon Schalow and Janet A. Walker, 425–457. Stanford, CA: Stanford University Press.

Craig, Albert M. 2009. *Civilization and Enlightenment: The Early Thought of Fukuzawa Yukichi.* Cambridge, MA: Harvard University Press.

Creighton, Millie. 1997. "*Soto* Others and *uchi* Others: Imaging Racial Diversity, Imagining Homogenous Japan." In *Japan's Minorities: The Illusion of Homogeneity,* edited by Michael Weiner, 211–238. New York: Routledge.

Crissey, Etsuko Takushi. 2017. *Okinawa's GI Brides: Their Lives in America.* Translated by Steve Rabson. Honolulu: University of Hawai'i Press.

Curtin, J. Sean. 2002a. "Making Japan a More Multi-ethnic Society is an Investment in the Future." GLOCOM Platform, September 25. http://www.glocom.org/debates /20020925_curtin_making/.

——. 2002b. "International Marriages in Japan." GLOCOM Platform, October 28. http://www.glocom.org/special_topics/social_trends/20021028_trends_s13/.

Doi, Takeo. 1985. *The Anatomy of Self: The Individual Versus Society.* Translated by Mark A. Harbison. Tokyo: Kodansha International.

Dower, John W. 1986. *War Without Mercy: Race and Power in the Pacific War.* New York: Pantheon.

——. 1999. *Embracing Defeat: Japan in the Wake of World War II.* New York: Norton.

Dozier, Raine, and Pepper Schwartz. 2001. "Intimate Relationships." In *The Blackwell Companion to Sociology,* edited by Judith R. Blau, 114–127. Malden, MA: Blackwell.

Ehman, Kenny. 2007. *Okinawa Explorer: A Complete Guidebook to Okinawa, 2nd ed.* Naha: Ikemiyashokai.

Enloe, Cynthia. 1989. *Bananas, Beaches, and Bases: Making Feminist Sense of International Politics.* Berkeley: University of California Press.

——. 2000. *Maneuvers: The International Politics of Militarizing Women's Lives.* Berkeley: University of California Press.

Ervin-Tripp, Susan, Kei Nakamura, and Jiansheng Guo. 1995. "Shifting Face from Asia to Europe." In *Essays in Semantics and Pragmatics: In Honor of Charles J. Fillmore,* edited by Masayoshi Shibatani and Sandra Thompson, 43–71. Amsterdam: John Benjamins.

Fackler, Martin. 2012. "Where the Songs Linger, but the Tune Is Different." *New York Times.* February 20. http://www.nytimes.com/2012/02/21/world/asia/in-okinawa -some-still-toast-era-of-us-control.html.

Faier, Leiba. 2009. *Intimate Encounters: Filipina Women and the Remaking of Rural Japan.* Berkeley: University of California Press.

Fentress, James, and Chris Wickham. 1992. *Social Memory: New Perspectives on the Past.* Oxford: Blackwell.

Figal, Gerald. 1997. "Historical Sense and Commemorative Sensibility at Okinawa's Cornerstone of Peace." *Positions* 5(3):745–778.

Fisch, Arnold G., Jr. 1988. *Military Government in the Ryukyu Islands: 1945–1950 (Army Historical Series).* Washington, DC: Center of Military History, United States Army.

Fitz-Henry, Erin E. 2011. "Distant Allies, Proximate Enemies: Rethinking the Scales of the Anti-Base Movement in Ecuador." *American Ethnologist* 38(2):323–337.

Forgash, Rebecca. 2009. "Renegotiating Marriage: Cultural Citizenship and the Reproduction of American Empire in Okinawa." *Ethnology* 48(3):215–237.

——. 2004. *Military Transnational Marriage in Okinawa: Intimacy Across Boundaries of Nation, Race, and Class.* PhD diss., University of Arizona.

Foucault, Michel. 1978. *The History of Sexuality, Volume 1: An Introduction.* Translated by Robert Hurley. New York: Random House.

Francis, Carolyn Bowen. 1999. "Women and Military Violence." In *Okinawa: Cold War Island,* edited by Chalmers Johnson, 189–203. Cardiff, CA: Japan Policy Research Institute.

Franklin, Sarah, and Susan McKinnon, eds. 2002. *Relative Values: Reconfiguring Kinship Studies*. Durham, NC: Duke University Press.

Gal, Susan. 2007. "'Circulation' in the New Economy: Clasps and Copies." Paper presented at the 106th Meeting of the American Anthropological Association, Washington DC.

Garon, Sheldon. 1997. *Molding Japanese Minds: The State in Everyday Life*. Princeton, NJ: Princeton University Press.

Giddens, Anthony. 1992. *The Transformation of Intimacy: Sexuality, Love and Eroticism in Modern Societies*. Stanford, CA: Stanford University Press.

Gillem, Mark L. 2007. *America Town: Building the Outposts of Empire*. Minneapolis: University of Minnesota Press.

Glacken, Clarence. 1955. *The Great Loochoo: A Study of Okinawan Village Life*. Berkeley: University of California Press.

Gottlieb, Nanette. 2006. *Linguistic Stereotyping and Minority Groups in Japan*. New York: Routledge.

Gray, John. 1992. *Men Are from Mars, Women Are from Venus: A Practical Guide for Improving Communication and Getting What You Want in Your Relationships*. New York: HarperCollins.

Hamabata, Matthews Masayuki. 1990. *Crested Kimono: Power and Love in the Japanese Business Family*. Ithaca, NY: Cornell University Press.

Harmon, B. A, W. D. Goran, and R. S. Harmon. 2014. "Military Installations and Cities in the Twenty-First Century: Towards Sustainable Military Installations and Adaptable Cities." In *Sustainable Cities and Military Installations, NATO Science for Peace and Security Series C: Environmental Security*, edited by Igor Linkov, 21–47. Heidelberg: Springer Netherlands.

Harootunian, H. D. 1998. "Figuring the Folk: History, Poetics, and Representation." In *Mirror of Modernity: Invented Traditions of Modern Japan*, edited by Stephen Vlastos, 144–159. Berkeley: University of California Press.

Harrison, Deborah, and Lucie Laliberté. 1997. "Gender, the Military, and Military Family Support." In *Wives and Warriors: Women and the Military in the United States and Canada*, edited by Laurie Weinstein and Christie C. White, 35–53. Westport, CN: Bergin & Garvey.

Hawkins, John P. 2001. *Army of Hope, Army of Alienation: Culture and Contradiction in the American Army Communities of Cold War Germany*. Westport, CN: Praeger.

Hein, Laura, and Mark Selden, eds. 2003. *Islands of Discontent: Okinawan Responses to Japanese and American Power*. Lanham, MD: Rowman & Littlefield.

Hellyer, Robert I. 2010. *Defining Engagement: Japan and Global Contexts, 1640–1868*. Cambridge, MA: Harvard University Press.

Hendry, Joy. 1981. *Marriage in Changing Japan: Community and Society*. London: Croom Helm.

Hicks, George. 1994. *The Comfort Women: Japan's Brutal Regime of Enforced Prostitution in the Second World War*. New York: Norton.

Higa, Mikio. 1963. *Politics and Parties in Postwar Okinawa*. Vancouver: University of British Columbia.

Ho, Engseng. 2004. "Empire through Diasporic Eyes: A View from the Other Boat." *Comparative Studies of Society and History* 46(2):210–246.

Höhn, Maria, and Seungsook Moon, eds. 2010. *Over There: Living with the U.S. Military Empire from World War Two to the Present*. Durham, NC: Duke University Press.

Ikeda, Kyle. 2014. *Okinawan War Memory: Transgenerational Trauma and the War Fiction of Medoruma Shun*. New York: Routledge.

Inoue, Masamichi S. 2004. "'We Are Okinawans, but of a Different Kind': New/Old Social Movements and the U.S. Military in Okinawa." *Current Anthropology* 45(1):85–104.

——. 2007. *Okinawa and the U.S. Military: Identity Making in the Age of Globalization.* New York: Columbia University Press.

Ishihara, Masaie. 2001. "Memories of War and Okinawa." In *Perilous Memories: The Asia-Pacific War(s)*, edited by T. Fujitani, Geoffrey M. White, and Lisa Yoneyama, 87–106. Durham, NC: Duke University Press.

Ishizuki, Kaorie. 2001. *"Yamatunchu yome shiron: gendai okinawa no 'seikatsusha-tachi' wo kangaeru tame ni."* Paper presented at the Okinawa Folklore Society, Naha, Okinawa, November 2001.

Ivy, Marilyn. 1995. *Discourses of the Vanishing: Modernity, Phantasm, Japan.* Chicago: University of Chicago Press.

Japanese Ministry of Health, Labour and Welfare. 2014a. "Vital Statistics of Japan 2013: Divorces." http://www.e-stat.go.jp/SG1/estat/GL38020103.do?_toGL38020103_&listID=000001127002.

——. 2014b. "2014 Wage Structure Survey Results." http://www.mhlw.go.jp/toukei/itiran/roudou/chingin/kouzou/z2014/dl/08.pdf.

——. 2016. "Vital Statistics of Japan 2016: Marriages." http://www.e-stat.go.jp/SG1/estat/ListE.do?lid=000001157966.

Japanese Ministry of Internal Affairs and Communications. 2015. "2015 Labour Force Survey." http://www.stat.go.jp/data/roudou/pref/zuhyou/02.xls.

——. 2016. "Social Indicators by Prefecture." http://www.stat.go.jp/english/data/shihyou/.

Japanese Ministry of Justice. 2017. "Status of Residence Foreigners Statistics." http://www.moj.go.jp/housei/toukei/toukei_ichiran_touroku.html.

Japan Times. 2002. "Editorial: Good Neighbors to Diversity." November 18. https://www.japantimes.co.jp/opinion/2002/11/18/editorials/good-neighbors-to-diversity/.

——. 2015. "Government Bypasses City to Subsidize Henoko Communities for U.S. Base Relocation." October 26.

Johnson, Sheila K. 1988. *The Japanese Through American Eyes.* Stanford, CA: Stanford University Press.

Junkerman, John. 2014. "Postwar Okinawa Through American Eyes: Thoughts on *The Teahouse of the August Moon*." *GITS/GITI Research Bulletin 2013–2014.* http://gits-db.jp/bulletin/2013/papers/2013-2014.web.17-23.pdf.

——, dir. 2016. *Okinawa: The Afterburn.* Tokyo: Siglo.

Kawahashi, Noriko. 2000. "Religion, Gender, and Okinawan Studies." *Asian Folklore Studies* 59(2):301–311.

Keene, Donald. 1969. *The Japanese Discovery of Europe, 1720–1830. Rev. Ed.* Stanford, CA: Stanford University Press.

Kelsky, Karen. 2001. *Women on the Verge: Japanese Women, Western Dreams.* Durham, NC: Duke University Press.

Kerr, George H. 2000 (1958). *Okinawa: The History of an Island People.* Clarendon, VT: Tuttle.

Keyso, Ruth Ann. 2000. *Women of Okinawa: Nine Voices from a Garrison Island.* Ithaca, NY: Cornell University Press.

Kim, Bok-Lim C., and Michael R. Sawdey. 1981. *Women in Shadows: A Handbook for Service Providers Working with Asian Wives of U.S. Military Personnel.* La Jolla, CA: National Committee Concerned with Asian Wives of U.S. Servicemen.

Kimura, Tsukasa. 2017. "New Volume Sheds Additional Light on Battle of Okinawa." *Asahi Shimbun*, August 30.

Kina, Ikue. 2016. "Postwar US Presence in Okinawa and Border Imagination: Stories of Eiki Matayoshi and Tami Sakiyama." *Japanese Journal of American Studies* 27:189–210.

Knauft, Bruce M. 1996. *Genealogies for the Present in Cultural Anthropology.* New York: Routledge.

Koshiro, Yukiko. 1999. *Trans-Pacific Racisms and the U.S. Occupation of Japan.* New York: Columbia University Press.

Kreiner, Josef. 2000. "Recent Developments in the Ethnography of Ryukyu/Okinawa: A Review Article." *The Ryukyuanist* 50(Winter 2000–2001):6–11.

Lavie, Smadar. 1990. *The Poetics of Military Occupation: Mzeina Allegories of Bedouin Identity Under Israeli and Egyptian Rule.* Berkeley: University of California Press.

Lebra, William P. 1966. *Okinawan Religion: Belief, Ritual, and Social Structure.* Honolulu: University of Hawai'i Press.

Lee, Diana S., and Grace Yoon-Kyung Lee. 1995. *Camp Arirang.* New York: Third World Newsreel.

Lee, Jinyoung. 1995. "*Okinawa ni okeru dentou no souzou ikkyokumen: 'munchu' to keizu no seisei o chūshin ni* [A case of invented tradition in Okinawa: focusing on the creation of 'munchu' and genealogy]." *Okinawa minzoku kenkyū* 15:11–30.

Leupp, Gary. 2003. *Interracial Intimacy in Japan: Western Men and Japanese Women, 1543–1900.* New York: Bloomsbury.

Lie, John. 2001. *Multiethnic Japan.* Cambridge, MA: Harvard University Press.

Linde, Charlotte. 1993. *Life Stories: The Creation of Coherence.* New York: Oxford University Press.

Littlewood, Roland. 1997. "Military Rape." *Anthropology Today* 13(2):7–16.

Liu, Christina. 2003. "Asian Fusion: Fashion, Stereotypes and Society, Portrayals of Asian Females in Film and Fashion." Paper presented at the Western Conference of the Association for Asian Studies, Tempe, AZ, October.

LMO/IAA (Labor Management Organization, Incorporated Administrative Agency). 2013. "USFJ Employment Guide." http://www.lmo.go.jp/recruitment/pdf/pamphlet_en.pdf.

Loo, Tze May. 2014. *Heritage Politics: Shuri Castle and Okinawa's Incorporation into Modern Japan, 1879–2000.* Lanham, MD: Lexington Books.

Lutz, Catherine E. 1988. *Unnatural Emotions: Everyday Sentiment on a Micronesian Atoll and Their Challenge to Western Theory.* Chicago: University of Chicago Press.

———. 2001. *Homefront: A Military City and the American 20th Century.* Boston: Beacon.

———. 2002. "Making War at Home in the United States: Militarization and the Current Crisis." *American Anthropologist* 104(3):723–735.

———. 2006. "Empire Is in the Details." *American Ethnologist* 33(4):593–611.

———, ed. 2009. *The Bases of Empire: The Global Struggle against U.S. Military Posts.* New York: New York University Press.

Ma, Karen. 1996. *The Modern Madame Butterfly: Fantasy and Reality in Japanese Cross-Cultural Relationships.* Tokyo: Tuttle.

Maher, Kevin (Consulate General of the United States, Naha). 2008. "Some Interest in, but No Local Demand for, Expanded Return of Foster, Unclassified Report." January 10. https://wikileaks.org/plusd/cables/08NAHA8_a.html.

Maretzki, Thomas W., and Hatsumi Maretzki. 1966. *Taira: An Okinawan Village.* New York: Wiley.

Markman, Howard J., Scott M. Stanley, and Susan L. Blumberg. 1999. *Fighting for Your Marriage: PREP Leader Manual.* Denver, CO: PREP Educational Products.

Martin, Jo Nobuko. 1984. *A Princess Lily of the Ryukyus.* Tokyo: Shin Nippon Kyoiku Tosho.

Matayoshi, Masaharu, and Joyce Trafton. 2000. *Ancestors Worship, Okinawa's Indigenous Belief System: A Traditional View of Ideal Family Relationships.* Toronto: University of Toronto Press.

Matsumura, Wendy. 2015. *The Limits of Okinawa: Japanese Capitalism, Living Labor, and Theorizations of Community.* Durham, NC: Duke University Press.

McCaffrey, Katherine. 2002. *Military Power and Popular Protest: The U.S. Navy in Vieques, Puerto Rico.* New Brunswick, NJ: Rutgers University Press.

McCollum, Chris. 2002. "Relatedness and Self-Definition: Two Dominant Themes in Middle Class Americans' Life Stories." *Ethos* 30(2): 113–139.

McCormack, Gavan. 1999. "Okinawan Dilemmas: Coral Islands or Concrete Islands?" In *Okinawa: Cold War Island*, edited by Chalmers Johnson, 261–282. Cardiff, CA: Japan Policy Research Institute.

———. 2016. "Japan's Problematic Prefecture—Okinawa and the US-Japan Relationship." *Asia-Pacific Journal/Japan Focus* 14(17–2):1–27.

MCCS Okinawa (Marine Corps Community Services). n.d. "Japanese Spouse Orientation Program." Accessed September 14, 2019. http://www.mccsokinawa.com/japanese_spouse_orientation_program/.

McCune, Shannon. 1975. *The Ryukyu Islands (The Islands Series).* Mechanicsburg, PA: Stackpole.

McNaughton, James C. 1994. "Nisei Linguists and New Perspectives on the Pacific War: Intelligence, Race, and Continuity." Paper presented at the Conference of Army Historians. https://history.army.mil/html/topics/apam/Nisei.htm.

Mershon, Sherie, and Steven Schlossman. 1998. *Foxholes and Color Lines: Desegregating the U.S. Armed Forces.* Baltimore: Johns Hopkins University Press.

Mie, Ayako. 2016. "U.S. Return of Okinawa Training Area Faces Harsh Criticism from Local Residents." *Japan Times*, December 21. https://www.japantimes.co.jp/news/2016/12/21/national/u-s-return-okinawa-training-area-faces-harsh-criticism-local-residents/.

———. 2017. "Japan and U.S. Sign Deal Clarifying Civilian Protection under SOFA." *Japan Times*, January 16. https://www.japantimes.co.jp/news/2017/01/16/national/politics-diplomacy/japan-u-s-sign-deal-clarifying-civilian-protection-sofa/.

Millard, Mike. 1999. "Okinawa: Then and Now." In *Okinawa: Cold War Island*, edited by Chalmers Johnson, 93–107. Cardiff, CA: Japan Policy Research Institute.

Miller, Roy Andrew. 1982. *Japan's Modern Myth: The Language and Beyond.* New York: Weather Hill.

Miyanishi, Kaori. 2012. *Okinawa gunjin-zuma no kenkyū.* Kyoto: Kyōto Daigaku Gakujutsu Shuppankai.

Mizumura, Ayako. 2009. *Reflecting [on] the Orientalist Gaze: A Feminist Analysis of Japanese-U.S. GIs Intimacy in Postwar Japan and Contemporary Okinawa.* PhD diss., University of Kansas.

Molasky, Michael S. 1999. *The American Occupation of Japan and Okinawa: Literature and Memory.* New York: Routledge.

Moon, Katherine. 1997. *Sex Among Allies: Military Prostitution in U.S.-Korea Relations.* New York: Columbia University Press.

Morris-Suzuki, Tessa. 1998. *Re-inventing Japan: Time, Space, Nation.* New York: Sharpe.

Moskos, Charles C. 1977a. "From Institution to Occupation." *Armed Forces and Society* 4(1):41–50.

———. 1977b. "The All-Volunteer Military: Calling, Profession, or Occupation?" *Parameters* 7.

Murolo, Priscilla. 2011. "Wars of Civilization: The U.S. Army Contemplates Wounded Knee, the Pullman Strike, and the Philippine Insurrection." *International Labor and Working Class History* 80:77–102.

Murphy-Shigematsu, Stephen. 2001. "Multiethnic Lives and Monoethnic Myths: American-Japanese Amerasians in Japan." In *The Sum of Our Parts: Mixed Heritage Asian Americans*, edited by Teresa Williams-Leon and Cynthia L. Nakashima. Philadelphia: Temple University Press.

——. 2002. *Amerajian no kodomotachi: shirarezaru mainoritii mondai (Amerasian Children: A Little-Known Minority Issue)*. Tokyo: Shueisha.

——. 2012. *Half Is Whole: Multiethnic Asian American Identities*. Stanford, CA: Stanford University Press.

Nakachi, Kiyoshi. 1996. *Ryukyu Islands and Okinawans: Sightseeing and Lifestyle*. Naha: Okinawa Times.

Nakasone, Ronald Y., ed. 2002. *Okinawan Diaspora*. Honolulu: University of Hawai'i Press.

Negishi, Mayumi. 2000. "Amerasian Kids Get Short Shrift in Divorce Capital of Japan." *Japan Times*, July 20.

Nelson, Christopher T. 2008. *Dancing with the Dead: Memory, Performance and Everyday Life in Postwar Okinawa*. Durham, NC: Duke University Press.

New York Times. 2002a "Airman's Rape Conviction Fans Okinawa's Ire over U.S. Bases." March 29. http://www.nytimes.com/2002/03/29/world/airman-s-rape-conviction -fans-okinawa-s-ire-over-us-bases.html.

——. n.d. "General Order Number 1, Prohibited Activities for Soldiers." Accessed September 14, 2019. https://www.nytimes.com/interactive/projects/documents /general-order-no-1-prohibited-activities-for-soldiers.

Nippon.com. 2015. "A Look at International Marriage in Japan." February 19. http:// www.nippon.com/en/features/h00096/.

Nishioka, Hachiro. 1994. "Effects of the Family Formation Norms on Demographic Behaviors: Case of Okinawa in Japan." *Jinko Mondai Kenkyū* 50(2):52–60.

Noiri, Naomi. 2003. "The Educational Rights of Amerasians." University of the Ryukyus Repository. http://ir.lib.u-ryukyu.ac.jp/bitstream/20.500.12000/9007/6/12871024 -6.pdf.

Ochs, Elinor, and Lisa Capps. 1996. "Narrating the Self." *Annual Review of Anthropology* 25:19–43.

Ogasawara, Yuko. 1998. *Office Ladies and Salaried Men: Power, Gender, and Work in Japanese Companies*. Berkeley: University of California Press.

Oguma, Eiji. 1995. *Tan'itsu minzoku shinwa no kigen—"nihonjin" no jigazou no keifu*. Tokyo: Shinyōsha.

Okada, Yasuhiro. 2011. "Race, Masculinity, and Military Occupation: African American Soldiers' Encounters with the Japanese at Camp Gifu, 1947–1951." *Journal of African American History* 96(2):179–203.

Okinawa Josei Zaidan (Okinawa Women's Foundation). 1999. *Beigun kichi kara hassei suru josei no sho mondai chōsa jigyō*. Naha: Okinawa Prefecture Women's Center [Tiruru].

Okinawa Prefectural Government. 2013. "*Okinawa no beigun kichi*." https://www.pref .okinawa.lg.jp/site/chijiko/kichitai/okinawanobeigunnkiti2503.html.

——. 2018. "*Okinawa no beigun kichi*." https://www.pref.okinawa.lg.jp/site/chijiko /kichitai/2018okinawanobeigunkichi.html.

——. 2018. "What Okinawa Wants You to Know about the Military Bases." http://dc -office.org/wp-content/uploads/2018/03/E-all.pdf.

——. n.d. "US Bases and Okinawa's Economy." http://dc-office.org/basedata.

Ong, Aihwa. 1996. "Cultural Citizenship as Subject-Making: Immigrants Negotiate Racial and Cultural Boundaries in the United States." *Current Anthropology* 37(5):737–762.

——. 2006. *Neoliberalism as Exception: Mutations in Citizenship and Sovereignty.* Durham, NC: Duke University Press.

Onishi, Yuichiro. 2013. *Transpacific Antiracism: Afro-Asian Solidarity in 20th-Century Black American, Japan, and Okinawa.* New York: New York University Press.

Osburn, C. Dixon, and Michelle M. Benecke. 1997. "Conduct Unbecoming: Second Annual Report on 'Don't Ask, Don't Tell, Don't Pursue.'" In *Wives and Warriors: Women and the Military in the United States and Canada,* edited by Laurie Weinstein and Christie C. White, 151–177. Westport, CN: Bergin & Garvey.

Ota, Masahide. 1984. *The Battle of Okinawa: The Typhoon of Steel and Bombs.* Nagoya: Takeda.

Ota, Masahide, and Satoko Norimatsu. 2010. "'The World is Beginning to Know Okinawa': Ota Masahide Reflects on his Life from the Battle of Okinawa to the Struggle for Okinawa." *Asia-Pacific Journal/Japan Focus* 8(38)4. http://apjjf.org/-Ota-Masahide/3415/article.html.

Peterson, Valerie. 2000. "Mars and Venus: The Rhetoric of Planetary Alignment." *Women and Language* 23(2):1–7.

Phillips, Kimberley. 2012. *War! What Is It Good For?: Black Freedom Struggles and the U.S. Military from World War II to Iraq.* Chapel Hill: University of North Carolina Press.

Potts, Annie. 1998. "The Science/Fiction of Sex: John Gray's Mars and Venus in the Bedroom." *Sexualities* 1(2):153–173.

Powledge, Fred. 2008. "Beyond the Fenceline: Partnerships with Surrounding Communities." In *Conserving Biodiversity on Military Lands: A Guide for Natural Resources Managers,* edited by N. Benton, J. D. Ripley, and F. Powledge, 144–153. Arlington, VA: NatureServe. http://www.dodbiodiversity.org/ch10/.

Pratt, Geraldine, and Victoria Rosner, eds. 2012. *The Global and the Intimate: Feminism in Our Time.* New York: Columbia University Press.

Rabson, Steve. 1996. "Assimilation Policy in Okinawa: Promotion, Resistance, and 'Reconstruction.'" *Japanese Policy Research Institute,* JPRI Occasional Paper No. 8. http://www.jpri.org/publications/occasionalpapers/op8.html.

——. 2003. "Memories of Okinawa: Life and Times in the Greater Osaka Diaspora." In *Islands of Discontent: Okinawan Responses to Japanese and American Power,* edited by Laura Hein and Mark Selden, 99–134. Lanham, MD: Rowman & Littlefield.

——. 2010. "The Politics of Trauma: Compulsory Suicides During the Battle of Okinawa and Postwar Retrospectives." *Intersections: Gender and Sexuality in Asia and the Pacific* 24. http://intersections.anu.edu.au/issue24/rabson.htm.

——. 2016. "Perry's Black Ships in Japan and Ryukyu: The Whitewash of History." *Asia-Pacific Journal/Japan Focus* 14(16)9:1–12.

Racel, Masako N. 2011. *Finding Their Place in the World: Meiji Intellectuals and the Japanese Construction of an East-West Binary, 1868–1912.* PhD diss., Georgia State University.

Radansky, Captain Robert M. 1987. *Ministry Models: Transcultural Counseling and Couples Programs.* Washington, DC: Department of the Navy, Office of the Chief of Naval Operations.

Renda, Mary A. 2001. *Taking Haiti: Military Occupation and the Culture of U.S. Imperialism, 1915–1940.* Chapel Hill: University of North Carolina Press.

Ricoeur, Paul. 1991. "Narrative identity." *Philosophy Today* 35:73–81.

Rogers, R. 2005. "Family Ties Even More Crucial to the Corps." *San Diego Union-Tribune.* April 21, A1.

Rosaldo, Renato, ed. 2003. *Cultural Citizenship in Island Southeast Asia: Nation and Belonging in the Hinterlands.* Berkeley: University of California Press.

Rosenberger, Nancy, ed. 1992. *Japanese Sense of Self.* Cambridge: Cambridge University Press.

———. 2001. *Gambling with Virtue: Japanese Women and the Search for Self in a Changing Nation.* Honolulu: University of Hawai'i Press.

Russell, John G. 1998. "Consuming Passions: Spectacle, Self-Transformation, and the Commodification of Blackness in Japan." *Positions* 6(1):113–177.

———. 2007. "Excluded Presence: Shoguns, Minstrels, Bodyguards, and Japan's Encounters with the Black Other." *ZINBUN* 40:15–51.

———. 2009. "The Other Other: The Black Presence in the Japanese Experience." In *Japan's Minorities: The Illusion of Homogeneity, 2nd ed.*, edited by Michael Weiner, 84–115. Sheffield, UK: Routledge.

Ryukyu Shimpo. 2016. "Over 40 Percent of Okinawans Want Bases Withdrawn and 53 Percent Want Marines Withdrawn." June 3. http://english.ryukyushimpo.jp /2016/06/10/25179/.

Saki, Ryūzō. 1986. *Koibumi Sanjūnen: Okinawa, Nakama Hon'yaku Jimusho no saigetsu.* Tokyo: Gakushū-kenkyūsha,

Sakihara, Mitsugu. 2006. *Okinawan-English Wordbook: A Short Lexicon of the Okinawan Language with English Definitions and Japanese Cognates.* Honolulu: University of Hawai'i Press.

Schneider, David M. 1980. *American Kinship: A Cultural Account, 2nd ed.* Chicago: University of Chicago Press.

Seck, Hope Hodge. 2016. "First Female Navy SEALs Could Get Assignments in 2017, Plans Show." http://www.military.com/daily-news/2016/03/10/first-female-navy -seals-could-get-assignments-in-2017-plans-show.html.

Segal, David R. 2007. "Current Developments and Trends in Social Research on the Military." In *Social Sciences and the Military: An Interdisciplinary Overview.* New York: Routledge.

Segal, Mady Wechsler. 1986. "The Military and the Family as Greedy Institutions." *Armed Forces & Society* 13(1): 9–38.

Sered, Susan. 1999. *Women of the Sacred Groves: Divine Priestesses of Okinawa.* Oxford: Oxford University Press.

Shimanaka, Makiko. 1999. "Shima-naicha—Mainland Japanese Who Live on Okinawa." *Okinawa Living* (October): 6–7.

Silliman, Stephen W. 2008. "The 'Old West' in the Middle East: U.S. Military Metaphors in Real and Imagined Indian County." *American Anthropologist* 110(2):237–247.

Silverstein, Paul. 2005. "Immigrant Racialization and the New Savage Slot: Race, Migration, and Immigration in the New Europe." *Annual Review of Anthropology* 34:363–384.

Sims, Calvin. 2000a. "3 Dead Marines and a Secret of Wartime Okinawa." *New York Times,* June 1. https://www.nytimes.com/2000/06/01/world/3-dead-marines-and -a-secret-of-wartime-okinawa.html.

———. 2000b. "A Hard Life for Amerasian Children: Okinawan Women Fighting for Support from U.S. Servicemen." *New York Times,* July 23. https://www.nytimes.com /2000/07/23/world/a-hard-life-for-amerasian-children.html.

Slotkin, Richard. 1992. *Gunfighter Nation: The Myth of the Frontier in Twentieth-Century America.* New York: Atheneum.

Smits, Gregory. 1999. *Visions of Ryukyu: Identity and Ideology in Early-Modern Thought and Politics.* Honolulu: University of Hawai'i Press.

Steiner, Kurt. 1987. "The Occupation and the Reform of the Japanese Civil Code." In *Democratizing Japan*, edited by Robert E. Ward and Sakamoto Yoshikazu, 188–220. Honolulu: University of Hawai'i Press.

Stoler, Ann Laura. 1989. "Making Empire Respectable: The Politics of Race and Sexual Morality in 20th-Century Colonial Cultures." *American Ethnologist* 16(4):634–660.

——. 2002. *Carnal Knowledge and Imperial Power: Race and the Intimate in Colonial Rule*. Berkeley: University of California Press.

Strathern, Marilyn. 1992. *After Nature: English Kinship in the Late Twentieth Century*. Cambridge: Cambridge University Press.

Sturdevant, Sandra P., and Brenda Stoltzfus. 1993. *Let the Good Times Roll: Prostitution and the US Military in Asia*. New York: New Press.

Suzuki, Nobue. 2003. "Of Love and the Marriage Market: Masculinity Politics and Filipina-Japanese Marriages and in Japan." In *Men and Masculinities in Contemporary Japan: Dislocating the Salaryman Doxa*, edited by James E. Roberson and Nobue Suzuki. New York: Routledge.

——. 2007. "Carework and Migration: Japanese Perspectives on the Japan-Philippines Economic Partnership Agreement." *Asian and Pacific Migration Journal* 16(3): 357–381.

——. 2009. "Why Filipinas? Capitalist Modernity, Family Formation, and Masculine Desires." In *Cross-Border Marriages with Asian Characteristics*, edited by Hong-Zen Wang and Hsin-Huang Michael Hsiao. Taipei: Center for Asia-Pacific Area Study, Academia Sinica.

Suzuki, Yuko. 1992. *Juugun ianfu, naisen kekkon: sei no shinryaku, sengo sekiknin o kangaeru*. Tokyo: Miraisha.

Taira, Koji. 1999. "The Battle of Okinawa in Japanese History Books." In *Okinawa: Cold War Island*, edited by Chalmers Johnson, 39–49. Cardiff, CA: Japan Policy Research Institute.

Takagi, J. T., and Hye Jung Park. 1995. *The Women Outside: Korean Women and the U.S. Military*. New York: Third World Newsreel.

Takara, Kurayoshi. 1994. "King and Priestess: Spiritual and Political Power in Ancient Ryukyu." *The Ryukyuanist* 27(Winter):1–4.

Takemae, Eiji. 2003. *The Allied Occupation of Japan*, translated by Robert Ricketts and Sebastian Swann. New York: Continuum.

Takeuchi, Michiko. 2010. "'Pan-Pan Girls' Performing and Resisting Neocolonialism(s) in the Pacific Theater: U.S. Military Prostitution in Occupied Japan, 1945–1952." In *Over There: Living with the U.S. Military Empire from World War Two to the Present*, edited by Maria Höhn and Seungsook Moon, 78–108. Durham, NC: Duke University Press.

Takezawa, Yasuko. 2015. "Translating and Transforming 'Race': Early Meiji Period Textbooks." *Japanese Studies* 35(1):5–21.

Takushi, Etsuko. 2000. *Okinawa umi wo watatta beihei hanayometachi*. Tokyo: Kōbunken.

Tanji, Miyume. 2006. *Myth, Protest and Struggle in Okinawa*. New York: Routledge.

Tomiyama, Ichirō. 1990. *Kindai Nihon Shakai to Okinawajin: Nihonjin ni Naru to Iu Koto*. Tokyo: Nihon Keizai Hyōronsha.

——. 1998. "The Critical Limits of the National Community: The Ryukyuan Subject." *Social Science Japan Journal* 1(2):165–179.

Triplet, William S., ed. 2001. *In the Philippines and Okinawa: A Memoir, 1945–1948*. Columbia: University of Missouri Press.

Tsunami, Kiyoshi, et al. 2001. *Sōgō Annai*. Itoman: Okinawa Prefectural Peace Memorial Museum.

Turnbull, Stephen. 1977. *The Samurai: A Military History*. New York: MacMillan.

Ueno, Chizuko. 2001. "*Yamatunchu kara mita okinawa*." In *Okinawa-teki jinsei: minami no shima kara nihon wo miru*, edited by Ueno Chizuko. Tokyo: Kobunsha.

Uezato, Kazumi. 1998. *Amerajian: mō hitotsu no okinawa*. Tokyo: Kamogawa.

Uno, Kathleen. 1999. *Passages to Modernity: Motherhood, Childhood, and Social Reform in Early Twentieth-Century Japan*. Honolulu: University of Hawai'i Press.

Urciuoli, Bonnie. 2011. "Semiotic Properties of Racializing Discourses." *Journal of Linguistic Anthropology* 21(S1):E113–E122.

U.S. Department of Defense. 2001. "Guide to Preparation for Marrying in Okinawa (including MARCORBASESJAPANO 1752.1A)."

U.S. Department of Defense (Defense Task Force on Domestic Violence). 2003. "Compilation of Reports 2001–2003." http://www.ncdsv.org/ncd _militaryresponse.html.

U.S. Department of Defense. 2015. *Base Structure Report—Fiscal Year 2015 Baseline*. http://www.acq.osd.mil/eie/Downloads/BSI/Base%20Structure%20Report%20 FY15.pdf.

U.S. Department of Health and Human Services. 2017. "List of Hague Child Support Convention Countries." https://www.acf.hhs.gov/css/partners/international.

U.S. Department of the Navy. 1998. "Marine Corps Values: A User's Guide for Discussion Leaders." https://www.marines.mil/Portals/1/Publications/MCTP%206 -10B%20(Formerly%20MCRP%206-11B).pdf.

Vine, David. 2009. *Island of Shame: The Secret History of the U.S. Military Base on Diego Garcia*. Princeton, NJ: Princeton University Press.

Vogel, Ezra F. 1971. *Japan's New Middle Class: The Salaryman and His Family in a Tokyo Suburb*. Berkeley: University of California Press.

Vos, Frits. 2014. "A Distance of 13,000 Miles: The Dutch Through Japanese Eyes." *East Asian History* 39:131–138.

Wacker, Monica. 2000. "*Onarigami. Die Heilige Frau in Okinawa.*" *University Studies, Series XIX, Section B: Ethnology* 55. Berlin: Peter Lang.

Wardlow, Holly, and Jennifer S. Hirsch. 2006. "Introduction." In *Modern Loves: The Anthropology of Romantic Courtship and Companionate Marriage*, edited by Jennifer S. Hirsch and Holly Wardlow, 1–31. Ann Arbor: University of Michigan Press.

Weiner, Michael. 1997. "The Invention of Identity: 'Self' and 'Other' in Pre-War Japan." In *Japan's Minorities: The Illusion of Homogeneity*, edited by Michael Weiner, 1–16. London: Routledge.

White, Merry Isaacs. 2002. *Perfectly Japanese: Making Families in an Era of Upheaval*. Berkeley: University of California Press.

Wilson, Ara. 2012. "Intimacy: A Useful Category of Transnational Analysis." In *The Global and the Intimate: Feminism in Our Time*, edited by Geraldine Pratt and Victoria Rosner, 31–56. New York: Columbia University Press.

——. 2016. "The Infrastructure of Intimacy." *Signs: Journal of Women in Culture and Society* 41(2):250–280.

Wortham, Stanton, Elaine Allard, Kathy Lee, and Katherine Mortimer. 2011. "Racialization in Payday Mugging Narratives." *Journal of Linguistic Anthropology* 21(S1):E56–E75.

Yamada, Eimi. 1985. *Bedtime Eyes*. Tokyo: Kawade Shobo Shinsha.

Yanagisako, Sylvia, and Carol Delaney, eds. 1995. *Naturalizing Power: Essays in Feminist Cultural Analysis*. New York: Routledge.

Yonetani, Julia. 2003. "Future 'Assets,' but at What Price? The Okinawa Initiative Debate." In *Islands of Discontent: Okinawan Responses to Japanese and American Power*, edited by Laura Hein and Mark Selden, 243–272. Lanham, MD: Rowman & Littlefield.

Yoshida, Reiji. 2015. "Economics of U.S. Base Redevelopment Sway Okinawa Mindset." *Japan Times*, May 17. https://www.japantimes.co.jp/news/2015/05/17/national /politics-diplomacy/economics-u-s-base-redevelopment-sway-okinawa-mindset/.

Yoshikawa, Hideki. 1996. *Living with a Military Base: A Study of the Relationship between a US Military Base and Kin Town, Okinawa, Japan*. MA thesis, Oregon State University.

Yoshino, Kosaku. 1998. "Culturalism, Racialism, and Internationalism in the Discourse on Japanese Identity." In *Making Majorities: Constituting the Nation in Japan, Korea, China, Malaysia, Fiji, Turkey, and the United States*, edited by Dru C. Gladney. Stanford, CA: Stanford University Press.

Young, James E. 1994. *Texture of Memory: Holocaust Memorials and Meaning*. New Haven, CT: Yale University Press.

Yuengert, Louis G. 2015. "America's All Volunteer Force: A Success?" *Parameters* 45(4):53–64.

Yuh, Ji-Yeon. 2002. *Beyond the Shadow of Camptown: Korean Military Brides in America*. New York: New York University Press.

Ziomek, Kirsten L. 2014. "The 1903 Human Pavilion: Colonial Realities and Subaltern Subjectivities in Twentieth-Century Japan." *Journal of Asian Studies* 73(2):493–516.

Zulueta, Johanna O. 2017. "The Occupying Other: Third-Country Nationals and the U.S. Bases in Okinawa." In *Rethinking Postwar Okinawa: Beyond American Occupation*, edited by Pedro Iacobelli and Hiroko Matsuda. Lanham, MD: Lexington.

Index

CPSIA information can be obtained
at www.ICGtesting.com
Printed in the USA
LVHW091911300720
661980LV00004B/36/J